STAGING *Habla de Negros*

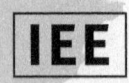

IBERIAN ENCOUNTER
AND EXCHANGE
475–1755 | Vol. 3

SERIES EDITORS
Erin Kathleen Rowe
Michael A. Ryan

The Iberian Peninsula has historically been an area of the world that fostered encounters and exchanges among peoples from different societies. For centuries, Iberia acted as a nexus for the circulation of ideas, people, objects, and technology around the premodern western Mediterranean, Atlantic, and, eventually, the Pacific. Iberian Encounter and Exchange, 475–1755 combines a broad thematic scope with the territorial limits of the Iberian Peninsula and its global contacts. In doing so, works in this series will juxtapose previously disparate areas of study and challenge scholars to rethink the role of encounter and exchange in the formation of the modern world.

ADVISORY BOARD
Paul H. Freedman
Richard Kagan
Marie Kelleher
Ricardo Padrón
Teofilo F. Ruiz
Marta V. Vicente

OTHER TITLES IN THIS SERIES:
Thomas W. Barton, *Contested Treasure: Jews and Authority in the Crown of Aragon*

Mercedes García-Arenal and Gerard Wiegers, eds., *Polemical Encounters: Christians, Jews, and Muslims in Iberia and Beyond*

STAGING
Habla de Negros

RADICAL PERFORMANCES OF THE
AFRICAN DIASPORA IN EARLY MODERN SPAIN

NICHOLAS R. JONES

THE PENNSYLVANIA STATE UNIVERSITY PRESS
UNIVERSITY PARK, PENNSYLVANIA

Library of Congress Cataloging-in-Publication Data

Names: Jones, Nicholas R., 1982– author.
Title: Staging habla de negros : radical performances of the African diaspora in early modern Spain / Nicholas R. Jones.
Other titles: Iberian encounter and exchange, 475–1755 ; vol. 3.
Description: University Park, Pennsylvania : The Pennsylvania State University Press, [2019] | Series: Iberian encounter and exchange, 475–1755 ; vol. 3 | Includes bibliographical references and index.
Summary: "An interdisciplinary exploration of white appropriations of black African voices in Spanish theater from the 1500s through the 1700s"—Provided by publisher.
Identifiers: LCCN 2019005860 | ISBN 9780271083469 (cloth : alk. paper)
Subjects: LCSH: Theater—Spain—African influences—History—16th century. | Theater—Spain—African influences—History—17th century. | Theater—Spain—African influences—History—18th century. | African diaspora in literature.
Classification: LCC PN2782.J66 2019 | DDC 792.0946—dc23
LC record available at https://lccn.loc.gov/2019005860

Copyright © 2019 Nicholas R. Jones
All rights reserved
Printed in the United States of America
Published by The Pennsylvania State University Press,
University Park, PA 16802-1003

The Pennsylvania State University Press is a member of the Association of University Presses.

It is the policy of The Pennsylvania State University Press to use acid-free paper. Publications on uncoated stock satisfy the minimum requirements of American National Standard for Information Sciences—Permanence of Paper for Printed Library Material, ANSI z39.48–1992.

If we are to believe the majority of writers of Negro dialect and the burnt-cork artists, Negro speech is a weird thing, full of "ams" and "Ises." Fortunately, we don't have to believe them. We may go directly to the Negro and let him speak for himself.
—ZORA NEALE HURSTON, "Characteristics of Negro Expression," 1934

Black English is the creation of the black diaspora. . . . A language comes into existence by means of brutal necessity, and the rules of the language are dictated by what the language must convey.
—JAMES BALDWIN, "If Black English Isn't a Language, Then Tell Me, What Is?," 1979

The history of blackness is testament to the fact that objects can and do resist. Blackness—the extended movement of a specific upheaval, an ongoing irruption that anarranges every line—is a strain that pressures the assumption of the equivalence of personhood and subjectivity.
—FRED MOTEN, In the Break: The Aesthetics of the Black Radical Tradition, 2003

Lumbe: Lumbe, Lumbe!
Lumbe: La cueva nganga.
Si Zarabanda tá seré, seré: Palo, kindiambo wé, sá, wé.
—AFRO-CUBAN CONGOLESE CONJURE SONG

Contents

LIST OF ILLUSTRATIONS ix

PREFACE: TALKING BLACK IN SPANISH xi

ACKNOWLEDGMENTS xvii

TRANSLATING BLACKNESS: AN EDITORIAL NOTE ON TRANSLATIONS xxi

Introduction: The *Habla de Negros* Palimpsest; Theorizing *Habla de Negros* 1

1 Black Skin Acts: Feasting on Blackness, Staging Linguistic Blackface 27

2 The Birth of Hispanic *Habla de Negros*: Signifying for the Black Audience in Rodrigo de Reinosa 85

3 Black Divas, Black Feminisms: The Black Female Body and *Habla de Negros* in Lope de Rueda 119

Afterword: B(l)ack to the Future; The Postmodern Legacy of *Habla de Negros*, or Talking in Tongues 159

NOTES 165

BIBLIOGRAPHY 185

INDEX 213

Illustrations

1. Alonso Sánchez Coello, *Vista de Sevilla*, 1576–1600. Photo: Wikimedia Commons   3

2. Rodrigo de Villandrando, *El príncipe Felipe y el enano Miguel Soplillo*, ca. 1620. Photo: Wikimedia Commons   32

3. Karel Dujardin, *Les Charlatans italiens*, 1657. Photo: Musée Paul-Dupuy   37

4. Woodcut from the broadside *Coplas de como una dama ruega a un negro que cante en manera de requiebro*, early 1500s   39

5. Frédéric Mialhe, *Day of the Kings*, ca. 1848. Photo: Beinecke Rare Book and Manuscript Library, Yale University   55

6. Domingo Martínez, *Carro del Aire: Máscara de la Fábrica de Tabacos con motivo de la exaltación al trono de Fernando VI*, 1747. Photo: Lipstick Alley   58

7. Engraving from an eighteenth-century chapbook pamphlet, *Nueva relación y curioso romance. . . .* Photo: Biblioteca Digital de Castilla y León   62

8. "Conguitos" postcard. Photo: Pinterest   82

9. Igrexa de San Fiz de Solovio, Santiago de Compostela. Photo: author   83

10. Early fourteenth-century romanesque portico, Catalonia. Photo: author   84

11. Sebastián de Covarrubias, *Emblema 98* "La mona," 1610. Photo: author   135

12. Sebastián de Covarrubias, *Emblema 78* "El papagayo," 1610. Photo: author   138

13. Cristóvão de Morais, *Portrait of Juana de Austria with Her Black Slave Girl*, 1553. Photo: author   140

14. Konrad Kyeser, *Bellifortis*, 1405. Photo: author   143

15. Promotional poster for "The Mrs. Carter World Tour," 2013–14. Photo: author   144

Preface
Talking Black in Spanish

Throughout my career, people—colleagues, friends, random strangers—have always asked me candidly: "How did a black dude from Seattle, Washington, get into studying black people and Black Spanish in Spain?" My answer to them revolves around the varieties of personal experiences that have deeply impacted my connection to the topic at hand. I explain to them that I convinced myself of the legitimacy of developing a book-length project on literary *habla de negros*—herein titled *Staging* Habla de Negros*: Radical Performances of the African Diaspora in Early Modern Spain*—I then forced myself to embark on a deep, introspective journey about the ideological and political investments surrounding my lived, racialized experience as a person of African descent, coupled with a coterminous set of politics and social codes pertaining to speaking a language—Spanish—that is not my native tongue. As I have analyzed my own personal experiences over the years (faced in both academic and nonacademic settings), I realized that an analogous experience was once lived by black slaves inhabiting the Iberian Peninsula. Such personal experiences ranged from condescending remarks such as "¡Ay, hiciste una negruda!" or, better yet, as a PhD candidate in my graduate seminar on the methodology of teaching the Spanish language: "¡Aquí, hablamos y pronunciamos el español *bien*!" As a result of these hurtful insults (often thrown around casually in academic settings, either "in jest" at parties or in formal classroom settings), it became clear to me that on an ontological level, Blackness—in its cultural, linguistic, and visual manifestations—throughout the Spanish-speaking world *is* and *has been* reduced to the geographical imaginary of the Caribbean, which has been categorically *raced* as "Black." While this book does not analyze Spanish Caribbean cultural and literary studies firsthand, I emphasize this geographical space in order to make the point that Blackness—again, artistically, culturally, linguistically, and visually—to many native and nonnative Spanish speakers somehow "belongs to," or stays within, the Caribbean or its coastal port cities. But, as we all know, not everyone from the Caribbean is of African descent nor claims or identifies with that ancestral genealogy. But, for some odd and inexplicable reason, the Hispanic Caribbean's non(black) African composition ultimately becomes overshadowed by the tendentious habit and fetishistic seduction of racializing, in very pejorative ways, the sociolinguistic legacy of the region. In my own life experiences, for example, this claim is best illustrated by the fact that no matter how neutral of a Castilian accent with which I may speak, I can never leave a conversation without the person with whom I am conversing inquiring, "Oh ... where in Puerto Rico, Cuba, or (maybe) Panama do you come from?" or, rather, "How did you learn to speak Spanish *so well; so clearly*?" As a great mentor of mine once explained to me, "Society assigns certain accents and dialects with a *prestige* that prizes and privileges them over other ones that are debased and frowned upon." Another prime example is the countless occasions where I would be present in an all-Spanish-language work setting, and those in the same space would refuse to speak to me in Spanish, yet when a nonblack person would enter that all-Spanish-language space, their Whiteness (or, perhaps, their perceived "mixed"-racedness)—physically and visually—somehow would inaugurate a bilingual moment where the native Spanish speaker would willingly converse in Spanish with the "white *gringo*" Other while speaking to me, the perceived "dark *negrito*" Other, in English. In summation, these personal anecdotes, despite the anger and pain they have caused me over the years, illustrate only but a few personal experiences that have compelled me to write this book on early modern literary habla de negros. As I have learned in carrying out research for this project, coupled with the specters of my personal experiences of inadvertently talking or sounding too "Black," this topic on literary habla de negros will never be separate from larger issues and questions of language and race in the Spanish-speaking world.

Staging Habla de Negros: *Radical Performances of the African Diaspora in Early Modern Spain* broaches new territory by illuminating the variety of ways Africanized Castilian animates black Africans' agency, empowers their resistance, and highlights their African cultural retentions in early modern Spain. As a result, the book dismantles the long-held belief by literary critics and linguists that white appropriations and representations of habla de negros language is "racist buffoonery" or "racist stereotype." The project calls for a specifically Black and gendered performance theory approach that challenges, revises, and radically reimagines the function, materiality, performance, and presence of black Africans' bodily, sartorial, and linguistic Blackness in early modern Spanish cultural and literary studies.

As Atlantic Africa and the Spanish Caribbean began to connect blacks and whites in unprecedented ways, black people, as Monica L. Miller observes, "expressed their own sense of style in relation to that which they perceived was operating in European societies with which they traded or in which they lived."[1] On the backs of those on the African coast and those imported into the Americas and other European destinations such as the Iberian Peninsula, a negotiation of identity was taking place, a visual and visible sign of how Africans cast into a diaspora would have to construct their identities literally and materially.[2] Early modern habla de negros texts allow us to glimpse under what conditions and societal pressures black Africans understood, negotiated, and reinvented the construction of their images through the acquisition, consumption, and, at other times, redeployment of clothing, cosmetics, gesture, and wit. In this book's three chapters, the image of the black body—via habla de negros speech and its cultural production and textual circulation—is an image that carries the weight of many centuries of forced labor, of coercive and violent sexual desire, and of ongoing political struggle.[3] As we will see, however, the control and gaze of white poetic and dramatic practitioners of habla de negros cannot sustain a seamless denigration of Blackness. Rather, the concept of "radical performances," which I stipulate here and elucidate in the introduction, points to the idea that the constitution of Whiteness via the most racist images and practices of Africanized Castilian is neither seamless nor easy. Although I trace the image of the black body in early modern Spanish texts between the sixteenth and early eighteenth centuries in Spain, at no point does my analysis understand the black body, and therefore black subjects, to be without agency. Developing in an early modern context the ideas of cultural performance theorist José Esteban Muñoz in *Disidentifications: Queers of Color and the Performance of Politics*, the motley crew of black African characters I study in this book—whose Africanized Castilian language is empowered by a corpus of texts that awakens unwritten speech—negotiates between a fixed identity disposition and the socially encoded roles that are available for such subjects.

"The *Habla de Negros* Palimpsest: Theorizing *Habla de Negros*" serves as the introduction to the book as a whole, furnishing a background on the cultural, historical, and sociolinguistic contexts of Castilian habla de negros. The main contention of this chapter is that literary depictions of habla de negros need to be theorized because there has been a lack of analysis due to racialized value systems of artistic expression. To that end, this introductory chapter lays out my critical interventions for studying habla de negros texts.

In chapter 1, "Black Skin Acts: Feasting on Blackness, Staging Linguistic Blackface," I argue that habla de negros speech cannot be separated from the act and practice of blackface performance. Analyzing the inability to detach linguistic Blackness from blackface practices on early Spanish stages—primarily in *teatro breve*—I proceed to rehearse my own theoretical conceptualizations of how blackface operates on early Spanish stages. What I hope to make clear in this chapter is that black skin *acts* in conjunction with the excessively deformed black corporeality of the *bozal*'s black mouth and the register of the sonic highlighted by "African" dances, lyrics, and songs. My theory of feasting (on Blackness), as a racially performative act that tantalizes the senses, fortifies the success of blackface's convincing entertainment to the audience enjoying its blackface performance.

In chapter 2, "The Birth of Hispanic *Habla de Negros*: Signifying for the Black Audience in Rodrigo de Reinosa," I look at Rodrigo de Reinosa's collection of habla de negros poems and situate them as the earliest example of literary habla de negros speech found in the Peninsular Spanish canon. The primary text for discussion is Reinosa's "Gelofe, Mandinga" (1501; 1516–20). Turning to the black vernacular expression of signifying, I argue in this chapter that "Gelofe, Mandinga" exemplifies performative elements of Black signification, particularly in the modes of call and response (antiphony), in the verbal game referred to as "Playing the Dozens," and in witty tongue-in-cheek responses. My reading practices in this chapter suggest that the poem illustrates, on the one hand, an inner dialectical quality of subversive black speech and, on the other, complicates the relationship between black spectators (the audience) and the performance of race, gender, and black diasporic self-fashioning.

I focus in chapter 3, "Black Divas, Black Feminisms: The Black Female Body and *Habla de Negros* in Lope de Rueda," on black feminist theory and offer a racially gendered critical analysis attuned to the intersectional discourse of gender, language, and race on display in early modern Spanish representations of black women in Lope de Rueda's *Eufemia* (1542/1554) and *Los engañados* (1538/1558). In these two plays, I treat the two black female characters—Eulalla and Guiomar—as authoritative black female subjects, or "divas." As divas, these characters' notoriety and marketability enables them to access the (Spanish) nation as so-called royalty and queens, which hinges on a savvy self-fashioning and somatic Blackness that are fluid and performative yet deceptive and paradoxical. Manifested in their habla de negros speech, Eulalla and Guiomar speak with witty verbal puns and exhibit audacious bodily performances representative of Renaissance self-fashioning in relationship to cosmetics, female agency, and material objects such as books and letter writing, hair and makeup, and foreign, exotic animals. I suggest in this chapter that Rueda's portrayal of these two characters might serve as a beacon for today's scholars of early modern Spain to augment their initial critical approach to analyzing black women in the literature of Renaissance Europe. Just as Eulalla and Guiomar stunned sixteenth-century Spanish audiences with their contestatory power, their worldly savvy illustrated in Rueda's theatrical works will also illuminate black women's claims to female authorship for present-day readers.

In response to sexually and morally pathologizing labels imposed on black female literary characters, this book echoes black feminist cultural critic Hazel Carby's caution against policing black women's bodies. In the interpretive act of literary and cultural analysis, I urge that black feminist theory must serve as a prime critical framework for analyzing black women characters in early modern Spanish literature and cultural history. Black feminist readings are not antithetical to the scholarly exercise of the literary analysis of early modern Spanish literary and cultural texts. Furthermore, it is incumbent upon early modern Iberian studies critics to privilege black feminist readings as valid forms of scholarly criticism. To this end, the theoretical framework of black feminism empowers this book to render visible black women characters' authoritative voices and complex identity positioning in their habla de negros language.

I conclude the book by looking ahead to the future. In its reexamination of the past, this book closes with an afterword titled "B(l)ack to the Future: The Postmodern Legacy of *Habla de Negros*, or Talking in Tongues." It concerns itself with the present, the future, and the inscription of "the past" within the future. The book closes by dialoguing with nineteenth- and twentieth-century Latin American *poesía negra*, as well as the ritual songs and scenes of trance possession associated with the Afro-Cuban Congolese- and Yoruba-based cosmologies and religious systems of *Las Reglas Congas* (more broadly referred to as *Palo Mayombe*) and *Lukumí* ("Santería"; *La Regla de Osha*)—each of which is heavily influenced and inflected by early modern habla de negros from early modern Spain. Both in this afterword and throughout this book's ruminations about the legacy and value of early modern Castilian habla de negros, I ask: Is the final racial-linguistic imprint of literary habla de negros solely a marker of the impoverishment of a language? Africanized Castilian symbolizes a multilayered model that encompasses the vernacular, the material, and that which is territorial. This book shall remind us how Blackness is subversively performative and paradoxical.

Acknowledgments

This book is but one outcome of the extraordinary friendships and mentorship I have been so honored to acquire, maintain, and enjoy over the years. Mentors, teachers, and sage interlocutors cleared the road for me, created opportunities for me, read drafts of this project, and provided guidance, advice, and critical insights at every juncture during the writing of this manuscript: Vincent Barletta, Josiah Blackmore, Kinitra D. Brooks, Pablo García Piñar, K. Meira Goldberg, Miles P. Grier, Chad Leahy, Adrián J. Sáez, Arek Samuels, and Cassander (Cassie) L. Smith.

I am enormously grateful to my colleagues at Bucknell University's Spanish Department and Africana Studies Program as well as to those at Emory University, Georgetown University, and New York University.

Friends and loved ones, colleagues, teachers, students, and acquaintances taught me, gave me things to think about, inspired me, encouraged me, and accompanied me on the journey to not only build this project but also to refine my scholarly interest in black Africans in Spanish early modernity. I give infinite thanks to: Ralph Bauer, Herman L. Bennett, John Beusterien, Jesús Botello, Margaret Boyle, Marina Brownlee, María Mercedes Carrión, Bruno Carvalho, Roberto Castillo-Sandoval, Vanessa Ceia, Marco Antonio Cervantes, Jeffrey K. Coleman, Ann Craig Befroy, Robert (Beto) de León, Ángel M. Díaz, Leah DeVun, Steve Dolph, Luis Duno-Gottberg,

Nicholas Durón, Toni Espòsito, Fernando Esquivel-Suárez, Hernán Feldman, Jim Fernández, Emily Francomano, Federico Fridman, Becky Goetz, Yinka Esi Graves, Derrick Higginbotham, David Jeffries, Ross Karlan, Aisha Khan, Rebecca Kumar, Ana Laguna, Jill Lane, Christina Lee, Ross Lerner, Lázaro Lima, Obed Lira, Jason McCloskey, Isaac and Zunera Mirza, Sandra Navarro, Fabio Parasecoli, Sarah J. Pearce, John Penniman, Stephanie Pridgeon, María Cristina Quintero, Susana Ramírez, Erin Roark, Dylon Robbins, Gabriel Rocha, Elizabeth Rodríguez, Jared Rodríguez, Tom D. Rogers, Renato Rosaldo, Miguel Ángel Rosales, Kathleen Ross, Joshua M. Rumley, P. Khalil Saucier, Grant D. Schleifer, Erika Serrato Chiprés, Víctor Sierra Matute, Stephen Silverstein, Rosi Song, Dianne M. Stewart, Karen Stolley, Ana Catarina Teixeira, Sarah Thomas, Zeb Tortorici, Henry Turner, Felipe Valencia, Yohan Vicente Ayala, Nicole von Germeten, Alicia Walker, Emily Weissbourd, David Wheat, Thelathia "Nikki" Young, and many others.

For more than a decade, I have been lucky enough to benefit from the friendship, mentorship, patience, and wisdom of the dynamic trio: Israel Burshatin, Gigi Dopico, and Mary Louise Pratt. It is to them that I owe my deepest gratitude for sharing their extraordinary intellectual support and vision. Since my time as an undergraduate student at Haverford College, Israel Burshatin has opened my eyes to a plethora of medieval and early modern Iberian texts. As a longtime friend, mentor, and advocate of my scholarly work, Gigi Dopico took me under her wing and never abandoned me. She is a gifted administrator and writer, and I thank her for teaching me the ins and outs of diplomacy, grace, humility, and patience in a scathingly cutthroat academia. And I will forever be indebted to Mary Louise Pratt for her erudition and wisdom. I cannot thank you all enough for believing in the merit of this project. I thank each of you for the many afternoon lunches and impromptu chats over coffee, for reading and editing my work, and for giving me many books to read. Israel, Gigi, and Mary: this book is for y'all—a testament to your trust in my intellectual risks and your faith in this project since its conception. ¡A vosotros, mis padres académicos, os agradezco desde las profundidades de mi ser!

I am very fortunate to have had this book chosen for publication by Penn State University Press under its Iberian Encounter and Exchange, 475–1755 series. My debts at the press begin with Eleanor Goodman and IEE series editors Erin Kathleen Rowe and Michael A. Ryan. I cannot thank them enough for their gracious enthusiasm and efficient efforts. I am truly honored and humbled by their support. And again, to Eleanor Goodman: *thank you* for contacting me, meeting me at the 2016 Annual Meeting of the Renaissance Society of America in Chicago, and for championing the project when I nearly lost sight of its importance and value. Many thanks to my esteemed classicist colleague Melissa Haynes for translating the Latin passage in Konrad Kyeser's *Bellifortis* Queen of Sheba painting. Infinite thanks to the book's marketing team and copyeditors Nicole Wayland and Janice North for their impeccable work. Much gratitude to Amyrose McCue Gill and Lisa Regan of Text*Formations* for their outstanding work on the index as well as the Museu Coleção Berardo for granting permission to use one of their paintings as this book's cover image. Deepest thanks to my generous anonymous readers for their brilliant, bountiful comments and suggestions. Because of their sage critical attention, this project will empower Black speech to be heard and listened to!

I dedicate this book to my parents, Peggy and Wendell Jones, as well as my big sister, Erica Myers. Thank you for keeping me centered, grounded, and humble.

Translating Blackness
An Editorial Note on Translations

Throughout this book, I work with a handful of terms and concepts, including the orthographical distinction between black and Black, the ideological constitution of Blackness, and reticence in using hyphenated terms such as "Afro-Hispanic," "Afro-Iberian," and so forth when referring to peoples of African descent living in the early modern period.

Let us begin with the orthographical differences between black and Black. I use "black," with a lowercase *b*, to speak of people and color: as in *black* Africans or *black* slaves. "Black," with an uppercase B, refers to concepts, ideology, and culture. In a more taxonomical sense, I also use "black" as an umbrella term that includes and refers to the racial hierarchies and identities of people. In addition to Iberian names and African ethnonyms, sub-Saharan Africans and their descendants are frequently described in early modern Iberia as either *negro* or *negra* ("black"), *moreno* or *morena* ("brown," and also sometimes "black" too), and *mulato* or *mulata* ("mulatto," which in the Caribbean usually meant a lighter-skinned person of mixed African and Iberian ancestry). As David Wheat explains: "In the Iberian world, race was not yet the primary factor determining who could or could not be enslaved and often appears to have been less important as a marker of personal identity than religious and political loyalties or association with a specific household or extended family."[1] "The categories of 'negro' and 'moreno,'"

Wheat adds, "were clearly mutable—the same person could be called 'negra' or 'morena' depending on the circumstances—and both terms were often used as a reference to general social categories rather than a straightforward description of an individual's skin tone."[2]

I am fully aware that my preference for and practice of referring to African-descended literary characters as "black" and, at other times, "black African" leave me open to the charge of reifying the very binarism I am trying to deconstruct. Audre Lorde, in her essay "Burst of Light," articulates this position with some sympathy while still suggesting its problems:

> I see certain pitfalls in defining Black as a political position. It takes the cultural identity of a widespread but definite group and makes it a generic identity for many culturally diverse peoples, all on the basis of a shared oppression. This runs the risk of providing a convenient blanket of apparent similarity under which our actual and unaccepted differences can be distorted or misused.... There must be a way for us to deal with this, if only on the level of language. For example, those of us for whom Black is our cultural reality, relinquishing the word in favor of some other designation of African Diaspora, perhaps simply *African*.[3]

As much as I recognize the validity in Lorde's reservations about the term "black," her suggested alternative, "African," carries similar problems. It replaces a generic term of color with a term of geography that is no less generic when we think about the organization of communities within the continent.[4] Lorde's "African" alternative provides even more vexed problems for the early modern period, since Africa, as we see in medieval and early modern cartography, did not exist for the writers with whom I am dealing.

As Lorde insists in her essay, I risk erasing very real and significant cultural differences, but in this study such a risk is superseded by the problem of working with representations of diasporic peoples whose self-determined cultural identity is largely lost to me. In *Staging* Habla de Negros: *Radical Performances of the African Diaspora in Early Modern Spain*, the categories of "black" and "Blackness" encompass the peoples of the African diaspora *without* having to make attributions of nationality and culture that have been erased from historical records or did not exist in the early modern period.

For instance, is a black African recently brought to the Iberian Peninsula "Afro-Hispanic," "Afro-Portuguese," or "Afro-Iberian"? Similarly, should newly arrived African slaves brought to Spain's many kingdoms in the Americas between the sixteenth and early eighteenth centuries be called "Afro-Mexican," "Afro-Peruvian," or "Afro-Argentine"? Rather than negotiate such tangled thickets in this space, I adopt a simple, albeit problematic (for some), nomenclature: black and black African.

In my translations of habla de negros texts—translating from Africanized Castilian and Africanized Portuguese to English—I will always use the "standard" English variety and will never utilize African American Vernacular English (AAVE) varieties, for the translation of habla de negros language into AAVE is not necessary. As a translator of habla de negros, my task, to echo Benjamin's "The Task of the Translator" (1923), ultimately consists of finding that intended effect upon the language into which I am translating that produces in it the echo of the original.

Units of currency will appear often throughout this book. By the late 1500s, the smallest and most basic unit of currency, against which all other monies of account could be measured, was the maravedi. From the maravedi, I will "translate" the following early modern Iberian monetary units to aid my readers' conversions. The real, worth 34 maravedis, was probably the most common silver coin in circulation. The peso of unassayed or common silver (*plata corriente*) was worth 8 reales, or 272 maravedis (the phrase "piece of eight" is derived from *peso de a ocho reales*). Pesos of assayed silver (*plata ensayada*) were worth the considerably higher sum of 450 maravedis. These values could change over time and from one location to another; by the 1570s, pesos of gold (*oro*) were used less commonly in the Caribbean but held values of approximately 400 maravedis or more. *Ducados*, or ducats, were the equivalent of 375 maravedis, or eleven reales. The silver mark (*marca de plata*) was worth 2,210 maravedis, or sixty-five reales.[5]

INTRODUCTION

The *Habla de Negros* Palimpsest: Theorizing *Habla de Negros*

I begin with a personal anecdote from spring 1999 on the Guadalquivir River in the Arenal district of Seville, Spain, the famous riverfront promenade and slave port heavily trafficked by Portuguese financiers and merchants involved in the auctioning and trading of black African slaves during the reign of Felipe II.[1] On that warm spring day—whose air was perfumed with jasmine and orange blossoms—I was purchasing a snack at a local ice cream shop. Upon exiting the confectionary, a frail elderly lady gently grabbed my shoulder and carefully stated in her *andaluz* Spanish accent while smacking the flesh of her forearm, "aunque no parezca, yo *sí* tengo sangre negra como *tú*; mis bisabuelos y tatarabuelos eran negros con sangre negra" (even though it doesn't appear so, I, in fact, have black blood just like *you*; my great-grandparents and great-great-grandparents were black; of black blood [lineage]). Pointing outward in a circular motion toward the Avenida de la Constitución through the Arco del Póstigo (currently the intersection of Paseo de Cristina and Paseo de las Delicias), as if she were a seasoned tour guide, the woman, whose name I never got that day, continued her quasi-autobiographical narrative by sharing with me that "muchos negros y sus descendientes vivían por toda esta zona aquí por el río Guadalquivir" (many blacks and their descendants lived all over this neighborhood here along the Guadalquivir River).[2] Ever since that day, the brief exchange with that kind *sevillana* stranger has changed the way I see, study, and talk about Seville, the Arenal, and early modern Spain at large. Her captivating comments and bodily movements empowered me to see what is *not* readily available for the eyes to detect regarding Peninsular Spanish ancestry, history, and space, acknowledging the marginalized and overlooked presence of black sub-Saharan Africans living in Iberia since their forcible *and* nonforcible arrival by medieval Islamic occupation forces from the Sudan and Ethiopia.[3]

This anecdote underscores the diasporic arrival and dispersal of black African cultural practices and languages across the Iberian Peninsula beginning in sixteenth-century Seville via Portugal. To put it another way, my anonymous guide's description of the Arenal—its wharves, public squares, and marketplaces—cannot be separated from this book's close examination of African diasporic culture as it manifests in habla de negros speech forms. In the sixteenth century, slaves from Africa, Asia, the Americas, and the circum-Mediterranean world made up a sizeable constellation and conspicuous part of the population of Seville (fig. 1).[4] The city's cosmopolitan atmosphere, global economic glory, and, at other times, rampant structural corruption earned it the ignominious epithet of the "Great Babylon." For example, literary works such as Lope de Vega's play *Servir a señor discreto* (1610/1615) and Luis Vélez de Guevara's prose work *El Diablo Cojuelo* (1641) refer to Seville as the "Gran Babilonia de España." The short-skit interlude *Los mirones* (attributed to Cervantes, 1623) casts Seville as the ancient Assyrian "Nínive," another kind of Babylon, whose infinite black population's Africanized Castilian rumbled in the streets of the Santa María de la Blanca neighborhood.[5] As a metaphorical Tower of Babel (a site used in the book of Genesis in the Hebrew Bible to explain the origin of different languages), Seville speaks to the plausibility of habla de negros language having flourished.[6] When historicizing the demography of Seville's sub-Saharan African population under the reign of Felipe II (1556–1598), I see a clear correlation between Seville's black population and the texts studied in this book that feature this community. (Luis Quiñones de Benavente, Lope de Rueda, Lope de Vega, Miguel de Cervantes Saavedra, Rodrigo de Reinosa, and Simón Aguado are among the authors who set their works in Seville with black protagonists.) The city of Seville and the kingdom at large had a voluminous black population that reached a height of 11 percent. In a one-year period, between 1569 and 1570, 1,100 slaves were sold annually, of whom more than

FIG. 1. Alonso Sánchez Coello, *Vista de Sevilla*, 1576–1600. Oil on canvas, 150 × 300 cm. Museo de América, Madrid, inv. no. 00016.

85 percent were purchased by neighboring cities across Andalusia.[7] Primarily dominated by Portuguese merchants and traffickers of black bodies (aided in turn by intermediary slave traders and buyers from the various kingdoms of Castile), Seville's black African population was ethnically diverse, originating from Angola and the Congo Basin, the Cape Verde Islands, the Kingdom of Dahomey, the Senegambia and its Rivers of Guinea, as well as Mozambique and neighboring Portuguese outposts in East Africa and Goa.[8] The overwhelming presence of blacks and their descendants in Seville gave way to the city's alias as the *tablero de ajedrez*, or chessboard table. For example, Lope's *Servir a señor discreto* references the black-and-white chessboard demographic of the metropolis, while the merchant Alonso Carrillo observes how "Sevilla parecía [como] los trebejos de ajedrez, tanto prietos como blancos" (Seville looked like chess pieces, black as well as white). Luis de Peraza in his sixteenth-century *Historia de Sevilla* renames the city's Barrio Santa Cruz district as the Varrio del Atambor because it was the place where black Africans—enslaved and free—gathered on Sundays to play music and sing.[9] Seville's ethnically diverse population of sub-Saharan Africans recurs in the dramatic and poetic materials examined in this book. Even the Spanish historical drama TV series *La Peste* (Alberto Rodríguez and Rafael Cobos, 2018) recognizes this history and its diasporic imprint on the Iberian Peninsula.[10] I would also propose that Renaissance Seville—as well as other cities of early modern Spain whose prominence ebbs and flows—serves as a source of

inspiration for early modern Spanish writers to capture and explore habla de negros speech forms in their works. This is what I call the habla de negros palimpsest, an oeuvre of cultural and linguistic Castilian Blackness that has been effaced and then modified, or overwritten, by subsequent authors.

The Habla de Negros Palimpsest: Its Genre, Its Corpus

Staging Habla de Negros: *Radical Performances of the African Diaspora in Early Modern Spain* centers African diasporic cultural studies in Spanish literature. It intends to explicate the need for a critical analysis of white appropriations of black African voices in Spanish literary and dramatic texts from the 1500s through the 1700s, when the composition and performance of Africanized Castilian—commonly referred to as habla de negros—were in vogue. The use of Black speech in Spanish literature goes part and parcel with its racialized construction of black Africans in early modern Spain. As linguist John Lipski has argued in numerous studies, "black Spanish must be understood as a linguistic fabrication used as a comic device [that] is a purely literary language."[11] Comic in its objective, with a bountiful representation of purely comical-burlesque aesthetic and dramatic possibilities,[12] Lipski's reading of Africanized Castilian further maintains that its authors portray black characters as "buffoons, mindless dancers, or simple victims of fate" whose habla de negros speech operates as an "exaggerated travesty."[13] André Belo summarizes the scholarly interest in and conclusion of Africanized Castilian (and Portuguese) as follows: "Scholars helped maintain the symbolic violence that was inherent in the use of such a speech: it was a language made by white authors, destined to be heard and/or read by a public dominated by white people, and with an intention of mockery expressing a strong social and racial prejudice."[14]

This book posits an alternative interpretation of habla de negros speech events that disrupts the aforementioned critical reception bestowed on literary appropriations of Africanized Castilian. While acknowledging the compelling research conducted by previous scholars, I aim to revise the dominant discourse they have established. My goal here is to highlight the agentive subject positions of habla de negros speakers and to examine their voices as viable discourses. To be clear, this book is a political project. Over the course of its three chapters, I set into motion a new scholarly precedent and trend that will place at the forefront a paradigm shift for scholars of Iberian studies, Latin American studies, and African diasporic studies. Although some scholars will contend that it is impossible for any white author of habla de negros materials to engage in nonracist characterizations of their black literary creations, the close readings performed throughout this book will suggest otherwise. Regardless of the ideologies espoused by these authors, I argue that their texts do, in fact, render legible the voices and experiences of black Africans in fundamental ways that demand our attention. Rodrigo de Reinosa's "Gelofe, Mandinga"—a poem directed specifically at the black population of Seville—highlights West African aesthetics and culinary practices. In Lope de Rueda's *Eufemia* and *Los engañados*, the black women who populate these dramatic works' intercalated *pasos* sass and subvert their white interlocutors' racist and misogynist epithets. At the turn of the seventeenth century, in 1602, Simón Aguado's *Entremés de los negros* stages the agentive voices of Dominga and Gaspar, who challenge their white masters by interrogating the institution of slavery and its infringement on the marrying of black slaves. Aguado's play is also a foundational work in early modern Spanish theater studies, for it lays the groundwork for other Spanish authors such as Francisco Avellaneda (*Entremés de los negros*, 1622) and Francisco de Quevedo ("Boda de negros," 1643) to explore the theme of black weddings, nuptials, and sub-Saharan African musical traditions and dance in Spain.[15] And even more fascinating are the ways in which practitioners of habla de negros link the language to African dances and music, which I do not treat entirely as a mockery nor an attempt to hypersexualize and denigrate blacks. Rather, when Spanish dramaturgs incorporate black dances and musical traditions—the *guineo*, *gurumbé*, *zarabanda*, and *zarambeque*, to name just a few—into their plays, a new aesthetic and exploration of African diasporic culture comes alive.

Just as much as the critique and deconstruction of "white" literary constructions of habla de negros are undoubtedly valid, my scholarly endeavor in this book is not centered around nor fixated on repeating a scholarly narrative that has tendentiously emphasized the way in which white Spanish poets and playwrights have excoriated Blackness through their putative antiblack stereotyping via habla de negros speech forms. I agree fully with my colleagues that many, if not all, of the extant habla de negros literary works depict black Africans in an artificially hackneyed manner. There is no dispute in their assessment. In this book, however, I seek to shed light on the recurring—*not* exceptional—instantiations where habla de negros texts showcase their black characters acting and speaking with agency and destabilizing the category of Whiteness—culturally, linguistically, and in terms of power relations—altogether. Similar to the scholarly interventions made by race studies scholars in early modern British literary and cultural studies (most notably in Shakespeare studies),[16] my hope is to change how we think about and teach habla de negros texts and the representations of the black body that shape them. Ultimately, this book will revolutionize theoretical conceptualizations and figurations of Blackness in a larger hemispheric Hispanophone purview.

In this book, I channel Black speech through the Bakhtinian paradigms of the carnivalesque and heteroglossia. I turn to these concepts in order to demonstrate how habla de negros texts empower the unwritten speech of their black African speakers. While not always evident in every single habla de negros work, this book aims to highlight the way in which practitioners of Africanized Castilian utilize their black characters to simultaneously reify and contest prevailing stereotypes while also speaking with an inherent expressive power, or heteroglossia, that situates them as subversive, thinking black subjects. If this book illuminates the variety of ways in which Africanized Castilian animates black Africans' agency, empowers their resistance, and highlights their African cultural retentions in early modern Spain, it also calls for a specifically Black and gendered performance theory approach that challenges, revises, and radically reimagines the presence of black Africans' bodily, sartorial, and linguistic Blackness in early modern Spain. My aim herein is to complicate the very apparent antiblack racist stereotyping in which habla de negros texts potentially engage. In three separate case studies, I analyze representations of a motley crew of speakers of habla de negros who illustrate the embodied materiality of Blackness in Castilian dramatic texts. As I show in the next chapter, for example, the black mouth who laughs, sings, and shouts in habla de negros combats the violent desire of white supremacy. In this book, laughter, singing, and Black speech are conjoined as tropes of African diasporic cultural presence and resistance. To that effect, the habla de negros speech forms analyzed herein show blacks speaking with an inherent expressive power that positions them as responsive—rather than merely *reactive*—agents.

The critical analytic and central term stipulated in the book's subtitle—"radical performances"—anchors my ideation of how early modern Spanish dramatic representations of habla de negros speech channel Black performance. Throughout this book, I argue that Black performance theory is a valid framework for reading early modern Spanish cultural and literary renderings of black Africans. What interests me here are the various ways in which habla de negros speech acts allow black expression and black sensibilities to emerge whether there are black bodies present or not. Thomas F. DeFrantz and Anita Gonzalez's intellectually arresting and stimulating volume *Black Performance Theory*, for example, uncovers a history of black performance that assists me in assembling a body of thought to theorize habla de negros language in this book. Zora Neale Hurston's prescient essay "Characteristics of Negro Expression" (1934) immediately comes to mind. Working from her fieldwork observations, Hurston theorizes Negro performance of the American South of the early twentieth century in provocative and unabashed style.[17] Describing Hurston's essay, DeFrantz and Gonzalez highlight the anthropologist's proclamation of Negro talk to be "dramatic" and embodying a characteristic willingness to use "action words"—words that paint pictures—as a stabilizing point of entry to understanding the expressive aesthetics of black language and gesture.[18] For the intents and purposes of this study, I do not treat Hurston's ethnographic findings of black language of the American South as mutually exclusive from Africanized Castilian spoken in early modern Spain and its representation in dramatic texts from that time period.

Each chapter in this book attests to Hurston's most notable quality of Negro Expression: the "will to adorn." Via the will to adorn, I see habla de negros language—as is the case in Hurston's study of African American Vernacular English of the American South—pushing forward toward an unprecedented space of expressiveness. Taking cues from Hurston, we can conclude that black expressive performance—in this context, habla de negros—springs from the need to communicate beyond the limited events of words alone. In addition to black linguistic expression, Hurston's "Characteristics of Negro Expression" highlights dancing, dialect, folklore, and imitation—salient themes I explore in the chapters ahead to animate the highly expressive and performative quality of habla de negros texts. Inspired by Hurston's Negro Expression theory, my close readings in this book allow black performance to be in dialogue simultaneously with itself, the world around it, and the lives of black people.[19]

The radical frame forged in this book underscores Fred Moten's charge stated in his *In the Break: Aesthetics of the Black Radical Tradition* that "the history of blackness is testament to the fact that objects can and do resist.[20] My research is motivated by Moten's theoretical premise that Blackness is "a strain that pressures the assumption of the equivalence of personhood and subjectivity."[21] The "radical" allows me to not only theorize the significance of habla de negros language but, more importantly, to arrive at a wider framework with which to *theorize* literary representations of black Africans in early modern Spanish texts. I employ the concept of "radical" to unabashedly account for this book's methodology and theoretical framework: it privileges and utilizes Africana critical thought, black feminist theory, and critical race theory to analyze and discuss textual representations of black Africans in addition to equally valid and necessary conventional Western approaches, such as those informed by philology. As a scholar whose work is deeply rooted in early modern Iberian studies *and* Africana studies, I enlist the strategies, methodologies, and insights of Africana studies in the service of Early Modern studies—and vice versa. In one sense, this book aims to mobilize corrective interventions to commonly held notions in Early Modern studies and Africana studies, and, in another sense, the project theorizes a synthetic methodology for the Early Modern/Africana studies discursive divide. Following Moten, and echoing Audre Lorde, I conclude by emphasizing my commitment to language and to the power of language in that I am reclaiming—via the prisms of agency, subjectivity, the radical, and black performance—black language that has been made to work against images of blacks and their Blackness in early modern Spain.[22]

*

The habla de negros literary corpus is vast. Over a span of two centuries, from the sixteenth to the eighteenth, more than thirty Spanish writers composed poems and staged plays featuring characters who spoke in habla de negros. In late Baroque and Enlightenment Spain, more than a dozen anonymous works circulated throughout Granada, Huesca, Lucena, and Madrid. In "Para saber todas las ciencias y artes mecánicas y liberales en un día," a chapter from *Libro de todas las cosas* (1631), Quevedo fashions an axiom indicating to his readers how to write (and talk) like a black African: "Si escribes comedias y eres poeta, sabrás guineo en volviendo las *r*, *l*, y al contrario: como Francisco, *Flancico*; primo, *plimo*" (If you are a playwright and a poet, you'll know to use guineo by interchanging *r*'s and *l*'s, and vice versa.[23] Such as Francisco, *Flancico*; primo, *plimo*). The satirist's audience understood the word "guineo" to mean habla de negros speech as well as the popular dance performed at royal feasts and on Catholic feast days. Quevedo's maxim typifies Bantu linguistic influences on early Portuguese and Castilian bozal speech, which involved the change of /r/ > [l]. There are many examples of this shift in early literary imitations of Africanized Portuguese and Castilian, as well as the Portuguese-based creole languages of São Tomé, Príncipe, and Annobón, in which the Bantu contribution was significant.[24] Interchange of /l/ and /r/ in the syllabic onset occurred sporadically in Ibero-Romance, although the shift of /l/ to [r] was much more frequent. In contemporary Andalusian Spanish, the same process occasionally occurs, but never with the frequency found in habla de negros texts.[25] As suggested and popularized by Quevedo's formula (*Francisco* > *Flancico*; *primo* > *plimo*), some stereotyping was involved. However, habla de negros texts should be interpreted not as indicating only the shift of /l/ > [r] among black Africans but also the fact that the opposite change, /l/ > [r], was unremarkable in rustic non-African Castilian.

The habla de negros palimpsest and its literary corpus to which I refer cannot be understood without taking into account the importance of genre—that is, the types of literary works characterized by a particular style, form, and purpose.[26] In prose fiction, narrativized constructions of habla de negros appear in Francisco Delicado's *La Lozana andaluza* (1528), Feliciano de Silva's *Segunda comedia de Celestina* (1534), Gaspar Gómez de Toledo's *Tercera parte de la tragicomedia de Celestina* (1536), Cervantes's exemplary novel *El celoso extremeño* (1613), and Mariana de Carabajal's eighteenth-century novel *La industria vence desmanes*. The most salient literary representations of habla de negros speech forms, however, were composed in poetry and staged in theater. To illustrate the multitude of these materials—borrowing from but also adding to Lipski's "Appendix to Chapter 3: Afro-Hispanic Texts from Spain" in *A History of Afro-Hispanic Language* (2005)[27]—I organize them alphabetically by author:

Poetry:
1. Anonymous: "Romancerillo" (Valencia, 1590), "Gurumbé" (1670), "Aquí za" (Huesca, 1661), "Hagámole plaça" (Huesca, 1661), "Desde Angola benimo" (Madrid, 1676), "¿Flasico? Ziol" (Madrid, 1676), "Tumbalá" (1670), "Ah mi siolo Juanico" (Lucena, 1694), "Con el zon zonezito del zarabuyi (Madrid, 1696), "A Belén han venido" (n.d.), and "Zarambeque" (n.d.).
2. Alonso de Blas y Sandoval: "Aquellos negros que dieron" (1694), "Qué gente, plima?" (1699), and "Azí Flaziquiya" (1701).
3. Ana Caro de Mallén: "Loa sacramental que se representó en las fiestas del Corpus de Sevilla" (1639).
4. Fr. Jesús Casano: "Los negros de manicongo vienes a la Noche Buena" (1709).
5. Francisco García Montero Solano: "¡Ah Flansiquiya!" (1673).
6. Luis de Góngora: "A la 'Jerusalem conquistada' de Lope de Vega" (1609), "En la fiesta de la adoración de los reyes" (1609), "En la fiesta del Santísimo Sacramento" (1609), and "A lo mismo [al nacimiento de Cristo nuestro señor]" (1615).
7. Antonio Navarro: "Los narcisos de Guinea" (1701).
8. Esteban Redondo: "Apalte la gente branca" (1783) and "Los negrillos esta noche" (1783).
9. Rodrigo de Reinosa: "Gelofe, Mandinga" and "Mangana, Mangana" (1501; 1516–20?).
10. Alonso Torices: "Negro de Navidad" (1680).

Theater:
1. Simón Aguado: *Entremés de los negros* (Seville, 1602).
2. Anonymous: *Auto de Tamar* (second half of the sixteenth century), *Égloga al Santísimo Sacramento sobre la figura de Melquisedec* (second half of the sixteenth century), *Entremés de los negros de Santo Tomé* (1609), and *La negra lectora* (1723).
3. Francisco Avellaneda: *Entremés de los negros* (1622).
4. Francisco Bernardo de Quirós: *El regidor* (Seville, 1674).
5. Pedro Calderón de la Barca: *La casa de los linajes, La pandera, La rabia* (Primera parte), *Las carnestolendas, La Sibila del Oriente y gran reina de Sabá* (1650–70), and *La negra* (attributed, Madrid, 1691–1708).

6. Miguel de Cervantes Saavedra: *Los mirones* (Seville, 1623?).
7. Andrés de Claramonte: *El valiente negro en Flandes* (1640).
8. Jaime de Güete: *Comedia intitulada tesorina* (first half of the sixteenth century).
9. Antonio Mira de Amescua: *El negro del mejor amo* (1653).
10. Luis de Miranda: *Comedia Pródiga* (Seville, 1554).
11. Agustín Moreto: *La fiesta de palacio* (1658).
12. Juan Pastor: *Farsa de Lucrecia* (mid-sixteenth century).
13. Luis Quiñones de Benavente: *El borracho, El negrito hablador, y sin color anda la niña*, and *Entremés famoso: Los sacristanes burlados* (1640s).
14. Lope de Rueda: *Comedia de Eufemia, Comedia de Los engañados, Comedia de Tymbria*, and *El coloquio de Gila* (1538–66).
15. Diego Sánchez de Badajoz: *Farsa de la hechicera, Farsa de la ventera, Farsa del moysen*, and *Farsa teologal* (1525–47).
16. Martín de Santander: *Comedia Rosabella* (1550).
17. Antonio de Solís: *Entremés del niño cavallero* (1658).
18. Lope de Vega: *El amante agradecido, El capellán de la virgen, El mayor rey de los reyes, El negro del mejor amo, santo negro Rosambuco, Segundo entremés de los negros de Santo Tomé, La limpieza no manchada, La siega, Madre de la mejor*, and *Vitoria de la honra* (1602–18).
19. Luis Vélez de Guevara: *El negro del seraphín* (1643).
20. Gil Vicente: *Cortes de Júpiter* (1521) and *Floresta de engaños* (1536).
21. Diego Ximénez de Enciso: *Juan Latino* (Madrid, 1652).

In his *Proemio e carta al condestable de Portugal* (Prologue and Letter to the Constable of Portugal), written at the threshold of the Renaissance, Íñigo López de Mendoza, the marqués de Santillana (1398–1458), placed poetry at the epicenter of human affairs: "Las plazas, las lonjas, las fiestas, los conbites opulentos sin ella así como sordos e en silencio se fallan. ¿E qué son o quáles aquellas cosas adonde—oso dezir—esa arte así como necesaria no intervenga e no sirva?" (Public squares, marketplaces, festivals, opulent feasts are as if deaf and silent without it. What are those affairs in which—I dare to say—this art does not intervene as if by necessity?).[28] In this book, I treat poetic constructions of Africanized Castilian as a human affair in the sense outlined by the marqués de Santillana. Habla de negros poetry gives voice to the culture that Renaissance Castilian poets such as Santillana, and those after him during the Baroque period, elevated and rendered. Poetic uses of habla de negros speech forms were so common because of the diversity of Renaissance poetic forms, genres, subjects, and other material factors. When written down, habla de negros poems circulated in manuscript anthologies whose varied formats and contents reflect heterogeneous tastes, goals, and audiences.[29] When printed, the medium of the press transformed verse into commodities of varied commercial and cultural status: from the popular, ephemeral *pliegos sueltos* (chapbooks) to the collected works of an individual nobleman.[30] Most notable examples originate in the Portuguese editor and poet Garcia de Resende's *Cancioneiro geral* (1516) and the chapbooks in verse by Rodrigo de Reinosa (1516–20?) that first depicted the Africanized Castilian spoken by enslaved West Africans, which I discuss more fully in chapter 2.

Circulated in chapbooks and heterogeneous collections such as the *Cancioneiro geral*, a majority of habla de negros speech varieties appeared frequently in *villancicos*. The villancico can be characterized in the following three ways: (1) by its musical character, (2) by its popular origin and appropriation in part by learned poets, and (3) by its restriction to religious settings.[31] I surmise that poets preferred the villancico form over others, not only to express burlesque Blackness via habla de negros speech forms but also to highlight the constitution of "popular" lyric altogether. By "popular," I am referring to the folkloric and musical aspects of lyric that open up a space for poets to define and to derive meaning out of the linguistic and somatic Blackness forged through poetic representations of Africanized Castilian. Such meanings range from, but are not limited to, dynamic "African"-inspired medleys and rhythms to the reliance on a common stock of symbols such as hair, lips, and skin color. These musicalized rhythms and tunes operated as if they were variations on a theme—an illustration of poets' ability to reinvent and riff on "African" sounds such as, for example, "Zambambé," "Zambambú," and "Zanguanga" in the anonymous "Villancico cantado en el real convento de la Encarnación de Madrid en los matines de navidad" (Madrid, 1689). In his recent study titled "El villancico de negro y su pertinente abordaje sociológico y literario," Octavio Páez Granados reveals that the villancico poetic tradition and popular lyric opened up a space for black authorship and the creation of habla de negros poetry's aforementioned African sounds. Citing the hypotheses of José Labrador Herraiz and Ralph DiFranco in their essay "Villancicos de negros y otros testimonios al caso en manuscritos del Siglo de Oro," we learn that many habla de negros villancicos might have been composed by blacks and mulatos who were literate and received formal education while working alongside clergymen and military officials, bankers and merchants, noblemen and noblewomen, monks and nuns, and painters and poets.[32]

Habla de negros speech events epitomize the Spanish Baroque. As Mary Malcolm Gaylord remarks, "Everywhere in Baroque verse contradictory impulses pull simultaneously in opposite directions."[33] If Africanized Castilian is a visceral deformation of "perfect" Castilian, then I turn this interpretation on its head by signaling the way in which poets (and playwrights) of the Spanish Baroque complicate our present-day understanding of Castilian Blackness. Seventeenth-century depictions of habla de negros are inflected by a taste for exaggeration, disproportion, violent contrasts, and paradox. And as such, what manifests in Baroque portrayals of this Black speech is a fascination with a perceived ugliness, deformity, and monstrosity that competes with the lure of hyperbolic beauty and grace. In my theorization of habla de negros, I maintain that its poetic and theatrical constructions demonstrate Spanish writers' ability to portray cultural and linguistic Blackness as a hyperbolic trope of nature's excess. Hyperbolism best characterizes habla de negros because it is a language that represents extraordinary things, experiences, and events. As they skillfully manipulate the literary traditions in which they have been trained by employing literary habla de negros in their own works, Renaissance and Baroque Spanish writers reinvent the art of exaggeration.

Nonliterary examples of Africanized Castilian have also been preserved in Madrid's National Historic Archive under the bureaucratic genre of Inquisition records. Produced by monks, notaries, priests, and scribes (men trained in the writing of bureaucratic of ecclesiastic forms and discourses), this genre recorded and transformed black African voices. At the beginning of the seventeenth century in Granada, an Inquisition testimony given by a black female slave who, speaking in Africanized Castilian, blackmailed her *judeo-conversa* owner: "si tu hacer yr a mí a la inquisiçión, yo diré que tu açotar Christo" (If you report me to the Inquisition, I'll tell them you whip Christ).[34] The language of sorcery and witchcraft—*hechicerías* and *brujería*—also offers insight into the racially gendered framing of language in

Inquisition dossiers. While not exact examples of habla de negros, the bureaucratic (mis)reading of Maghrebi and Morisco women's voices is noteworthy and deserves more scholarly attention. Triply marked by their ethnicity, gender, and speech, scribes often annotated paratextually, on the margins of their parchment, these women's accents and dialects under the guise of "sin dejarse entender" (unable to be understood), "sin menear los labios" (mumbling), or "entre dientes" (muttering).³⁵ Other descriptions of Castilian Muslim women's voices fall under the category of "en lengua arábiga" (in Arabic), reciting the *"hamdululey,"* or invoking the Prophet Muhammad in their language. When inquisitorial scribes speak of this invocation of Muhammad, or the "hamdululey," they are referring to the Arabic phrase that praises and gives thanks to God: *al-ḥamdu lillāh* or *alḥamdulillāh* (in Arabic, الحمد لله). In addition, in conversational Arabic, when one is asked "How are you?," a common reply is "al-ḥamdu lillāh." To that end, while these examples are not habla de negros phrases (nor do I wish to elide them as if they were), they do allow us to imagine those contexts in which Black speech might have been documented by Inquisition scribes. The archive of the Inquisition, and its documentation and prosecution of African-descended and Iberian Muslim women's language, shows how these women molded their voices and stories in response to their audience and circumstances.

The African Diaspora in Early Modern Iberia: What Is Africa to Me?

If the first argument of this book is to highlight the agentive subject positions of habla de negros speakers in literature, then the second argument of this book claims that black populations of early modern Spain actively participated in the formation of a so-called Black Experience that thrived *outside* of Brazil, the Caribbean, and the United States. Historian James H. Sweet's pioneering book *Recreating Africa: Culture, Kinship, and Religion in the African-Portuguese World, 1441–1770* has been instrumental to my theoretical framing of the African diaspora in relation to early modern Iberia. What I find compelling about his work in *Recreating Africa* is its strength in stressing the centrality of the African past in African diasporic studies. Like Sweet, I also argue that resistance among African slaves did not always manifest itself in the ways in which scholars have typically understood their bondage and subordination.³⁶ And by no means do I fetishize black people's agency and resistance to oppression. Historically, in early modern Iberia (as well as in the variety of texts I examine throughout this book), black Africans and their descendants frequently addressed the institution of slavery and its attendant uncertainties and pressures with the most potent weapons at their disposal—not muscle and might but the materiality of clothing, food, hair, makeup, religion and spirituality, and song and dance. These performative embodiments of black expression are deeply embedded in habla de negros speech, and I treat them as evidence for Africans addressing their condition.

Following Sweet's work, I even dare to say that African diasporic cultural survivals and life began in Europe, specifically the Iberian Peninsula, at the start of the initial phases of the Portuguese slave trade from 1441 to 1521.³⁷ I am referring to a diasporic identity formation three hundred years before its typical chronology and on the other side of the Atlantic Ocean. Habla de negros speech forms spoken by black literary characters ultimately exemplify the dispersal of sub-Saharan African linguistic retentions in early modern Spanish texts. In addition to Sweet, my critical stance here is indebted to several historians who have catapulted strong theoretical statements that depart from the broader debate over the emergence of a "creolized" Atlantic world.³⁸ According to Paul E. Lovejoy, a new generation of diaspora scholars whom he calls the "revisionist" school shifts the focus of African diaspora studies away from the explicit study of creolization and toward an emphasis on placing Africans and their descendants at the center of their own histories. I urge readers of this book to include Iberia in their narratives and cartographies of the African diaspora. And as Sweet explains: "Africa arrived in the various destinations of the colonial world in all of its social and cultural richness, informing the institutions that Africans created and providing them with a prism through which to interpret and understand their condition as slaves and as freed peoples."³⁹ I would extend Sweet's assertion here to understand the "colonial world" as including the Iberian context that anteceded the emergence of transatlantic colonial structures. Part of my work on this project is to uncover the various ways in which white literary appropriations, mediation, and reconstructions of habla de negros speech end up, in fact, privileging black African aesthetics, culture, and racial identifications in early modern Spanish literature and society. To avoid static, homogenized notions of an essential "Africa," habla de negros texts make Africa the starting point for the study of Africans in the diaspora, especially during the era of the slave trade. In tracing the trajectory of slaves from Africa to the diaspora, scholars should ultimately chart the processes of social, cultural, and political change from specific African ethnic homelands to slave communities in the colonial Americas and Europe. Ultimately, as a revisionist project, this book does not submit to an ideological scholarly leaning that reduces black literary characters to insignificant stereotypical, monolithic entities.[40] Following Lovejoy's "revisionist" school, my aim is to provide present-day readers with a more holistic portrayal of black Africans and their descendants in Spain. By placing early modern Iberia in conversation with discourses on African diasporic studies, my hope is that readers will appreciate how black Africans and their descendants not only developed but, more importantly, *created* black diasporic communities in early modern Spain.

In the 1920s, the Harlem Renaissance poet Countee Cullen asked: "What is Africa to me?" The diasporic origin of Cullen's question, posed in the name of racially discriminated and socioeconomically disenfranchised blacks in the United States, grounds the diasporic focus of this book. Africa to me—as I invoke Alexandre Dumas's romantic yet contested maxim "Africa begins at the Pyrenees"—begins in Iberia.[41] As a black person of African descent, Alexandre Dumas, père, I surmise, acknowledged this historical fact. My conceptualization and vision of an "African" Spain consists of dark-skinned sub-Saharan Africans who also brought their memories of sub-Saharan Africa with them—memories rooted in cultural, linguistic, and religious traditions and survivals. To be clear, I am not linking the categories of black "Africanness" and "Spanishness" to the Black Legend's propaganda. "Africa," to me, *cannot* be separated from our theoretical conceptualizations and practical (con)figurations of early modern Iberia. To recognize this, we must recall the history of al-Andalus (Islamic Iberia). During the Umayyad dynasty under the Caliphate of Córdoba, for example, black Africans lived and worked as royal bodyguards, emissaries, envoys, and slaves.[42] Since the Almoravid dynasty's trade routes and expansion in the eleventh century, black Africans actively participated in the Almoravid trans-Sahara trade of Akan gold shipments and animals entering the Iberian Peninsula.[43] In the thirteenth century, after Fernando III of Castile's Reconquest of Seville in 1248, Christians first came to possess black slaves, which continued well into the era of the Catholic Monarchs. The presence of black Africans in medieval Islamic Iberia—enslaved and free—offers an alternative narrative that offsets the assumption that the visibility of black lives in early modern Spain began with the Portuguese-initiated Atlantic slave trade. As John Lipski has shown, this complex network of the trading of black bodies and sub-Saharan African materials has a rich cultural and intellectual history that manifests, I argue, in literary representations of habla de negros.[44] When examining the corpus of habla de negros texts, ancient African city-states are named, thereby displaying authors' knowledge of sub-Saharan African kingdoms. For instance, Timbuktu (in habla de negros "Tumbucutu" or "Tambucutú") appears in Simón Aguado's *Entremés de los negros* (1602) and Lope de Vega's *Limpieza no manchada* (1618). An anonymous Nativity carol from Huesca, Spain, circa 1661, uses the word "Malia" to reference the kingdom of Mali.[45] The land of Angola is highlighted in two anonymous texts: a villancico titled "Desde Angola benimo" (Madrid, 1676) and the short-skit play *La negra lectora* (1723). The same ways in which Spain, in its popular perceptions and scholarly conceptions, has been in Saidian terms Orientalized as Europe's exotic Other, this book offers new readings of black historical and literary figures' Blackness that have long been marginalized and studied in opposition to the cultural and literary representations of Iberian Jews and Muslims in medieval and early modern Spain.[46]

I am also indebted to the courageous and rigorous work produced by anthropologist Stephan Palmié. Borrowing from his 2008 collection *Africas of the Americas*, the tentative goal of my book also "indicates the potential of historical and literary approaches that deliberately question the assumption that the 'Africanness' of places, people, and practices represents an objective quality whose presence or absence could be empirically based."[47] In this book, I advocate instead for a systematic focus on the diverse (and sometimes contradictory) ways in which conceptions of "Africa" and "Africanity" are socially deployed in the construction, reflexive validations, or at times critique or rejection of contextually specific modes of identification, forms of practice, collective visions of morally salient pasts, or futures to which the actors we will encounter throughout this book aspire.[48] "To do so," as Palmié notes, ". . . allows us to circumvent an all-too-common tendency which, in the words of Wilson Moses, reduces the 'designation African' to a range of biogenetic meanings associated with 'the *idea* of "blackness" as it has been institutionalized in the history, customs, and legal traditions of the United States' and thereby unwittingly implicates us in the reproduction of essentially racist forms of discriminatory knowledge."[49] Rather, I offer new critical readings about early modern Spanish constructions of black Africans and their Blackness that address "Africa" and "Africanity" as theoretical problems and *not* ontological givens. This approach will therefore pressure, in the most productive and self-interrogating ways, my readers to ask how and to what extent these terms have variously come to take on ethically, morally, and politically salient meanings not only in the African diaspora but also among individuals and groups located on the African continent itself.[50]

Buffoonery Disavowed: Theorizing Habla de Negros

Buffoonery disavowed implies that within habla de negros speech acts exist modes of dissidence, resistance, and self-reflection. Literary depictions of habla de negros need to be theorized because there has been a lack of analysis due to racialized value systems of artistic expression. My subject position as a black scholar born in the United States who has lived in Spain and also identifies both as a Hispanist *and* an Africana studies scholar shapes the way I sense the representation of black lives and voices in early modern Spanish texts. To that end, I turn to critical race theory as a strategy to diffuse meaning and value into the cultural production, embodied materiality, and the playful performativity of Castilian habla de negros.

The madman's speech! I align the implications embedded in such critical receptions of habla de negros language with Michel Foucault's description of how historiography, institutions, and society at large devalue the madman's language and voice. In Foucault's lecture "The Discourse of Language" (1971), he explains that "from the depths of the Middle Ages, a man was mad if his speech could not be said to form part of the common discourse of man. His words were considered [null] and void, without truth or significance, worthless as evidence, inadmissible in the authentication of acts or contracts[.] Whatever the madman said, it was taken for mere noise; he was credited with words only in a symbolic sense, in the theatre, in which he stepped forward, unarmed and reconciled, playing his role: that of masked truth."[51] In addition to the rendering of Africanized Castilian as artifice and fabrication, the ideological forces behind the cultural and literary criticism of habla de negros in Spanish texts treat the representation of habla de negros speakers as mad. And if the language of black Africans, fabricated or not, is indeed a reflection of the madman's verbal antics, I then, in this book, dare to turn the marginalization of the madman's speech on its head in relation to early modern Spanish habla de negros, suggesting it embodies a dialectical and performative masked truth that has the potential to disavow antiblack racism and stereotyping.

All groups of people, not only those "of color," are classed, gendered, raced, and (hyper)sexualized based on *how* they do and do not speak. I submit to the fact that there exist social orders that assign prestige and disrepute to nonstandard(ized) accents, lexicon, and speech forms. Analyzing the role of Arabic in Castilian vernacular, the language that the humanist Antonio de Nebrija sought to codify as the handmaiden of empire in his 1492 *Gramática de la lengua castellana*, Barbara Fuchs calls us to challenge the notion of literary maurophilia in local vernacular.[52] "The social issues of language," as Pierre Bourdieu persuasively argues in *Language and Symbolic Power*, "owe their specifically social value to the fact that they tend to be organized in systems of differences . . . which reproduce, in the symbolic order of differential deviations, the system of social differences."[53] The literary use of habla de negros speech teaches us this. As John Beusterien insightfully remarks, "Despite the tendency to systematize Castilian, [poets] and dramatists created a [black language] filled with inconsistencies and flux."[54] Habla de negros language is the exact site where the terms of economy, language, and race allow us to disassemble a Eurocentric project that theorizes nonwhite Others in depreciating ways. Bourdieu's insights concerning language are rendered evident when we acknowledge that ethnic groups including diverse black Africans, but also Roma people, Basques, Iberian Muslims, Amerindians, and others, are routinely racially marked and marginalized by reference to their forms of "talk(ing)."[55]

In response to persistent critical lacunae in the work of linguists and literary critics, in this book I situate Africanized Castilian as a linguistic site shaped by accents, grammar, and cultural expression that give voice to the historical experiences of diasporic Africans living in Spain. Habla de negros texts provide numerous illustrative examples that indicate black characters positioning themselves as agents who subversively contest the oppressive lot in which they exist, thereby allowing them as black subjects, through their Africanized language, to *have* language, a language that is both symptom and sign of their lived experience. This study seeks to empower subjects whose voices have been rendered nonsensical and characterized as incomprehensible "jumbled baby-babble" or "crude infantile mumble." To this end, Giorgio Agamben's *Infancy and History: On the Destruction of Experience* (1978), on language in relation to animals, humans, and infancy, proves useful. Agamben deploys the term "infancy" in his early work to describe an interim state between our pure state of grace in language, echoing that of the animal, and our acquisition of a voice.[56] An Agambenian reading of linguistic, literary, and philological critical ideations of black literary characters' habla de negros speech as "animallike" and "infantile" will reveal how—when exploring the idea of Africanized Castilian as a type of "animalized" and "infantilized" distortion of Castilian—animals are not, in fact, denied language and, on the contrary, are always and totally imbued with language.[57] My point here is to highlight the subjectivity of habla de negros speakers. "Animals do not enter language," argues Agamben; "they are already inside it."[58] Agamben notes that "if language is truly man's nature . . . then man's nature is split at its source, for infancy brings it discontinuity and the difference between language and discourse."[59] Both the Castilian authors of habla de negros texts and the black Africans who speak it in their works destabilize present-day readers' assumptions about the cultural and literary constitution of black African racial difference in the early modern world. Thus, if "the historicity of the human being has its basis in this difference and discontinuity,"[60] then the white appropriations of Blackness I analyze in this book—which undoubtedly have the potential to dehumanize blacks in violent ways—demonstrate the slippery polymorphousness of racist depictions of blacks in early modern Castilian literature and cultural productions. And because race and voice are elusive and culturally charged and contextual, it is the polymorphous, slippery quality of Black Spanish that I contend will illuminate textual articulations of agency, resistance, and subversiveness in black African cultural expression and modes of speech in early modern Spain. In this book, I aim to demonstrate how the numerous ways in which blacks in early modern Spain speak with a Black language that challenges abjection and diffuses the supposed "power" invested in Western racist antiblack anxieties, stereotypes, and subjective insecurities on which Frantz Fanon comments in "The Negro and Psychopathology" in *Black Skin, White Masks*.⁶¹

Borrowed from the language of economics, Bourdieu uses the terms "market," "capital," and "profit" to describe fields and properties that are not "economic" in the strictest sense of the word. For Bourdieu, "capital" encompasses not only "economic capital" in a limited way (i.e., material wealth in the form of money, stocks and shares, and property) but also "cultural capital" (i.e., knowledge, skills, and other cultural acquisitions) and "symbolic capital" (i.e., accumulated prestige or honor).⁶² To be clear, for Bourdieu the field of cultural production operates on an antieconomic logic. As a *prise-de-position*, the rejection of the economic is viewed as part of a strategy to amass symbolic capital in the literary field. In the case of early modern Spanish poetry in particular, there is a huge tension between the commercial and the need to reject the commercial. So, in truth, very few people actually published their lyric verses—Lope de Vega, for example, is probably the best example with his *Rimas, Rimas sacras, Rimas de Tomé de Burguillos*, and so forth—whereas much of the lyric of Góngora and Quevedo circulated in manuscript form. An aristocratic prudence could be at work too, for the noble class is founded explicitly on the rejection of their own labor. Aristocratic otium is what makes lyric possible. In other words, there was an active discourse in the period that viewed theater as directly commercial in an economic sense—a huge tension apparent in Lope's 1609 academic treatise *Arte nuevo de hacer comedias*—versus lyric poetry, which was overtly anticommercial, restricted mostly to manuscript circulation.⁶³ Lope's success as a dramatist is, in the first instance, of economic significance.⁶⁴

I use the term "capital" to capture the ways in which Castilian habla de negros became a mass-produced commodity in early modern Spanish literature. As an example, let us consider Góngora's poetic battle with Lope de Vega in the sonnet "A la 'Jerusalem Conquistada' que compuso Lope de Vega" (1609):

> Vimo, señora Lopa, su Epopeya,
> e por Diosa, aunque sá mucho legante,
> que no hay negra poeta que se pante,
> e si se panta, no sá negra eya.
> Corpo de san Tomé con tanta Reya.

¿No hubo (cagayera fusse o fante)
morenica gelofa, que en Levante
as Musas obrigasse aun a peeya?
¿Turo fu Garcerán? ¿Turo fu Osorio?
Mentira branca certa prima mía
do Rey de Congo canta don Gorgorio,
la hecha si, vos turo argentería,
la negrita sará turo abalorio,
corvo na pruma, cisne na harmonia.⁶⁵

[Ms. Lope: we saw your Epopee, and, for the love of God, even though it's elegant, there's no black woman poet whom it scares (and if it does frighten her, she's no black lady at all). You've got the body of St. Thomas, but you're more of a Queen (woman). Little black Wolof chick (supposed Knight you were, or maybe a Fante knave): were there no Muses in the *Levante* to laud you? Not even a bitch? Was it all Garcerán? Was it all Osorio? Don Gregorio sings about the King of the Kongo's liar white cousin. And if she is a liar—ornate and pompous as you are—the little black chick will remain a trinket: a black-feathered crow; white as a swan like Harmonia.]

Góngora's fourteen-line sonnet trashes Lope's *Jerusalén conquistada*—subtitled as "Epopeya clásica"—composed in twenty cantos in the *octavas reales* meter. Lope's self-proclaimed "Classic Epic" is a text that was itself written in direct imitation of Tasso's *Gerusalemme Liberata*. Lope's imitation of Tasso thus establishes him within the humanist tradition in terms of the text's content and chosen mode of composition. But as David Quint and others have noted, Lope was a latecomer to the historical position of the Italian Renaissance. Thus, his (bad) imitation of Tasso reveals Lope's rumination on a kind of historical loss and displacement. To that end, Lope's reputation as a writer derives not so much from works in the high style of epic such as the *Jerusalén conquistada* but rather from his extraordinary output as a playwright.⁶⁶

Long-standing rivals, Góngora, in the aforementioned sonnet, monopolizes habla de negros language (Africanized Castilian superimposed with Portuguese *lusismos*, coupled with a quick reference to Fante, an Akan dialect and ethnic group of Ghana) and constructs his image of the black female body (paralleled with Harmonia's bereft white female body and cursed necklace) to benefit him as a superior practitioner of habla de negros. Góngora deploys these tropes of embodied and linguistic Blackness to berate and effeminize his nemesis Lope de Vega. In this context, habla de negros takes on a paradoxical meaning of Bourdieu's "symbolic capital." The paradox is that literary habla de negros accrues a material wealth in the work of Spanish Baroque writers. Even though the poetic battle between Góngora and Lope indeed mocks and capitalizes on habla de negros speech, the very exercise of Góngora's poetic might and deliberate use of Africanized Castilian ultimately transforms it, thus revealing that a concurrent "economic" interest exists in the literary portrayal of black African voices. Just as black bodies are indicative of a genealogy and history of African-based slavery (one that is closely connected to an assortment of economic appraisals, systems, and values), Bourdieu's "economic" value and capital of literary habla de negros parallels that of the economic constitution of (enslaved) black bodies.[67] And just as black bodies are for sale, the *language* uttered from their mouths is also *sold* in poetry and plays.

The ligature between race, language, and the "economic" constitutions of habla de negros allows the speech form to operate as a site of tension in which Castilian writers try to maintain, and at other times alter and mask, their cultural and symbolic capitals. Habla de negros practitioners sustain a rhetoric of cultural capital—knowledge, skills, and language acquisition—that renders black Africans culturally bankrupt because of the so-called deformed language they are made to speak. Bourdieu argues that "the individual [writers] who participate in these struggles will have differing aims—some will seek to preserve the status quo, others to change it—and differing changes of winning or losing, depending on where they are located in the structured space of positions."[68] This means that Castilian authors of habla de negros confront a dilemma—or, as Bourdieu puts it, a "struggle"—as to *how* to portray the Africanized language spoken by blacks. One such struggle appears in Pedro Calderón de la Barca's play *La Sibla del Oriente y gran reina de Sabá* (1634–36), where only one black character speaks in habla de negros and the rest of the cast (primarily black women) speak in a "standard" Castilian. In the play *Servir a señor discreto* (1610/1615), Lope de Vega illustrates the struggle between debasing habla de negros language through mockery and ultimately elevating it. Elvira, a code-switching *mulata indiana* from the Spanish

American West Indies, for example, chooses carefully when (and when not) to speak in habla de negros in the presence of both blacks and whites.

Another aspect of Bourdieu's "economics" metaphor that I employ in my theorization of habla de negros is his corollary motifs of "game," "playing," "winning," and "value." I turn to them in an attempt to make sense of how early modern Spanish writers imagine Africanized Castilian. For instance, habla de negros speech forms sometimes appear randomly in poetry and drama. I read this so-called randomness as analogous to playing a game. Bourdieu asserts that "all participants must believe in the game they are playing, and in the value of what is at stake in the struggles they are waging."[69] The participants here are Spanish practitioners of habla de negros. Their game is *writing* and *plotting* how, when, and where habla de negros speech forms and words will appear and under what circumstances. Africanized Castilian held a prominent place and esteemed popularity among court poets and playwrights, as well as in historical documents that have preserved this language as an archived antechamber of African diasporic culture and language. Habla de negros language was, in fact, alive and breathing on ships docked at trading ports in the Rivers of Guinea of the Senegambia region and cosmopolitan Renaissance urban centers such as Lisbon and Seville. And I argue that Bourdieu's theoretical framing of "game," "playing," and "winning"—demonstrated most notably in Góngora and Lope's poetic battles—offers a critical optic for reimagining how sixteenth- and seventeenth-century Spanish writers represented habla de negros in this context where the stakes were high.

To theorize further the impact habla de negros had on early modern Spanish society, I suggest we also avail ourselves of the concept of "cool" or "Black coolness." My concept of Black coolness can be conceptualized as a European attraction to and fascination with the alterity of habla de negros, its musicality, and the accompanying dance movements and sounds that embody it. My thinking behind Black coolness can also be analogized to the global popularity of hip-hop culture and music. Linguist and hip-hop scholar Marcyliena Morgan states that "[hip-hop] is the preferred music for 67% of Black and 55% of all non-White youth and is steadily becoming a staple of rock performances and recordings."[70] In an analysis of twenty billion tracks, the music streaming company Spotify announced, in an article published by *Complex* on 14 July 2015, that hip-hop is the most listened to genre in the world.⁷¹ Writing on "cool hip-hop blackness" from a sociological perspective, American studies scholar Michael Jeffries, in *Thug Life: Race, Gender, and the Meaning of Hip-Hop*, remarks on how "the dominant narrative of cultural appropriation and absorption of hip-hop into the mainstream avows that white people, and specifically white men, enjoy a voyeuristic relationship with irreverent and spectacularly cool hip-hop blackness."⁷² To be clear, the transtemporal connection I am tracing here between the notoriety of hip-hop culture in non-African-descended communities and the prolific circulation and production of habla de negros in print culture and on stage is the idea that the proliferation of habla de negros occupied a "mainstream" status in early modern Spain. And as a result, the speech form's widespread exposure captured the attention of dozens of writers of varying levels of success as well as their audiences. And it is for this reason I ultimately position Africanized Castilian as "cool" in the eyes of its nonblack consumers and spectators, thus creating an aesthetic and literary culture for the image of habla de negros to be "in vogue" during sixteenth- and seventeenth-century Spain.

As a "cool" cultural and linguistic phenomenon, Africanized Castilian overlaps with Bourdieu's terms "value" and linguistic *habitus*—"the set of dispositions that generate practices, perceptions and attitudes which are 'regular' without being consciously co-ordinated or governed by any 'rule.'"⁷³ The linguistic habitus characterizes the literary production—and the "cool" appeal—of habla de negros language, for the linguistic utterances it constitutes is always produced out of the context and market of the institutions of literature, slavery, and theater. While I do not deny whatsoever that the appropriation of habla de negros by elite (white) male writers such as Góngora and Lope de Vega operated as an effort to dominate this speech form and absorb it into their own poetic enterprises, I, however, propose that the Castilian literary and cultural absorption of habla de negros endows this language with a "value," or "linguistic capital," representative of the ways in which black Africans "incorrectly" spoke Castilian and appear in the early modern Spanish literary canon. Further, I also encourage the comparative study of habla de negros with other marginalized communities' language varieties such as the rustic Leonese *sayagués* (commonly used in the theatrical works of Lucas Fernández and Diego Sánchez de Badajoz, as well as in Sancho Panza's proverbial speech acts in *Don Quixote de la Mancha*),⁷⁴ the language of Roma people (as evidenced in Cervantes's exemplary novel *La*

Gitanilla and Nativity carols performed at La Capilla Real de Granada),[75] and the varieties of Morisco speech forms and *aljamiado-morisco* narrative texts.[76] Ultimately, by acquiring and reproducing these forms of literary and cultural capital, Africanized Castilian challenges and complicates the perception of antiblack discrimination and the infantilized racist buffoonery many critics have insisted on privileging.

The next chapter looks at sixteenth- and seventeenth-century theatrical representations of habla de negros language on early Spanish stages. At the center of this case study is the contention that habla de negros speech cannot be separated from the act and practice of blackface performance. In the analysis of lesser-known works written by playwrights such as Francisco Bernardo de Quirós, Luis Quiñones de Benavente, Pedro Calderón de la Barca, and Simón Aguado (among others), I argue that black skin *acts* in conjunction with the excessively deformed Black corporeality of the bozal's black mouth and the register of the sonic highlighted by "African" dances, lyrics, and songs. The overarching goal therein is to provide readers with a clearer sense of and feel for the performance history—costuming, director's logs, makeup, stage directions, and wardrobe—of habla de negros dramatic works, which will then serve to orient the theatrical performativity of African diasporic language and black bodies in early modern Spain. As we shall see throughout this book, the dances, musicality, and sounds that are directly linked to racial impersonation on early Spanish stages go part and parcel with the performance of habla de negros language.

I

BLACK SKIN ACTS
Feasting on Blackness, Staging Linguistic Blackface

This chapter is an entrée, in its panoply of innuendo and meaning, if you will, that seeks to animate and extract the roles of the black mouth, black dances, and the sonic in the habla de negros texts we examine throughout this book. I argue in this chapter that habla de negros language *cannot* be separated from the act and practice of blackface performance, which I link not only to the bozal slave's black mouth but also to the dances and (sonic) onomatopoeia and vocalization of habla de negros speech forms' signature "African"-inspired, if not also derived, grunts, hums, musicality, sounds, and vocables. The textual repertoire that activates most vividly my rendering of blackface performance in habla de negros texts appears in the *baile*, the *entremés*, and the *mojiganga* subgenres of the teatro breve.

Teatro breve encompasses several forms of theater, some of ancient origin, others newly born, which became satellites of Lope de Vega's redefined and revamped *comedia nueva* (any full-length, three-act play combining comic and dramatic elements).[1] The best known of these is the entremés, the short-skit play (or interlude) performed by members of the troupe between the acts of a full-length *comedia*. "A typical afternoon at the theatre," elaborates Jonathan Thacker, "might begin with music (perhaps the singing of a ballad) to welcome the audience, then continue with a *loa*, which preceded Act 1 of the *comedia*, then an *entremés*, Act 2, a *baile* or *mojiganga*, then Act 3, and the *fin de fiesta* consisting in further music and dancing."² I would also add, although Thacker omits this important tidbit of early modern Spanish theatre history, that Peninsular playwrights often integrated African dances and songs—performed in blackface and sung in habla de negros language—to close out their comedias. Marcella Trambaioli in her 2002 study "Apuntes sobre el guineo o baile de negros: Tipologías y funciones dramática" confirms my point when she insists that "el baile de negros, pues, resulta funcionar como micro-texto significativo, al igual que los cuentecillos, los refranes, las canciones y todo texto 'citado' que los dramaturgos áureos solían intercalar en sus versos"³ (African dance, then, seems to function as an important microtext—just like the short stories, proverbs, songs, and all "cited" texts commonly intercalated in the [theatricalized] verses of Spanish Golden Age playwrights). Félix Lope de Vega y Carpio and Pedro Calderón de la Barca were some of the more well-known seventeenth-century dramatists who inserted the rhythms and sounds of sub-Saharan Africa, as salient microtexts, into their comedias. A notable, yet understudied, example appears in the third act of Calderón's burlesque play *Céfalo y Pocris* (1691), when the play's Giant character comes out on stage to dance the guineo, in a closing mojiganga, with all actors available.⁴

Just as blackface lends itself to the teatro breve's popular elements of carnival and dance forms in the baile, entremés, and mojiganga that unquestionably mock, infantilize, and stereotype racially impersonated black Africans,⁵ I propose in this chapter that we complicate and nuance our critical reception of said racial impersonations by exploring the analytic of how black skin *acts* in the baile, the entremés, and the mojiganga subgenres of teatro breve in seventeenth-century Spain. As I have underscored explicitly in the introduction, at no point does my analysis understand the black body and therefore black subjects—albeit via white appropriation and racial impersonation—to be *without* agency. For I contend theoretically that black skin embodies—via the link I forge between habla de negros speech and blackface performance—with the excessively deformed black corporeality of the bozal's black mouth and the register of the sonic highlighted by "African" dances, lyrics, and songs.

So, what is (black) skin? How does black skin act on early Spanish stages? How do early modern Spanish playwrights experience the black skin of the characters and the white skin of the actors who have "blackened-up"? To borrow Michelle Ann Stephens's tantalizing explanation:

> The skin provides a boundary between self and world that serves as both an entryway to the outside world and an enclosure of interior space. It provides us [and the sixteenth- and seventeenth-century Spanish dramatists studied in this book] with our most immediate, sensual engagement with the world and others through touch, and yet, it is often the organ we think about the least, invisible and taken for granted. The skin we see, upon which so many signs of difference can be projected and inscribed—tattoos, skin colors, ornaments, birthmarks, scars—does not feel the way it looks; no matter how different two people may look their skins feel virtually the same. The skin reminds us of ourselves in a way that differs from how we think about ourselves in the abstract; the skin brings us back in touch with ourselves, literally, as bodies.[6]

What is fascinating about early modern Spanish dramatic representations of black skin—as constructed by blackface practices and the habla de negros speech acts that activate them aurally—are the recurring tropes of feasting on and performing "African"-derived dances, music, and sounds that, on the one hand, rely on the theatricalized black skin to entertain adequately and, on the other hand, to fortify the success of its convincing entertainment to the audience enjoying its blackface performance. In an African diasporic context, the skin operates as a master signifier for the particularity of race. It is the object produced by what Frantz Fanon and Paul Gilroy call "epidermalization."[7] It is the sign for race understood purely as a scopic sight and the skin as the object of a specularizing gaze. And it is to these scopic signs and specularizing gazes of blackface performance on early Spanish stages that I conjoin the sonic reverberations of habla de negros speech forms' signature "African"-inspired, if not also derived, grunts, hums, musicality, sounds, and vocables.

Before Blackface: Casting Black Actors on Early Spanish Stages

While I concentrate, in this chapter, on the blackface performance of black characters on early Spanish stages, it would be responsible of me to point out first that not all theatrical representations of black Africans occurred as racial impersonation. Comedia historian José María Ruano de la Haza, for instance, argues that it would not be surprising that sixteenth- and seventeenth-century theater companies hired black African actors.[8] To support his claim, Ruano de la Haza, citing Luis Fernández Martín in *Comediantes, esclavos y moriscos en Valladolid: Siglos XVI y XVII*, tells us that "in 1585, Antonio Torres, a Portuguese trader in linens and lingerie from Lisbon, sold a black female slave (either 19 or 20 years old) named Esperanza to the *madrileño* playwright Bernardino Velázquez."[9] Relying on demography and the historical record of Seville's large sub-Saharan African population between the sixteenth and seventeenth centuries, Vern Williamsen insists that actual black actors could have been cast to play the roles of black characters, in particular that of Juan de Mérida in Andrés de Claramonte's *El valiente negro en Flandes*.[10]

But even more compelling is the role of the Portuguese black actress cast in the Conde de Villamediana's *La Gloria de Niquea* on 15 May 1622, Day of the Pentecost, in Aranjuez to celebrate Felipe IV's birthday and ascension to the throne (even though he had been crowned the year before and the royal court was still mourning the sudden death of Felipe III) at the age of seventeen.[11] Villamediana set his *La Gloria de Niquea* at the Jardín de la Isla—an island on the Tagus River located on the premises of the Aranjuez royal gardens—whose preparations took three months to complete. Villamediana collaborated with the Italian captain and engineer Julio César Fontana to design the work's portable wooden stage and to transform the palace into a Renaissance wonderland in order to capture and recreate the play's medieval and mythological themes. In a sense, present-day readers can liken this theatrical production's extravagance and appeal to the audience's senses (music, painting, poetry, sculptures, and singing) to a Broadway show or an opera performance—similar to what we find in the theater of Calderón de la Barca. Inspired by Feliciano de Silva's *Amadís de Grecia* (Cuenca, 1530) and *Florisel de Niquea* (Valladolid, 1532), *La Gloria de Niquea* extols, on the one hand, and lauds, on the other hand, Felipe IV as a new (mythological) Apollo who will inaugurate a new and glorious Golden Age of Spanish imperial reign as (knightly) Amadís de Grecia whose shield will reflect rays of (sun)light:

> Cuarto planeta español,
> luz de uno y otro polo
> del árbol sale de Apolo
> Dafne a ser Clicie en tu Sol. (vv. 252–55)[12]

[Fourth Spanish Planet:
Light from one and another pole
from Apollo's tree emerges
Daphne to be Clicie in your Sun.]

A grand-scale production, the showpiece casts the noblewomen and girls of the Aranjuez court as its actresses, among them María de Guzmán (youngest daughter of the Count-Duke of Olivares, prime minister and royal favorite to Felipe IV); Leonor de Guzmán (Olivares's sister); the Tábara sisters, Margarita and Francisca; Margarita Zapata (most likely related to the powerful Cardenal Zapata); and the Princess (*Infanta*) Margarita Teresa (daughter of Felipe IV, central figure of Diego Velázquez's famous *Las Meninas* painting, and none other than the one who protagonized Niquea, the play's queen and goddess of beauty [la Hermosura]). And of primary concern to our interests in this section on black actors on early Spanish stages, Villamediana casts Felipe IV's African-descended dwarf Don Miguel Soplillo as his shield (*escudo*), dressed in "trage antiguo, negro y plata" (black and silver ancient garb) (fig. 2).[13] Finally, portraying the Night (la Noche) in *La Gloria de Niquea* is an unnamed black actress from Portugal. Antonio Hurtado de Mendoza describes her wardrobe as follows:

> Salia la Noche que la representaba una portuguesa negra, excelentíssima cantora, criada de la Reina, vestida con saya entera de tafetán negro, sembrada de estrellas de plata, y manto derribado de los ombros, quaxado de las mismas estrellas.... Baxaba en una nube resplandeciente la Aurora que la representaba la señora doña Maria de Aragón, vestida con basquiña y vaquero de tela de plata blanco forrada en encarnado, y quaxado de perlas, y un manto de velo de plata sembrado dellas.[14]

> [Portrayed by a Portuguese black woman, Night emerged. An exquisite songstress and maid to the queen, she was draped completely in black taffeta that fell from her shoulders. The garment she wore was glittered with embossed silver-plated stars.... Descending on a gleaming cloud came Aurora (Dawn), portrayed by Doña María de Aragón, dressed in a *basquiña* of white-silver serge with red lining, embossed with pearls and fitted with a silver veil beaded in pearls.]

FIG. 2. Rodrigo de Villandrando, *El príncipe Felipe y el enano Miguel Soplillo*, ca. 1620. Oil on canvas, 204 x 110 cm. Museo del Prado, Madrid, PO1234.

The black actress who performed in *La Gloria de Niquea* allegorizes the personification of the Night. A conventional reading of her nightly Blackness would claim that Villamediana recreates and positions it in the mind of the aristocratic audience, appealing to their perceived racially gendered anxieties, fears, and exoticism. But in addition to this interpretation, I find that the material conditions of her astral, chromatic, and somatic Blackness in the play allow for the possibility of the actress's black beauty and humanity to manifest not only visually but also rhetorically through the sound of her voice. Her sonorous voice and skill as a singer—"excelentíssima cantora"—coupled with her stellar wardrobe, gilded in embossed stars, must not be downplayed in our scholarly reading of her, for these attributes aid in the simultaneous construction and elevation of her black beauty and humanity.

Theorizing Blackface on the Early Spanish Stage

Blackface performance in early modern comedia studies is not only undertheorized, but the corpus of dramatic works that feature it is also understudied and obscure. I am both indebted to and building on John Beusterien's pioneering work on blackface performance in *An Eye on Race: Perspectives from Theater in Imperial Spain*. Beusterien is the first scholar to reconstruct a theater history of blackface performance on early Spanish stages. He argues that "blackface performance needs to be understood through Franz [sic] Fanon's perspective rather than read as a performance of Spanish otherness in the psychoanalytic sense."[15] "In light of the study on blackfacing in the U.S. cultural history over the past years," he legitimately adds, "... it is surprising that no one has examined the practice of blackfacing in the imperial Spanish context."[16]

Beusterien's critical attention to blackface in imperial Spanish theater has helped me to think through and thereby continue the groundwork he has laid on the subject. In this chapter, I aim to shed further light on *how* blackface activates and thus catalyzes a theoretical reading of habla de negros speech via blackface performance on early Spanish stages. I am less interested in rehearsing the conventional conclusive analysis that blackface abjectly denigrates black people—which, to be clear, I do not negate or wish to subdue—but rather implicates the history of Whiteness and its white gaze, whose cultural, ideological, and racial hierarchies become sustained by the very racist mockery and stereotyping of blacks inaugurated by blackface performance itself. Echoing Bridget Orr's sentiment in *Empire on the English Stage, 1660–1714* that critics have approached black characters in seventeenth-century drama with a too "static view of race," I also maintain that the theatricality of black characters served a primary importance in negotiating the increasing "absolute difference" of black characterization and its relationship to Spanishness and Whiteness.[17]

Blackface performance on early Spanish stages parallels blackface minstrelsy of the mid-nineteenth century in US-American popular culture. Demonstrating "Manichaeanism at the heart of minstrelsy," I highlight critic

Saidiya Hartman's work in *Scenes of Subjection: Terror, Slavery, and Self-Making in Nineteenth-Century America*, where she argues, "[Blackface minstrelsy] was the division between races. The seeming transgression of the color line and the identification forged with the blackface mask through aversion and/or desire ultimately served only to reinforce relations of mastery and servitude."[18] Hartman illuminates the ways that minstrelsy posited multiple and yet mythically separate and competing bodies in the blackface figure. This duality, as I see it manifest in early modern Spanish blackface practices, is frequently reproduced and reinforced through the distillation of racially impersonated black-(faced) Africans' diasporic dance, music, sounds, and print culture (I am specifically thinking about the Cromberger woodcuts of the fifteenth and sixteenth centuries, which depicted their Blackness and genealogical ties to "Guinea," or sub-Saharan Central and West Africa).

In this study's implication and indictment of Whiteness and its gaze (specifically the performance of white men masquerading as black caricatures whose blackface act is therefore controlled and mediated by the playwright), I am underscoring blackface performance's promotion of "white self-exploration" through what Hartman identifies as the "elasticity of blackness and its capacious affects" that led to an inevitable method of performance that depended on containing difference and dissonance in one (acting) body.[19] To explicate my overarching claim that habla de negros cannot be separated from blackface performance, I am establishing a theoretical premise that we can, in fact, productively resituate scholarly criticism on blackface performance on early Spanish stages. It is my goal herein to disentangle the knotty assumptions and investments in some comedia studies scholars' tendentious overemphasis on the racist mockery and stereotyping of habla de negros and its representation of blacks and their Blackness in Spanish early modernity. My proposed reframing of early modern Spanish blackface—as I will uncover in the pages ahead—focuses on the form's material and sonic qualities: (1) its cosmetic practices and technology, (2) its "Africanized" dances and sounds, and (3) its hyperbolic representation of the black mouth. In doing so, I am relying on blackface—and the various "Africanized" sounds that accompany it—as the epitome of theatrical excess, a proxy for exhibiting the linguistic excess of habla de negros for early modern Spanish actors, playwrights, and theatergoers. This "excess," rooted in the mythical black body, ultimately provides the crucial link between blackface performance in teatro breve.

Prêt-à-porter! Costuming Race, Wearing Blackface

The costume of Blackness proved difficult to remove from conceptions of actual black people, those for whom Blackness seemingly comes prêt-à-porter.[20] Staging somatic Blackness on early Spanish stages—or instructing an actor to blackface through costumes and makeup—was indicated in a play's stage directions. What the function of these stage directions shows us is that blackface performance then becomes an artfully perfected staging of Blackness that takes form in the blackface performer's facial expressions, hand movements, gait, and other forms of body language that are particularly expressive.[21] In this sense, race functions as a costume that could be put on and taken off but never really abandoned. The idea of racial characteristics functioning like attire is reinforced by the fact that early stage blacks actually put on black costumes, using makeup, masks, gloves, and other fabric to mimic the blackness of skin.[22] Writing about the actor's body and racial impersonation on the Shakespearean stage in her essay "Shakespeare, Other Shakespeares and West Indian Popular Culture: A Reading of the Erotics of Errantry and Rebellion in *Troilus and Cressida*," postcolonial studies critic Curdella Forbes notes how "the moving actor's body negotiates relations among multiple levels of consciousness and experience," and Virginia Mason Vaughan adds that the actor then "feeds upon the audience's responses, creating 'kinetic energy' in the playing space."[23] Masquerading as black caricatures speaking in habla de negros language, the moving (white) actor's body then encapsulates Hartman's rendering of blackface as embodying "grotesque bodily acts like rolling eyes, lolling tongues, obscene gestures, [and] shuffling."[24] In order to achieve the grotesque bodily act observed by Hartman, I argue that the cosmeticized practice of staining the skin with darkening agents such as burnt cork or soot characterizes cultural obsessions with the physical metamorphoses of blackface practices on early Spanish stages.

Like early American minstrelsy show productions, early modern Spanish blackface performance valorized a grotesque humorous and often erotic exhibition of racial transformation, structuring entertainment elaborately around the titillating display of bodies in distortion and the corporeally transfigured white male figure—especially demonstrated by the high number of blackface plays featuring black women leads.[25] (On the opposite end of the spectrum, in the practice of whiteface, the application of flour was used to whiten the skin of the actor.²⁶) Juan Cortés de Tolosa's 1620 *Lazarillo de Manzanares* (reprinted in Madrid, 1901) illustrates an uncanny transatlantic and cross-temporal overlap with the image of the *commedia dell'arte* figure Ganassa's grotesque blackface act: "Era tan negro como mis culpas; y como los dientes fuesen muy blancos y los labios colorados, y lo demás tan negro, parecía riéndose Ganasa" (He was just as black as my sins, and as his teeth were so white and his lips so red, and the rest of his face so black, it seemed Ganassa was laughing).²⁷

*

In 1657, the Dutch painter Karel Dujardin (1626–1678) in *Les Charlatans italiens* depicts a commedia dell'arte show displaying Ganassa's blackface performance (white teeth, pronounced red lips, and playing a guitar), which operates as a visual foil to Cortés de Tolosa's Spanish picaresque description of the blackfaced Ganassa in *Lazarillo de Manzanares* (fig. 3).²⁸ Dujardin's painting is important to this study because it confirms for early modern Spanish comedia studies scholars and students that blackface performance in early modern Spain shared similar modes of textual and visual representation that must not be ignored.

Dujarin's painting, like Cortés de Tolosa's narrativized image of blackface, evidences the cosmeticized practice of transfiguring the blackface performer into a visceral spectacle. I see this aspect manifesting explicitly in early Spanish theater stage directions' use of the verb *teñir* (to dye or to darken [in color]). The Real Academia Española defines the verb "teñir" as follows: "(1) Dar cierto color a una cosa, encima del que tenía; (2) Dar a algo un carácter o apariencia que no es el suyo propio, o que lo altera; (3) *Pint.* Rebajar o apagar un color con otros más oscuros" ([1] To give a certain color to a thing, on top of what it already has; [2] To transfer to something a character or appearance that is not its original, or that alters it; [3] In painting, to mute or to cancel out a color with other darker ones).²⁹ As Beusterien notes, "Many plays explicitly put blackfacing as part of the stage directions,"³⁰ and in those instructions, I would like to add, appear lexical variants of the word "teñir." In Luis Vélez de Guevara's play *Virtudes vencen señales* (ca. 1620) (*Virtues Overcome Signs*), the actor is instructed to come out "teñida la cara de negro" (the face dyed, or stained, black).³¹ Manuel Coelho Rebelo's 1658 archival

FIG. 3. Karel Dujardin, *Les Charlatans italiens*, 1657. Oil on canvas, 45 × 52 cm. Musée du Louvre, Paris, inv. no. 1394.

document housed in the National Library of Spain, *De dos alcaldes y el engaño de una negra* (*Two Mayors and Their Trick on a Black Woman*), indicates that the actress comes out backstage with her face dyed black ("sale en lo alto la señora con la cara teñida de negro").[32] The scenographic presence of *teñir* in these stage directions shows how blackface performance negotiates a duality between embodied cosmetic practices—that is, blackening up the white body with burnt agents, dyes, and ink—and the technological modernity inscribed within them therein.

The materials of and recipes for cosmetic Blackness were often not complex preparations. To blackface white actors, professional theaters used pigments made of *betún* or *zulaque*—consisting of materials ranging from burnt cork and ivory, an assortment of gums, as well as coal and charcoal— to which bases of animal fats, dyes, egg whites, grease, tallow, and water

BLACK SKIN ACTS 37

were added. In addition to the Real Academia Española's aforementioned definitions of teñir, as I relate them to blackface makeup, I am also inclined to include the application of ink (*el tinte*) to circumscribe the cosmeticized practice and technological aspect of blackface performance. In the sixteenth- and seventeenth-century Spanish literary imaginary, ink profoundly impacts the ways in which the corporeality of sub-Saharan Blackness is codified. In Francisco de Quevedo y Villegas's *romance* "Boda de negros" (1643), line 12—"algodones y tintero" (cotton and the inkwell)—exemplifies Quevedo's metaphorical allusion to material culture and slavery.[33] The plural form of "algodones," as explained in the *Diccionario de Autoridades*, refers to material fabrics such as silk and wool. Metonymically, "tintero" (inkwell) analogizes the color of ink to black skin, which facilitated a logic vetted within white actors and playwrights to produce their mutated black-faced bodies. "Tintero," I argue, highlights Quevedo's knowledge of imperial Spain's deep investment in sub-Saharan African slave trading. The poet satirizes Blackness, through the motif of ink, by way of alluding to the proverb "sobre negro no hay tintura" (on top of black [color or persons] there is no [blackness of] ink), as stated in Sebastián Covarrubias's 1611 *Tesoro*.[34] Together, Covarrubias's refrain and Quevedo's passage from "Boda de negros" call into question an issue of ontology as perpetrated through what is most difficult to correct: the bad temperament (*mal genio*), ugly condition (*natura; natural; naturaleza*), and distasteful ways customarily aligned with people of African ancestry. Quevedo's usage of cotton (*el algodón*) and ink (el tinte) addresses larger issues related to material culture—the production and importation of goods produced under specific market relations, for example, that then are assigned value within a system of exchange—and its role in transatlantic slavery. Printing houses such as the one owned by the Cromberger family of Seville had black slaves work with inks and fabrics for its printing tasks (fig. 4).[35] Quevedo's symbolic triangulation of black bodies, cotton, and ink demonstrates the poet's critical and shrewd ability to liken Blackness to the imperial legacy of transatlantic European imperial mercantilism and commerce.

I do not see this history as mutually exclusive from the performative enterprise of blackface on early Spanish stages. "It is this shared field of blackface performance, tattooing, writing, and printing," writes Miles P. Grier, "that I call *inkface*."[36] "By relating the histories of racial thought and

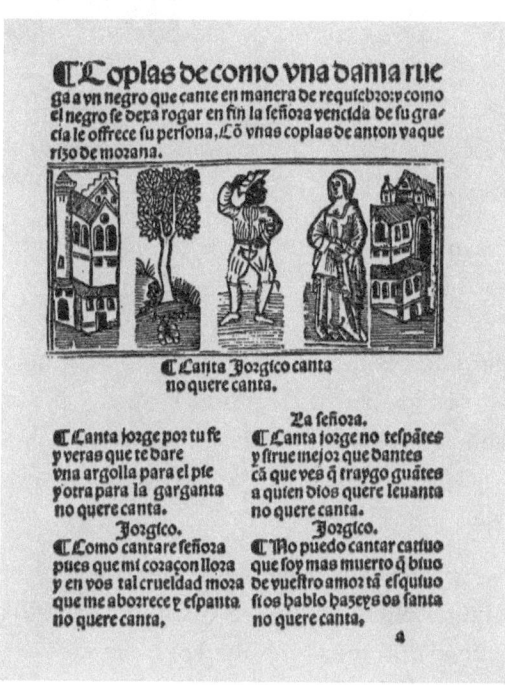

FIG. 4. Woodcut from the broadside *Coplas de como una dama ruega a un negro que cante en manera de requiebro* (Seville: Cromberger, early 1500s), fol. 1.

the technologies of reading and writing," Grier rightfully contends, "the inkface concept enables a rich account of performances of literacy as rituals that invented an elastic racial category of illiterate, legible blacks."[37] Grier's brilliantly perceptive inkface terminology also manifests in my analysis of Góngora's poetic representation of black female beauty and humanness in the *letrilla* "En la fiesta del Santísimo Sacramento" (1609).[38]

Emphasizing the makeup article of eyeliner, or kohl, Góngora underscores the power of black beauty through cosmetics, fine clothing, and the allegorical exegesis of the Song of Songs's well-known message: "I am black but beautiful." The poet's staging of cosmetics' ideological and rhetorical formulations illustrates how black women construct their own racial identity through the subversive assertion of their natural beauty and humanity, specifically by reclaiming cosmetic practices and stylizations of the body typically available to European women. Góngora rehearses the materiality of cosmetic Blackness, via a metatheatrical blackface performance, in "Santísimo Sacramento," set in the Cathedral of Córdoba during Corpus Christi festivities sponsored by Bishop Diego de Mardones. To support this claim, I begin with Covarrubias's dictionary entries on "alcohela" and "alcohol" from his *Tesoro*:

> ALCOHELA. Nombre arábigo diminutivo *quhiletum*, negrillo, del verbo *quehale*, que vale ser negro.[39]
>
> [The diminutive Arabic name for *quhiletum*, black in color, from the verb *quehale*, which means (to be) black.]
>
> ALCOHOL. Es cierto género de polvos, que con un palito de hinojo teñido en ellos le pasan por los ojos para aclarar la vista y poner negras las pestañas y para hermosearlos. Y es así que con el alcohol parece agrandarse los ojos, y por eso le llaman *plathyophthalmon*, producidor y dilatador de los ojos.[40]
>
> [KOHL. Is a kind of powdery substance with which a small stick of dyed fennel is used to outline and highlight the eyes and darken the eyelashes for beautification. And thus with the kohl, the eyes are enlarged and widened; that is why they call it "*plathyophthalmon*," the producer and enhancer of eyes.]

"En la fiesta del Santísimo Sacramento" contains only two very short lines that reference cosmetic application: "Alcoholemo la cara / e lavémono la vista" (vv. 3–4) (Let us make up [blacken] our faces with kohl liner and wash our eyes [white]). Yet in these poetic statements resounds, as I will argue henceforth, Góngora's strategy for underscoring larger ideological perceptions of Blackness, cosmetics, gender, and slavery—perceptions that dramatize, in poetic terms, the paradoxical belief that black beauty is undesirable yet at the same time functions as a sign of spiritual beauty.[41]

Góngora's use of the word "alcohol" is revealing. To speak of cosmetic adornment, he could have chosen a noun such as "afeites" (makeup; cosmetics) or the verb "pintar" (to paint). But instead he turns "alcohol" into a verb—"alcoholar"—in order to reproduce a form of cosmetic representation that, on the one hand, exaggerates black beauty—in hyperbolic form as an effective reading of "alcoholemo la cara"—and, on the other, creates a racially charged textual production when examined from a material perspective. The fine powder antimony sulfide, also known as "alcohol," is slathered on top of black skin to blacken it even more. It is important to note that the circulation of the words "tinte" and "tizne"—ink—also plays a central role in early modern Spanish writers' textual productions of material perspectives on cosmetic representation in relation to bodily perspiration, as conveyed in Clara's abject racialized claim in lines 24 and 25: "Mas tinta sudamo, Juana, / que dos pruma de crivana" (But we sweat more black ink, Juana, than a scribe's two quills). The same materials used to make black ink—alum and galls—figured prominently as ingredients in cosmetic recipes and preparations for darkening both black and white skin.

"Alcohela," as defined by Covarrubias, and as an etymological variant of "alcohol," points to a suggestive reading of Góngora's canny usage of "alcohol" to describe Juana and Clara's cosmetic work. Covarrubias tells us that "alcohela" literally means *to be* black. In the opening lines of "Santísimo Sacramento," Góngora has his two black female characters—particularly through Juana's voice—announce their racial blackness by physically blackening their faces with "alcohol." This is what I regard as Góngora's cosmetic ontology for black women. Góngora's cosmetic production of race manifests itself in what might be called cosmetic subversion—that is, black women's subversive ways of asserting their racial identities by reclaiming cosmetic practices and material culture. The poet's inversion of the verb "alcoholar," through the rhetorical figure of chiasmus, for example, is a noteworthy example of this cosmetic subversion. Instead of the expected "alcoholemo *la vista [los ojos]* / e lavémono *la cara*" (vv. 3–4; emphasis added) (Let us make up [blacken] our *eyes* with kohl liner and wash our *faces*), Juana presents a different model—one opposite to that of white women—that is, blackening the face with a kohl utensil and washing away the whiteness from their eyes. My reading of Juana and Clara's "incorrect" way of adorning themselves suggests possibilities of building on other scholars' considerations of Góngora as a Baroque poet who redirects Petrarchist codes. As Ignacio Navarret argues, "[Góngora] must be taken into account, for his redirection of the Petrarchist tradition subverted its canons to the point that they were nearly redefined."[42] If in his lyric love poetry Góngora is already subverting the Petrarchist codes, canons, and topoi in the way Navarrete describes, "Santísimo Sacramento" goes even further, completely turning them on their head.

Góngora defends black beauty by indirectly contrasting its naturalness with the facial cosmetics typically linked to white women. Although the cosmetic practices of white Spanish women do not appear in "Santísimo Sacramento," I would argue that the poem does, in fact, reference them indirectly by highlighting black beauty through superimposing black-colored cosmetics—as both a satirical questioning of and an alternative ideal to white beauty—in order to praise the *plainness* of black skin as that which is true and valuable, for it is not painted white. Góngora leads by example, in that he disavows his fellow contemporary poets' and playwrights' tendentious measures to denigrate and tease black women as "*galguinegras*" and hideous harlots.[43] Nor does Góngora's depiction of blacks as simple and plain perpetuate the reading of the happy-go-lucky bozal simpleton stereotype overemphasized by scholars. Instead, Góngora's poetic representation of Juana and Clara's cosmetic subversion upholds black women's beauty as exemplary in comparison to the received wisdom that warned against the adulterous and dangerous effects of cosmetics on white women.

Cosmetic application, according to the anticosmetic tracts propagated by the moralists and theologians of the time, betrays the natural beauty God supposedly bestowed upon women. In early modern Spain, for example, moralists, literary figures, and theologians alike perceived (white) women's use of cosmetics to be a peculiarly feminine vice. Like the Stoics and early Christian theologians previously mentioned, Juan Luis Vives, in his *De institutione feminae christianae* (1524), condemns the practice of face-painting in both England and Spain by ascribing diabolic origins to it. Vives's Spanish translation *Instrucción de la mujer cristiana* (1528) cautions that "los ángeles malos . . . enseñaron alcoholar los ojos, arrebolar la cara, enrubiar los cabellos y trastocar toda la naturaleza y forma del guesto y cuerpo" (bad angels instructed [women] how to outline their eyes in black pencil, to put on rouge, to bleach their hair, and to disturb the entirety of Nature's bodily and facial form).[44] In the eleventh chapter of *La perfecta casada* (1583), Fray Luis de León also berates those women who waste "tres horas afilando la ceja, y pintando la cara, y negociando con su espejo que mienta y la llame hermosa" (three hours threading their eyebrows, painting their faces, and negotiating with their mirror, who lies by calling them beautiful).[45] Góngora engages his contemporaries' anticosmetic sentiments by way of Juana and Clara's unseemly application of black eyeliner to accentuate their plain black skin.

Plain black faces—either without makeup or cosmetically adorned (blackfaced) with black-colored makeup—inadvertently buttress the anticosmetic tradition propelled by Christian apologists since antiquity. Tertullian's "On the Apparel of Women," for instance, associates cosmetics and hairdressing with deceitful devilish deeds that betray the very roots of Christian devotion. Citing Tertullian, de León, in his *La perfecta casada*, warns, "Salid, salid aderezadas con los afeites y con los trajes vistosos de los Apóstoles. Poneos el blanco de la sencillez, el colorado de la honestidad; alcoholad con la vergüenza los ojos, y con el espíritu modesto y callado" (Go forth to meet those angels, adorned with the cosmetics and ornaments of the Prophets and Apostles. Let your whiteness flow from simplicity, let modesty be the cause of your rosy complexion; paint your eyes with demureness, your mouth with silence).[46] Góngora echoes Fray Luis's caution against the dangerous and alluring subject of cosmetic excess by focusing on black women's unadorned black faces. The *negras alcoholadas* of the poem must be modest and simple, for they must adequately prepare their bodies for Christ on the Corpus Christi feast day. If Juana and Clara's blackened faces symbolize paradoxically an ideal of modesty and simplicity that is traditionally referenced through Whiteness, then the cosmetic ontology of Juana and Clara sustains itself.

Black skin color operates as a literary trope that supports anticosmetic discourse, especially when black women are using cosmetics to make their skin blacker.[47] Aurelia Martín Casares's analysis of the word "negro," and its link to an inalterable, stable human condition, grounds historically the simplicity and naturalness that the cosmetic alcohol provides for Juana and Clara as black women in my reading of "Santísimo Sacramento." The quote also nods to a larger anticosmetic project that, as the Gongorine text underscores, alludes to the durability of Blackness. In relation to the black body and black beauty (especially a hyperbolically cosmeticized, *blackfaced* beauty), Blackness as a concept is durable because it is not ephemeral or susceptible to decay (especially if Spanish Baroque society understands the black body to be resilient and robust under domestic servitude and enslavement).

Ultimately, in arguing that in "Santísimo Sacramento" Góngora treats cosmetic adornment as a multilayered hyperbole (which Góngora constructs in two ways: [1] by the black-colored alcohol superimposed over Juana and Clara's black skin and [2] by the hyperbolic habla de negros language they speak), I am not suggesting that Góngora depicts the image of cosmetics vis-à-vis Juana and Clara in order to exacerbate xenophobic fears among his audience, although anxieties surrounding the so-called racial Other in early modern Spain certainly recur as a salient discursive element in Renaissance-Baroque texts and treatises. Instead, his representation of cosmetics in the poem addresses cultural forms and practices that differ from those to which early modern Spanish society might be accustomed. Nor does Góngora's portrayal of Juana and Clara communicate the notion of their face painting as a desire to hide their Blackness, which would implicitly categorize their souls as strange and deformed.

Just as blackface performance on early Spanish stages embodies the cosmeticized practices of staining the skin black with dyes and ink, I reiterate the salient role of the costume in early modern Spain's material archive of the *vestuario teatral*, or the theater dressing room, to trace the performance history of blackface on early Spanish stages. As I argued before that race functions as a costume that could be put on and taken off, I now turn to the earliest evidence where the racial characteristics of blackface, vis-à-vis attire and other props, appears in a registry dated in 1525 from Toledo, Spain. In Emilio Cotarelo y Mori's *Colección de entremeses, loas, bailes, jácaras y mojigangas desde fines del siglo XVI a mediados del XVIII*, the philologist describes the document as "La más antigua descripción completa de estas danzas que hemos hallado, es una que en 1525 presentaron en Toledo Bautista de Valdivieso y Juan Corica, en la fiesta de la Asuncion (15 de agosto)"[48] (The oldest and most complete description of these dances we have found is performed in 1525 in Toledo by Bautista de Valdivieso and Juan Corica, during the feast day of the Assumption on August 15). Cotarelo y Mori's redacted tract cites the *Cuenta del libro de gastos del año 1525* on the last page of *Archivo que fué de la Obra de la cal de Toledo (Papeles de Barbierz)*. The ledger, approximately ten short passages in length, explains the cost and usage of masks, paints, and other materials utilized in blackfacing the roles of black characters:

> La cuenta que para su cobro entregaron al cabildo, dice:
> "De la hechura de estas sayas y de estos santos negros, llevó a sastre 1 ducado;
>
> 1. Del molde en que se amoldaron los negros, que era de nogal, 3 reales;
> 2. Llevó el pintor por pintar los carros y cuatro máscaras de negros, y por el betún para teñir las piernas y los brazos, un ducado;

3. De platear los cuatro escudos y las cuatro porras de los negros y las cuatro flechas y los cuatros navajones y las argollas y las cuatro cadenas, por todo esto igualado, 6 reales;
4. De hilo para poner en trenzas el cáñamo de los salvajes y para coser los vestidos de los negros, 1 real y 9 maravedises;
5. De cola y trapos y arija para hacer las máscaras de los negros, 1 real y 6 maravedises;
6. De huevos y aceite para sentar el betún negro en las piernas y brazos siete huevos á 3 blancas, y 2 maravedises de aceite, que montan 14 maravedises;
7. De cuatro pares de zapatos blancos para los negros, á 30 maravedises cada par, que montan 120;
8. De cuatro pañetes para los negros, cada par á medio real, el par que son 2 reales;
9. De 14 danzantes, que fueron 4 salvajes y 4 negros y 4 amazonas y un rey de los negros y unas reinas de las amazonas, los 12 que iban a pie á 3 reales, á real por la víspera y a 2 reales por el día, y á 2 reales por los que eran rey y reina, que monta todo 40 reales." (clxxii)

[The bill that they handed over to the cabildo for payment says:

To make these skirts and those of the black saints, a tailor was paid 1 ducat;

1. To make black characters from a walnut mold: 3 reales;
2. To paint the chariots and four black masks, and for the bitumen to dye the actors' legs and arms, the painter was paid 1 ducat;
3. To line in silver the black characters' four shields, four batons, four arrows, four daggers, the shackles, and four chains: 6 reales;
4. For the thread to make hemp braids for the savages and to sew the black characters' dresses: 1 real and 9 maravedis;
5. For the tail, rags, and soil to make the black characters' masks: 1 real and 6 maravedis;
6. For the eggs and oil to apply the black bitumen on the legs and arms: seven eggs at 3 *blancas* and 2 maravedis of oil, which totals 14 maravedis;

7. For four pairs of white shoes for the black characters, at 30 maravedis each pair, for a total of 120;
8. For the four scarves for the black characters, each pair at half a real, the complete pair costs 2 reales;
9. For fourteen dancers—four savages, four blacks, four Amazons, one king of the blacks, one queen of the Amazons—twelve who went on foot were paid 3 reales, 1 real for the day before and 2 reales for the day, and 2 reales for the king and queen roles, reaching a total of 40 reales.]

In her study "El hato de la risa: Identidad y ridículo en el vestuario" (2000), Evangelina Rodríguez Cuadros confirms what we have already seen in blackening up with makeup at the height of Spanish Golden Age theater. But in an appendix to her chapter, concerning racialized casting and costuming practices, Rodríguez Cuadros lists the accessories, clothes, shoes, and other garments typically worn by, and for, black characters (in and out of blackface):

Vestido: Jaquetillas coloradas y calzones de seda abiertos. Calzones marineros colorados y vaquero de colores. Bandas de color. Vestido *a lo guineo*. Casacas de catalufa de Flandes de colores. Vestido de sempiterna encarnada. Jubones de cotonía blanca y mantellines.
Zapatos: Zapatos blancos y medias de estambre.
Tocado o Sombrero: Diadema con plumas de colores. Casquillos de pelo. Diademas de hoja de lata. Bonete *a la africana*. Bonete de grana o colorado. Sombrerillos blancos. Cofias.
Accesorios: Mascarilla. Sonajas. Tamborino. Guantes. Toallas blancas. Cestillas.[49]

[*Costumes*: Short-length red jackets and loose silk breeches. Red sailor's trousers and colored serge. Colored cummerbunds. Guinea-style clothing (like a black African). Colored Flemish-style *casacas de catalufa*. Clothing of red wool. White cotton or hemp doublets and silk or lace head shawls.
Shoes: White shoes and woolen breeches.

Hats and Headbands: Diadems with colored feathers. Hairpins. Metal crowns. African-styled caps and hats. Red birettas, caps, and hats. Small white hats. Plain caps.

Accessories: Masks and visors. Rattles. Tambourines. Gloves. White towels. Small baskets.]

Here Blackness operates as an actual costume—its popularity seemingly indelible.[50] These documents reveal the extent to which blackface performance on early Spanish stages operated as an institutionalized and professionalized system—an undoubtedly modern enterprise where merchant capitalism and the circulation of material culture was central. As illustrated in the aforementioned passage, the economic exchange of and investment in valuable sixteenth-century coins—the blanca, the real, and the maravedi—show a Renaissance Spanish investment in a commodification of goods, materials, and objects that gauged the value and the extent to which the representation of not only black African bodies but also those of Amerindians, Frenchmen, Germans, Italians, Iberian Muslims, Portuguese, and the Roma people fell into the theatrical enterprise of racial impersonation. As demonstrated by the aforementioned archival and performance history documents, the act of *dressing* blackface performers underscores Karen Tranberg Hansen and D. Soyini Madison's treatment of the materiality of accessories, fabrics, and garments as "clothing savvy" and "clothing competence."[51] What the archive of blackface performance reveals about the materiality of clothing and props on early Spanish stages is the extent to which playwrights and stage managers—among many other persons involved behind the scenes—maintained and practiced an immaculate scrutiny over racial impersonation. As illustrated by the aforementioned documents, the material culture surrounding the packaging and staging of Blackness becomes highly professionalized and streamlined. And to that end, we learn that the materiality of Blackness and blackface performance were always ready to be worn on early Spanish stages.

"They Are Chatterboxes with Their Feet!": *Bailes de Negros*, Conjure, Folklore

In his *Premática del Tiempo* (1628; 1648), Quevedo attacks black African slave culture flourishing on Spanish soil. What he denigrates in particular is the guineo, a West African dance known for its quick and brisk movements. In his own words, he scoffs: "Item, vista la ridícula figura de los criados cuando dan a beber a sus señores, haciendo el *coliseo*, el *guineo* inclinando con notable peligro y asco todo el cuerpo demasiado, y que, siendo mudos de boca, son habladores de pies de puro hacer desairadas reverencias, declaramos sea eso tenido por descortesía e irreverencia"[52] (*Item*. Given the ridiculous figure of the servants when they serve drinks to their masters, dancing the coliseo and the guineo, hunching their whole body over in a notably dangerous and disgusting manner, and that, being mute of mouth, they are chatterboxes with their feet from making so many unattractive reverences, we declare this to be discourteous and irreverent). As if he were peering in on a masquerade ball or party, Quevedo's satiric commentary in this passage, as well as in the rest of the *Premática*, possesses an ethnographic and folkloric flavor. Transporting us to some kind of ritual or folkloric performance (yet also legalistic and inquisitorial, hence the repetition of "Item" throughout the treatise), Quevedo conjures an image of a deformed and grotesque black body qua *co[u]liseo* (derived from *culo*, or ass), guineo (the dance), and habla de negros (speech impediment). Riffing off his axiomatic construction of Africanized Castilian—guineo—in 1631 in *Libro de todas las cosas*: "Si escribes comedias y eres poeta, sabrás guineo en volviendo las r, l, y al contrario: como Francisco, Flancico; primo, *plimo*" (If you are a playwright and a poet, you will know to use guineo by interchanging r's and l's, and vice versa, such as Francisco, *Flancico*; primo, *plimo*).[53] Quevedo forges a link between habla de negros language and sub-Saharan African dances and musicality. The so-called chatter that Quevedo ascribes to Blackness—linguistically, musically, and somatically—also operates as a foil to the oeuvre of the quintessential *entremesista* of the Spanish Golden Age, Luis Quiñones de Benavente (1589?–1651) in *El negrito hablador, y sin color anda la niña, El borracho*, and *Los sacristanes burlados*. Quiñones de Benavente's portrayal of the habla de negros register and sub-Saharan African songs captures Quevedo's trope of chatter, or a scatological verbal diarrhea.

Quevedo's remark "they are chatterboxes with their feet" also stems from a larger cultural legacy and history of West-Central African dances that traveled to and from the continent of Africa, the Spanish Caribbean, and the Iberian Peninsula. At this juncture in the chapter, we will examine more closely sub-Saharan African dances—or *bailes de negros*, as they were called in early modern Spain—that influence habla de negros dramatic works and, as I contend, enhance the performativity of habla de negros language and the "African" sounds these performances purported to replicate. To acquire a fuller understanding of black dances in early modern Spain, we must go back to early modern continental Africa and colonial Cuba in order to trace these dances' transatlantic maritime journey to Spanish shores. Dance historian and flamenco scholar José Luis Navarro García, in *Historia del baile flamenco*, explains the indelible imprint of sub-Saharan African dances on Iberian soil. He is the first scholar, to my knowledge, who links black African dances, music, drumming styles, and ceremonial rituals coming from colonial Cuba to early modern Spain well into the eighteenth and nineteenth centuries. Navarro García explains that a variety of African dances, songs, and rhythms crossed the Atlantic, from Havana, brought by mariners and other travelers, arriving to the ports of Cádiz and Seville. In Seville, for instance, census reports and ecclesiastic records document the large presence of blacks and mulatos—"un elevado número de *morenos*"[54]—attending and participating in the Corpus Christi procession that welcomed Queen Isabella's arrival at the gate of the Macarena on 24 July 1477. Twenty years later, on 27 June 1497, for instance, during Queen Isabella's appearance at Seville's Corpus Christi festivities that summer, the city issued an order requesting that "all blacks in the city" participate in celebrating the Catholic Monarch's arrival.[55] This civic gesture, in the historical archive, of including and signaling "*all blacks*" in Seville to partake in *sevillano* citizenry repeats itself in the early 1500s in Rodrigo de Reinosa's literary archive of "Gelofe, Mandinga." In the Municipal Archive of Jérez de la Frontera (Cádiz), complaints circulated in response to predominantly black parties, or fiestas, where black and white slave "fandangueros," or partygoers, caused a lot of ruckus with their tambourines, barrel drums, and other instruments.[56]

The critical reception bestowed on these black dances—primarily expounded by Aurelia Martín Casares and Marga G. Barranco in their coauthored essay "The Musical Legacy of Black Africans in Spain: A Review of Our Sources"—claims that "while the cultural legacy of sub-Saharan Africa in terms of music has been better studied in Latin America and the Caribbean more generally, it is too little known in Spain. The relationship with ancestral styles in sub-Saharan Africa has yet to be analysed, for even if we have a relative abundance of literary references, we cannot imply that because a performer was black, they were necessarily playing or dancing African music."[57]

The way in which these two historians myopically position Black cultural expression in Spain contributes to some of the reasons why the cultural legacy and heritage of black Africans in Spain remain nebulous. Similarly, Beusterien contends that "[black] dances in Hispanic theater should not be considered African, but appropriated entertainment in a context that forgets their religious significance as well as the contexts in which they were performed, such as *plazas*, homes, or slave ships."[58] I depart respectfully from these scholars' critical approach. I dare to privilege the fact that black performers of bailes de negros in early modern Spain were, in fact, aware of the African-derived chants, music, and rhythms which they enacted. (Another way to look at the scenario: for the sake of authenticity and purity, do we question whether white performers were aware of the "Whiteness," or the "Europeanness," of the minuets or pavanes they performed? Is the reticence and scrutiny with which we speak of black Africans' cultural forms and practices in early modern Europe measured to the same standards, or, rather, authenticity politics, that are applied to the cultural appropriation of European art forms and culture?) Based on my ethnographic research conducted in Cuba (Havana, Matanzas, and Pinar del Río) on Afro-Cuban folklore and the spiritual-religious systems of the Congo and Lukumí peoples, I recognize an uncanny overlap between colonial Afro-Cuban folkloric performances *and* those portrayed in early modern Spanish habla de negros texts. Musicologists such as Rogério Budasz, Peter Fryer, and Gerhard Kubik have shown that during the seventeenth and eighteenth centuries, many dances of African influence appeared almost simultaneously at different points of the so-called Atlantic triangle, a region that comprised coastal cities of the Congo-Angola, Iberian Peninsula, and Latin America.[59] As these contacts took place across the sea, sailors and dockworkers played an important role in this cross-fertilization between the sounds and rhythms of three continents.[60] Budasz, in his essay "Black Guitar-Players and Early African-Iberian Music in Portugal and Brazil," elucidates this claim as follows: "Coming originally from different musical cultures in Africa, slaves and free blacks came into contact with Africans from other regions and with blacks already born in the Iberian Peninsula and the New World, and gradually incorporated elements of their new environment."[61] "In such a scenario," he adds, "Iberian secular music—especially the guitar repertory—would be enriched with structures, rhythms and melodic formulae from Central and Western African music traditions, resulting in a kind of musical *lingua franca*, comparable to the language used by Iberian merchants and their suppliers along the African coast."[62] The guitar repertory to which Budasz refers articulates an important counternarrative that ruptures extant scholarly readings—Cervantes's black character Luis from *El celoso extremeño* immediately comes to mind—that only see black guitar players' relationship to their instrument as a stereotypical preference and proclivity.

Borrowing from the critical vocabulary of black feminist and religious studies scholars such as Angela Davis (*Blues Legacies and Black Feminism*, 1998), Yvonne Chireau (*Black Magic*, 2003), Kameelah L. Martin (*Conjuring Moments in African American Literature*, 2012), and Kinitra D. Brooks (*Searching for Sycorax*, 2017),[63] I employ the concepts of "conjure" and "conjuring" in order to advocate for, on the one hand, and to illuminate, on the other hand, the presence of what I like to call a "parasacred" reality that cannot be spliced from secular modes of black expression and performance. Contrary to the assertion that literary texts do not provide sufficient evidence for proving the "relationship with ancestral styles," or the notion that from literary texts "we cannot imply that because a performer was black, they were necessarily playing or dancing African music," I maintain that for African diasporic peoples—both enslaved and free—the sacred and the secular are not separate(d). In sub-Saharan African cosmologies, there are no binaries nor separation of energies. In the poetic corpus of Nativity carols, or villancicos, for example, black Africans conjure meaning out of their Peninsular Spanish lives while also conjuring the (re)memory of their respective sub-Saharan lives. In a villancico performed at the Cathedral of Cádiz in 1693, José Pérez de Montoro recreates a work song intoned by a group of Arará slaves unloading a ship at a dock:

> Eya, Plimos, aplisa, aplisa,
> acábense de juntá,
> arrerá, arrerá,
> y samo acá, arerrá.[64]

> [Hurry up, cousins! Faster, faster!
> The cargo from the ship just arrived,
> Arará, Arará,
> and we are here to unload it, Arará.]

The Arará were an ethnic group from the Kingdom of Dahomey of southwest Benin, a part of the larger Yoruba kingdom. Characterized by its percussive style, Arará music consists of body percussion, drumming, and hand-clapping. A minority group in colonial Cuba (as well as in Brazil, Grenada, Haiti, and Trinidad and Tobago), the Arará formed their own *cabildos de nación* (ethnic association; town council) in the sixteenth and seventeenth centuries, establishing a well-preserved musical and religious legacy in Cuba and throughout the rest of Latin America.[65] To sustain their cultural traditions and improve their conditions, slaves, along with free people of color, participated in these socioreligious and cultural mutual aid organizations in order to conserve the core of African belief systems, dances, ritual practices, languages, instruments, chants, and songs.[66] Cabildos de nación stemmed from *cofradías de negros* (African confraternities)—like those portrayed in the TV series *La Peste*, which I reference in the introduction—organized in early sixteenth-century Seville and in many ways paralleled socioreligious organizations in West Africa.[67] As the population of African descent grew, Spain established cabildos de nación to provide assistance and cultural activities for slaves and freed women and men.[68]

Foregrounded in this villancico is a representation of sonic Blackness via the repetition of the word *"arrerá"* at the end of each verse in the rest of the poem:

> Plimo de mi vida, arrerá,
> vamo, pue, calgando, arrerá,
> que a esso vene e Niño, arrerá,
> pol nuestros pecaros vamo a calgá
>
> [My brothers, Arará,
> Let's push ahead and pick this load up, Arará,
> so that the Holy Child comes, Arará,
> (and) on behalf of our sins we're going to carry this load.]

This passage constructs a rhythmic pulse, a synchronized and well-coordinated beat, to which these workers would have moved in order to lift and carry heavy loads. Pérez de Montoro's imitation of this black slave work song must not be downplayed, for it is reminiscent of the work songs found in US-black American slave culture and society. Regardless of its imitation (after all, something so specifically unique to African diasporic slave culture could not have sprung out of thin air), Pérez de Montoro's villancico provides us with a glimpse into early modern Andalusian slave culture operating outside of the plantation society of the Americas. As James Cone reflects in *The Spirituals and the Blues* (1972), "The social mind of the slaves was a reflection of their African background . . . and their encounter with slave masters, overseers, auctioneers, and buyers. The [work] songs were a reflection of this existence and of the measures used to deal with the dehumanization inherent in it."[69] To that end, Pérez de Montoro, more broadly, negotiates the meaning of his Arará subjects' humanity as thinking subjects in a more nuanced fashion than what we may readily expect.

A document from 1493 held in the Municipal Historical Archive in Málaga corroborates a similar cultural phenomenon of black slave songs. At a town hall meeting held at a local cabildo, for example, city council members discussed the labor activities of black slaves who carried loads of grain to the *alhóndiga* (a distribution warehouse; market) from far distances. In addition to black slave work songs, Navarro García, in *Historia del baile flamenco* (an expanded version of his 1999 classic *Semillas de ébano: El elemento negro y afroamericano en el baile flamenco*), lays the foundation for us to consider the likelihood of conjuring moments to manifest in the presence of diasporic African dances in early modern Spain (fig. 5). He declares that "since the fifteenth century, African dances did not cease to arrive at our [Iberian] ports."[70] Navarro García further elaborates: "In their origin, from African lands, ritual dances were performed in honor of African gods and goddesses. In Cuba, still today, the execution of these dances is accompanied by the *conjuring* of these gods, whose altars have not been forgotten."[71] Arriving from the Spanish Caribbean, dances such as *el retambo, la cachumba*, and *la gayumba* became categorically marked, or racialized, as "Black" due to (1) their genealogical origins as "moreno" ("dark"; "black"; "African") from the Spanish West Indies and (2) their ritualized African roots.[72]

Even more compelling is Navarro García's speculative dare to link the Cuban Congo religious veneration of the *mpungo* Zarabanda to early modern Spain. He asserts,

Posiblemente el más popular de cuantos bailes de negros llegando a nuestra península. Se cantaba en forma dialogal, una fórmula típica de toda la música africana, y decía así:

> *Solo*: Sarabanda me dá . . .
> *Coro*: Mi Sarabanda para curá.
> *Solo*: Sarabanda me vá . . .
> *Coro*: Mi Sarabanda curá
> *Solo*: Sarabanda me verá.
> *Coro*: Mi Sarabanda para curá.

[Possibly the most popular of the many black dances arriving to our [Iberian] peninsula. Sung in dialogic form, a common form found in African music, it went like this:

> *Solo*: Sarabanda provides for me.
> *Chorus*: My Sarabanda heals.
> *Solo*: Sarabanda works for me.
> *Chorus*: My Sarabanda heals.
> *Solo*: Sarabanda watches out for me.
> *Chorus*: My Sarabanda heals.]

Following in the methodology and tradition of ethnography and folklore, this book's interdisciplinary scope takes inspiration from Zora Neale Hurston's corpus of ethnographic work—in particular, *Mules and Men*, *Tell My Horse*, and her autobiography *Dust Tracks on a Road*—to explore the way in which early modern Spanish dramatists and writers link their construction of habla de negros to the performance of African diasporic folklore via sixteenth- and seventeenth-century African dances—or bailes de negros, as they were called on both sides of the Atlantic, both in Spain and Cuba—such as the guineo, the zarabanda, and the zarambeque. These folkloric dances and the habla de negros sounds and songs performed with them lead me to recall the Congolese-derived ritual song "Lumbe, Lumbe," briefly quoted as an epigraph to this book. The word "lumbe" cannot be translated literally but instead operates as an exclamatory announcement that conjures one's ancestors, ancestral home, and spirits of the dead (in the diasporic Congolese context of the mpungo or *nkisi*) who inhabit and possess the force of an *nganga*.[73]

FIG. 5. Frédéric Mialhe, *Day of the Kings*. Plate in *Viage pintoresco al rededor de la Isla de Cuba: Dedicado al Escmo. Gov. Conde de Villanueva / dibujado y litografiado por D. Federico Mialhe* (Havana: Litografía de Luis Marquier, ca. 1848), fol. 24. Beinecke Rare Book and Manuscript Library, Yale University.

The source of "lumbe" comes from the Afro-Cuban religious traditions of *Regla de Palo*—several branches of Congo-based cultures and cosmologies subsumed under the general rubric of "Regla de Palo Monte Mayombe," including Regla Vriyuma, Regla Musunde, Regla Quirimbaya, and the Regla Kimbisa del Santo Cristo del Buen Viaje. Considered the most syncretized of Afro-Cuban practices, Congo religions in Cuba derive elements from Yoruba and other West and Central African practices, Islam, and Roman Catholicism. My close reading of lumbe is not necessarily a quicksilver fabulation. In one sense, it serves to both connect and dialogue with the salience of habla de negros words—primarily dances and ritual phrases—ending in the -(c)umbe suffix, such as *gurumbé* and *paracumbé*. In another sense, as a counterpoint to theoretical vocabularies such as "necrocapitalism" or "necropolitics," coined by Bobby Banerjee and Achille Mbembe,[74] which underscore the abuse and exploitation of enslaved black bodies via social death and the wane of African diasporic culture in the West, I highlight the importance of lumbe and other -(c)umbe suffixes in order to contest such paradigms. To do so, I utilize the term "necromancy" as a means to employ the lens of African cultural survivals—the manifestation and representation of sub-Saharan African folk practices, language and speech, religious and spiritual practices, as well as dance and music—in order to return, on the one hand, and to animate, on the other hand, an inherent agential voice to the habla de negros speakers whom we will encounter in this book. If, according to the *Oxford English Dictionary*, "necromancy" embodies "the art of predicting the future by supposed communication with the dead; (more generally) divination, sorcery, witchcraft, enchantment,"[75] then I, as the necromancer, aim to awaken the memory of early modern Spanish black lives via placing Hispanism in dialogue with Black studies.[76]

The habla de negros repertoire studied throughout this book references a variety of sub-Saharan African dances. From this corpus—primarily consisting of dramatic works and at other times villancicos—we encounter black dances such as the guineo, the zarabanda, the *chacona*, and the zarambeque, all of which were huge hits in early modern Spain well into the nineteenth century due to their transatlantic voyages from Havana.[77] My treatment of these dances in early modern Spanish society—performed not only on theatrical stages but also in cathedrals, dockyards, royal and religious sanctioned processions, palaces and courtyards, public squares, and in the intimate quarters of black cofradías and *hermandades* (confraternities and guilds)—originates from the fact that their popularity, especially as folkloric performances, cannot be disassociated from a cognitive and cultural threshold. Across class, ethnic, and racial divides, early modern Spanish audiences would have acquired an awareness of, appreciation for, and, if nothing else, a taste for the Black sounds (music), rhythms, and dances.

The first African dance most likely to have arrived to Andalusia would have been the guineo, whose name indicates quite clearly its origin: the Rivers of Guinea region of the Senegambia (fig. 6). Referenced by numerous writers of the sixteenth and seventeenth centuries, Covarrubias comments on the dance's abrupt, swift footwork and movements. Quevedo, as we have seen earlier in this section, attacks its perceived offensive gesticulations. Fernando Ortiz, in *Los negros brujos* (1906), *Glosario de afronegrismos* (1924), and his criminological treatise *Los negros curros* (1975), attributes Covarrubias's definition of the guineo to black dances performed in early colonial Cuba and Spain. Luis Vélez de Guevara, in *Diablo cojuelo* (1641), also references the guineo and other African-derived dances as both meta- and subtexts for talking about witchcraft and conjuring the Devil. Finally, in 1670, an anonymous poem titled "Gurumbé" collapses prior definitions of the guineo into one text:

> GURUMBÉ
> Como ven que todo es jira,
> todo bureo y contento,
> dos negrillos bailar quieren;
> y así empieza el *Guineo*:
> NEGRA. ¡Gurumbé!
> LOS DOS. ¡Gurumbé, gurumbé, gurumbé!
> Que fase nubrado y quiele yové.[78]

> [GURUMBÉ
> For them, everything is about festivity and joy;
> full-time entertainment and satisfaction.
> Two young blacks want to dance,
> and so begins the *Guineo*:
> NEGRA. ¡Gurumbé!
> LOS DOS. ¡Gurumbé, gurumbé, gurumbé!
> It is cloudy outside and it wants rain.]

Like lumbe, the context of the word "gurumbé" is highly specific. With respect to the poem just cited, the phrase signals glee and rejoicing. A term often misread by critics, one aligned with abject black buffoonery and idiocy, I situate gurumbé, and its relation to the guineo, in a larger symbiotic dialectic of the spirituals. Just as much as the sacred and the secular are not separate entities in sub-Saharan African cosmologies, Black music has a history of social commentary on the experiences of those who create it. The experience of slavery inspired—for better or worse, confined to a plantation or a domestic space—the creative musical endeavors of enslaved Africans. A dance transported from the Senegambia to the Iberian Peninsula, the guineo shows us—via the repetition of the exclamatory "¡gurumbé!"—the possibility of African slaves to conjure the affective modes of happiness and joy. And it is through the tropes of Black joy and Black entertainment where habla de

FIG. 6. Domingo Martínez, *Carro del Aire: Máscara de la Fábrica de Tabacos con motivo de la exaltación al trono de Fernando VI*, 1747, detail. Oil on canvas, 137 × 292 cm. Museo de Bellas Artes, Seville, CE0553P.

negros speakers respond to their lot with song and dance. If we are to accept "Gurumbé" as a textual example that parallels African American spirituals (emerging from sites of mourning, resistance, and pleasure), then we can begin to appreciate how the thematic content of "Gurumbé" comprises both lyric and sound that is embedded within habla de negros language.

At the turn of the sixteenth century arrived a new African dance called the zarabanda. Coming from the Spanish West Indies to Spain, this dance received harsh backlash for its presumed lascivious nature and sensuality. For example, Cervantes, in *El celoso extremeño*, refers to the dance as "*endemoniado*" (possessed; trancelike), noting its new arrival to Spain.[79] Prior to the Cervantine reference, in 1558, the *jácara* titled *La vida de Zarabanda, ramera pública del Guayacán* called the dance scandalous for its obscenity.[80] Later, in 1592, Fray Marcos Antonio de Camos, in his *Microcosmia* (Barcelona, 1592), aligns the zarabanda with diabolical acts. Alonso López Pinciano, in the *Filosofía antigua poética* (1596), expresses his disapproval of the dance by attacking the poetic content and lyrical form of its accompanying *coplas*. Well into the seventeenth century, pejorative remarks about the zarabanda did not cease. In Vélez de Guevara's *El Diablo Cojuelo*, the Devil speaks, if you will, claiming affinity with and ownership over *all* dances (of African origin or otherwise):

demonio más por menudo soy, aunque me meto en todo: yo soy las pulgas del infierno, la chisme, el enredo, la usura, la mohatra; yo truje al mundo la zarabanda, el déligo, la chacona, el bullicuzcuz, las cosquillas de la capona, el guiriguirigay, el zambapalo, la mariona, el avilipinti, el pollo, la carretería, el hermano Bartolo, el carcañal, el guineo, el colorín colorado; yo inventé las pandorgas, las jácaras, las papalatas, los comos, las mortecinas, los títeres, los volatines, los saltambancos, los maesecorales y, al fin, yo me llamo el Diablo Cojuelo.[81]

[Even though I meddle into all affairs, I am a common, younger demon. I am the fleas of Hell, the gossip, the entanglements, the usury, and the fraud. I brought into the world the *zarabanda*, the *déligo*, the *chacona*, the *bullicuzcuz*, the *cosquillas de la capona*, the *guiriguirigay*, the *zambapalo*, the *mariona*, the *avilipinti*, the *pollo*, the *carretería*, the *hermano Bartolo*, the *carcañal*, the *guineo*, the *colorín colorao*. I invented the *pandorgas*, the *jácaras*, the *papalatas*, the *comos*, the *mortecinas*, the *títeres*, the *volantines*, the *saltambancos*, and the *maesecorales*.]

But despite such long-standing ridicule and pushback against the zarabanda by grammarians, theologians, and writers, the zarabanda—like many, if not most, African dances—was an overnight hit among Spanish audiences, which, in turn, catapulted its popularity. What I find particularly fascinating about the zarabanda appears in Covarrubias's remarks on its kinetic energy, or kinesis: "Aunque se mueven todas las partes del cuerpo, los brazos hacen las más ademanes, sonando las castañetas"[82] (Even though all body parts are moving, the arms make most of the gestures, playing the castanets). In many respects, this definition hints at what one could presume to be a state of trance. The bodies dancing the zarabanda, who are simultaneously singing in habla de negros, reveal out-of-body experiences and physical states that both complicate and transcend euphemisms for sex.

If the zarabanda embodied hyperkinetic, provocative movements, then chacona exceeded the zarabanda, according to Francisco Fernández de Córdoba in his *Didascalia multiplex* (Lyon, 1615), as the "más provocativa" (most provocative). Usually danced with castanets and involving vivacious footwork, the chacona acquired its fame for symbolizing the good life, or *la bona vida*. Like the zarabanda, early modern Spanish writers link the chacona to sub-Saharan Africa. For example, in Lope de Vega's auto-sacramental *La isla del sol* (Madrid, 1616), the dance originates in Africa.[83] In the exemplary novel *La ilustre fragona*, Cervantes references the mixed-race, transatlantic African diasporic origins of the chacona, thereby personifying the dance as an "indiana amulatada." His personification of the chacona as a "mulata indiana" (*mulata* from the Indies) makes the etymological semantics behind the dance move transatlantically similar to *indiano*, but more closely to the indiano's slave or negra, an Africa-descended woman who has moved in a triangular trajectory from Africa to the Americas to the European metropolis.[84]

Around 1650, a new black dance from the Spanish Indies traveled to Andalusia with African-descended persons, mariners, and sailors, revitalizing and updating, if you will, the choreography and footwork of bailes de negros performed by blacks and mulatos during feast days and local gatherings at town squares. This newly arrived dance was called the zarambeque, and other times the *zumbé*. The entremés titled *Los gorrones*, for instance, uses these two names simultaneously in its stage directions: "Sale la negra y el negro y bailan el Zumbé o Zarambeque" (The black woman and the black man come out [on stage] and dance the zumbé and zarambeque). Often confused for the guineo, due to its vivacious rhythms and suggestive gyrations, the seventeenth-century zarambeque immediately replaced the once-infamous guineo. The *Autoridades* dictionary roots the zarambeque in rhythmic and sonic Blackness, defining it as "tañido y danza muy alegre y bulliciosa, la cual es muy frecuente entre los negros" (jingling in sound, an animated, lively, and boisterous dance, which is common among blacks).[85] Sebastián de Villaviciosa's short-skit play *Bayle de los sones* (1661) corroborates these characteristics in the following lines:

> El Zarambeque, que salta,
> pica y brinca más que todos
> los sones de la guitarra.[86]
>
> [The *Zarambeque*! It jumps,
> stings, and skips more than all of
> the guitar's beats.]

The zarambeque's fame and textual saturation reached its peak in the seventeenth century, most notably in the refrain "Teque, teque, teque, vaya el zarambeque" in Jerónimo de Cáncer's *El portugués*, as well as in the *Mojiganga de Don Gaiferos* (vv. 175–76; 181–82), Francisco de Castro's entremés *El destierro del hoyo*, and the *Sainete del matemático* (ca. 1663). Suárez de Deza's *Baile entremesado de los borrachos* modifies de Cáncer's refrain as follows: "Teque, teque, teque, vaya, Heráclito, un zarambeque" (Teque, teque, teque, c'mon Heraclitus, a *zarambeque*). The entremesista Antonio de Solís also repeats the formulaic "teque, teque, teque" in one of his loas (an opening dramatic piece for the play *Las amazonas* [1681]) and *El niño caballero* (1658).[87] Performed in cathedrals on both sides of the Hispanic Atlantic, the zarambeque appeared in dozens of Nativity carols, or villancicos, throughout the seventeenth century.[88] The execution of the zarambeque on early Spanish stages was primarily performed in blackface and spoken in habla de negros, de Villaviciosa's *Los sones* serving as one example. Other instances also existed where actual black actors performed on stage with blackfaced white actors. For example, the anonymous *Baile de la noche de Carnestolendas* (1660) casts the white actresses Isabel de Gálvez and Manuela de Escamilla, donning blackface, performing alongside "dos negritos verdaderos" (two real black actors) who dance and sing the zarambeque.

What I find particularly fascinating about zarambeque performances in seventeenth-century Spain is its creation of a visibly porous theatrical stage that troubles our present-day understanding of the racial impersonation and the cultural appropriation of Blackness. In many ways, to one's surprise, zarambeque performances blur the binarized fixity of gender, ethnicity, race, and sexuality. As Navarro García insists, white performers reflect a deep knowledge of black dances and study them seriously in order to perform them convincingly on stage (fig. 7).[89]

Dances originating from Angola—*bailes de Angola* known as the cumbé and the paracumbé—populated teatro breve works during the late seventeenth and early eighteenth centuries. Coming directly from Angola into Portugal, settling and being performed in Cádiz and the Port of Saint Mary on the banks of the Guadalete River, and then subsequently spreading into nearly all of Spain's provinces, the repertoire of bailes de Angola consisted of antiphony (call-and-response) and vibrant footwork, and boasted new, upbeat melodies of a $3 \times 4 + 6 \times 8$ rhythm. In 1708, an anonymous work

NUEVA RELACION, Y CURIOSO ROMANCE, EN QUE
se refiere la celebridad, galanteo, y acaso de una Boda de
Negros, que se executò en la Ciudad de el Puerto
de Santa Maria. Sucediò el año passado.

CEsse todo regocijo,
paresse todo recreo,
dilatense los festines,
suspendanse los burèos,
interin mi lengua explica
el mas gracioso sucesso,
que han oido los oyentes
contar en el Mundo entero;
y porque sea notorio,
quiero, que de passa tiempo
les sirva à los circunstantes,
por mofa, risa, ò festejo.
En la celebre Ciudad
de Santa Maria el Puerto,
se criò un Negro famoso,
que le dicen Thomàs Melo;
esse tal se enamorò
de una Negra, à quien el Cielo
se esmerò en darle mil gracias,
desde la planta al cabello;
cuyo pelo, por lo obscuro,
creo, que ha dudado el Pueblo;
si es de carnero merino,
ò si es del Sol el passeo;
Su frente, por lo espaciosa;

y por sus concavos densos;
ha llegado la badana
à menospreciar su precio:
Sus cejas, puedo decir,
que no son de terso pelo,
porque esto se le quedò
al Maestro en el tintero:
Sus ojos, los gatos tienen
mucha quexa contra ellos;
pues relumbran como asquas,
y solo se alumbran ellos.
Su nariz, es corta, y ancha;
de gran trabajo, al resuello;
gran caudal de ventanage;
de mal aliento lo mesmo.
Su boca parece bolsa,
los dientes como becerro;
la lengua como una baca;
la barba como un tablero;
el pescuezo gordo, y corto;
pero largo en los fideos.
Los pechos sirven de muestra
à todos los tinajeros:
llega à llenar su cintura
quatro varas, poco menos;

FIG. 7. Engraving from an eighteenth-century chapbook pamphlet, *Nueva relación y curioso romance* . . . (Seville). Biblioteca Digital de Castilla y León.

titled *Baile del paracumbé, a lo portugués* certifies the dance's origins and genealogy in Iberia:

> ¿Pues qué? ¿No me conoces?
> El paracumbé de Angola
> ciudadano de Guiné,
> casado a la Amorosa
> que escogí yo por mujer.
> Si queréis saber quién soy
> en este baile atended,
> y acompañad mi romance
> en estilo portugués.⁹⁰

> [Say what now? You don't know who I am?
> I'm the *paracumbé* from Angola,
> citizen of Africa,
> husband of the Amorosa,
> whom I chose as my wife.
> If you want to know who I am,
> pay attention to this dance
> and follow my ballad
> in Portuguese style.]

Assertive and direct in its tone, the interrogative questions "¿Pues qué?" and "¿No me conoces?" summon the audience to recenter and recognize continental Africa—Angola in particular—as progenitor of the paracumbé that is performed in Spain and Portugal. In a diasporic and transatlantic sense, these two opening questions also resemble the Afro-Cuban Palo Mayombe conjure song: "¿Pa'qué tú me llama, si tú no me conoce?" (Why are you calling [conjuring] me, if you don't know who I am?), which would have been sung around the same time as the passage just cited.

Seventeenth-century dramaturgs Francisco Bernardo de Quirós and Pedro Calderón de la Barca, for instance, collapse, if not also hybridize, Angolan dances and the zarambeque in the *mojigangas El regidor* (1674) and *La negra* (1691–1708). In the lesser-known and understudied *El regidor*, set in Seville on 28 May at five o'clock in the afternoon, Quirós introduced dramatic skits that reflected his local community and surroundings.[91] Consisting of 221 verses, *El regidor* takes place in Seville (as stated in lines 101, 175, and 184) and occurs during the feast day of the Corpus Christi. Written in hendecasyllabic and heptasyllabic rhyming couplets, totaling 124 verses, the first part of the mojiganga begins with a procession of the skit's *dramatis personae* (*un alcalde* [a mayor], *un regidor* [a town councilman], *un hombre* [a man], *una beata* [a mystic], *un gallego* [a Galician man], Doña Jimena, *un moro* [a Moor], *unos portugueses* [some Portuguese], *una negra* [a black woman], and musicians). The second part, more varied in its meter, corresponds directly to the mojiganga itself and is made up of octosyllabic verses. The final part of the skit is sung exclusively and consists of a couplet, seven *seguidillas*, and a final closing couplet.

Reiterating Navarro García's claim that white performers consciously express an interest in black dances and music, the mayor of Seville in *El regidor* does so by discarding European music, arguing that the best music for drama comes from Angola:

> Cantaremo lo teque teque,
> teque, reteque, reteque, teque,
> pidiendo el perdón Angola,
> porque no hay instrumento en la Europa con que yo no
>   sirva a Sevilla
> en auto, entremés, mojiganga y pandorga. (vv. 180–85)[92]

> [Let's sing: teque, teque
> teque, reteque, reteque, teque
> with our apologies to Angola,
> because there's no instrument in Europe
> that I haven't mastered well enough for Seville
> in its plays, *entremeses*, *mojigangas*, and *pandorgas*.]

In this scene, the regidor and the alcalde characters trot about town calling on different people to take on various roles in the town's mojiganga. The boisterous and loquacious dancer Juan Danzante—referred to as "el buen cascabelillo" (v. 90) (the good scatterbrained one)—performs the role of a black woman, reciting his lines in habla de negros.

Like Quirós's *El regidor*, Calderón de la Barca's *La negra*—performed in Madrid's Retiro Park in honor of Carlos II's nuptials and wedding festivities of Felipe V and María Luisa de Saboya—calls on different actors on stage to take on the roles of marginalized figures. In the second part of the play (vv. 49–240), dancing and singing are fundamental components to its performance, where an unnamed black woman introduces herself as Angolan—"Aunque en Angola nacimo" (v. 109)—and addresses the king directly:

> NEGRA   Al Retiro
> con tura la vira y alma,
> a llevalle a nuezo Rey
> cunfita, culambazata,
> rozquetilla, peladilla
> y una linda papangaya,
> y unaz panzillaz que busco,
> que no laz hallamoz.
> *Canta.*
> Aunque negla, no tiznamo,
> a ver a nozo Rey vamo,
> que ez lo que máz dezeamo
> como zabe bozanzú.
> Zangulú, zangulú, zambambú,
> loz negros y blancoz le hazemoz el buz. (vv. 123–38)[93]

> [I'm headed to the Retiro
> with all my life and soul,
> to present to our new king
> marmalades, pumpkins,
> *roscas*, candied almonds,
> a beautiful parrot,
> and some raisins that I'm looking for,
> none of which I can find.

> *She sings*:
> Even though I'm a black woman, I'm not blackfaced (or
>   dirty),
> We go to see our king,
> whom we favor most
> because he knows *bonzanzú*.
> Zangulú, zangulú, zambambú,
> blacks and whites make music together.]

Recapitulating the biblical maxim "nigra sum, sed fermosa" (I am black and/but beautiful) from the Song of Songs (a literary imagery deployed not only by Góngora in "Santísimo Sacramento" but also by a variety of early modern Spanish poets and playwrights), Calderón inverts the negra's racialized status in the play. Her Blackness is not up for ridicule—"Aunque negra, no tiznamo" (v. 133), she asserts—hence aligning her personhood with an allegorical Christianity that relates back to amicability, cleanliness, and charity.[94]

In closing this section, I would like to direct our attention to the "lower frequencies" that Ralph Ellison famously evoked in *Invisible Man*. If we are to read the bailes de negros corpus as examples of Black communication, then, as Tavia Nyong'o affirms in his essay "Afro-philo-sonic Fictions: Black Sound Studies After the Millennium," the radical tradition of Black communication on the lower frequencies is what enables me in this chapter to challenge Western epistemic illiteracy in the field of black sound— or, at least, the sounds emitted not only by black mouths but also by the dances and sonic Blackness of habla de negros speech forms' signature grunts, hums, musicality, and vocables. Appearing in the baile, entremés, and mojiganga subgenres of the teatro breve, the variety of black dances explored herein represent most vividly instances in which Black communication and expression manifest in early modern Spain. I turn to an analysis of the lower frequencies in order to make better sense of Western (mis) perceptions of the hypersexuality of these dances. Moving forward in our analyses of Black cultural expression, we must tread carefully when analyzing and describing these dances. We must also take with a grain of salt Western derogatory descriptions of them, most notably in seventeenth- and eighteenth-century Spanish dictionaries, as well as contemporary literary criticism and historical commentary. Characterized by suggestive hip and pelvic movements, sultry gyration, and the poking and provoking of one's dance partner and audience, the category of the lower frequencies allows us to pivot our focus on the hypersexuality of black dances and their sounds from the carnal to, instead, the hypervisible and the hyperkinetic. The hypervisibility of black dances lends itself to the fact of the regularity of their performance and fame. Yet, in haptic, scopic, and visual contexts, dancing black flesh—blackfaced or not—mesmerized and titillated Spanish audiences, and, at other times, disgusted moralists. But I also believe that dances like the zarabanda and the zarambeque also give evidence to the realm of the hyperkinetic (so nicely nuanced in Covarrubias's definition of the zarabanda in the *Tesoro*), which highlights the impactful dynamism of these black dances in early modern Spanish culture and daily life. As hyperkinetic entities, black dances not only served the immediate role of performance but also anchored, on the one hand, and connected, on the other hand, African diasporic dance culture to Black sounds reverberating on both sides of the Hispanic Atlantic world.

While I concentrate in this book on habla de negros and the African diaspora in early modern Spain, it is also important to place the category of Blackness in conversation with the dances, musical traditions, and sounds of the Roma people and Iberian Muslims. Javier Irigoyen-García has gifted early modern Iberian studies with important scholarship on the *leilas* and the *zambras* in religious festivities as well as the prohibition of them in general efforts to uproot Morisco cultural practices.[95] Cervantes even makes these Afro-Islamic and Afro-Romani connections apparent in his exemplary novels such as *La gitanilla, La ilustre fregona,* and *El celoso extremeño.* At the turn of the eighteenth century and well into the nineteenth century, the repertoire of sub-Saharan African dances in Spain—especially the zarabanda and zarambeque—became flamenco-ized, or were "aflamencándose," becoming intimately linked to the term *zorongo*.[96] In her recent monographic study *Sonidos Negros: On the Blackness of Flamenco,* K. Meira Goldberg traces how, in the span between 1492 and 1933, vanquished Iberian Muslims became black and how the image of the "Moor," enacted in terms of a minstrelized *gitano*, paradoxically came to represent Spain itself. In his essay "'Quiero llorar': Lorca and the Flamenco Tradition in *Poeta en Nueva York*," Rob Stone offers an astute reading of flamenco *cante* in Federico García Lorca's *Poeta en Nueva York*. Comparing the vernacular expression of Black songs with that of the gypsies, Stone remarks, "[There was] specific appreciation of the affined songs of the Blacks and Gypsies, with their comparable techniques of humming, moaning, chorus, clapping, percussion, improvisation, hollers, repetition, colloquialisms and interjected *ayes*."[97] In more recent years, activists and scholars have dedicated their time to the study and preservation of Afro-Flamenco studies. Among them are Goldberg (flamenco dancer, dance historian), Miguel Ángel Rosales (anthropologist, film director of the documentary *Gurumbé: Afro-Andalusian Memories*), Yinka Esi Graves (flamenco dancer, scholar), and Alberto del Campo Tejedor (anthropologist), among many others. Thanks to their recent endeavors, the history of bailes de negros in Spain will continue to receive global attention.

A final meditation. I would like to bring my readers' attention to the Grammy Award–winning early music interpreter Jordi Savall's performance of "La negrilla: San Sabeya Gugurumbé" (1535; 1550), written by the Aragonese Renaissance composer Mateo Flecha "el Viejo."[98] In Savall's studio recording of "La negrilla," accompanied by Hespèrion XXI and La Capella Reial de Catalunya, Savall's album *Villancicos y danzas criollas de la Iberia antigua al Nuevo Mundo (1550–1750)* does not ridicule habla de negros speech. Rather, the early international music ensemble highlights and utilizes beautifully African polyrhythmic structures—hemiola shifts and sharp syncopation—with percussive and stringed instruments from sub-Saharan Africa, *and* African-descended performers and singers to re-present and reproduce African diasporic artistry, rhythms, and sounds in Flecha's "La negrilla." Contrary to common assumptions, Savall's interpretation of habla de negros language is *not* a burlesque caricature or contrived mockery of Black Spanish. I emphasize this point because I do not believe that the Renaissance Iberian composers, musicians, and playwrights I study in this chapter caricaturized or denigrated Africanized speech forms conclusively. In fact, Savall's reproduction of African rhythms reflects the Aragonese composer's song's defining quality as a potpourri of folkloric dance. On 1 November 2018, I attended Jordi Savall's Philadelphia premiere, titled "The Routes of Slavery," a musical memoir that honored the journeys and lived experiences of enslaved black Africans through the musical legacy they imparted. In doing so, Savall's ethical decision to center *visibly* black performers on stage to emphasize artistically sub-Saharan African rhythms and sounds in his "The Routes of Slavery" debut further illustrates my point that it behooves us to refrain from the easy seduction of uncritically imposing and swiftly reinforcing the notion that the usage of habla de negros and sonic Blackness automatically instantiate modes of bereft and derogatory Blackness. To that end, Jordi Savall reminds us that there still exist responsible efforts to convey and produce on stage and in a recording studio the complex beauty of the sonic Blackness of habla de negros.

Feasting on Blackness: The Bozal's Black Mouth in Simón Aguado's *Entremés de los negros*

Simón Aguado invites his audience to feast on Blackness in the one-act skit *Entremés de los negros*, signed and dated 10 August 1602 in Granada, Spain. The play discloses the problem of marriage between black African slaves, specifically the union between the couple Dominga and Gaspar. In the essay "Nuptials Gone Awry, Empire in Decay: Crisis, *Lo Cursi*, and the Rhetorical Inventory of Blackness in Quevedo's 'Boda de negros,'" I explain that "the recurring motif of the weddings of black people has a rich literary history traceable in a series of satiric burlesque texts in seventeenth-century Spain."[99] A historical case that parallels Aguado's *Los negros* as well as other early modern Spanish texts that explore the theme of black weddings and marriage practices appears in the Archivo de la Curia Episcopal de Granada. Housed in this archive is a massive file that documents the life, marriage, and legal proceedings of the black slaves Esperanza de Horozco and Francisco Mejía. Esperanza was the slave of Juana de Orozco, the wife of a *receptor* (auditor; debt collector) for the Real Audiencia de Granada. Francisco was the slave of the Inquisitor Mejía de Lasarte. The file explains that Esperanza was captured at the age of ten and arrived in Granada when she was twelve. Concerning the agency of black Africans in early modern Spain, Esperanza and Francisco both initiated a legal proceeding in 1579, petitioning the court to grant their marriage when they were twenty. In 1582, Esperanza and Francisco won the trial and were granted a license to marry.[100] In addition to Aguado's *Entremés de los negros*, I list these other works that add to the early modern Hispanic literary canon of black African weddings: "Francisco de Quevedo y Villegas's 'Boda de negros' (1643), Francisco de Avellaneda's *Baile entremesado de negros* (Madrid, 1663), the anonymous *Nueva relación y curioso romance, en que se refiere la celebridad, galanteo y acaso de una boda de Negros, Mojiganga de la negra, Entremés del negro, Entremés Segundo del negro*, and the ballad [romance] 'Por una negra señora' (attributed to Luis de Góngora y Argote)."[101]

Aguado's *Los negros* is set in seventeenth-century Seville, a fascinating and volatile time in the city's history, when a heightened fear of blacks' recalcitrance existed.[102] The consequences and implications of an African's perceived obstinance becomes reflected in the playwright's depiction of Dominga's and Gaspar's slave masters, Rubio and Ruiz, who are infuriated that their slaves have neglected their domestic duties because they have fallen in love. To prevent Dominga and Gaspar from marrying, Rubio and Ruiz threaten to singe their flesh—*pringar*—with melted lard. The two slaves respond to their masters' violent threats by relying on song and dance to assuage their owners' ire, but, more importantly, through the medium of music—a form that grants them greater artistic and intellectual freedom than direct discourse.[103]

Despite the work's recurring racist epithets that align blacks with buffoonery, hypersexuality, promiscuity, and rabid dogs (as constituted and informed by seventeenth-century Seville's hyperawareness of its black population's defiance), I find the historic verisimilitude of Black rebellion directly coterminous with Dominga and Gaspar's misread "proclivities" for song and dance as an illustration of Black agentive voices and resistance. Through performance, the two slaves protest their masters, as bastions of the institution of slavery, to reclaim all aspects of their destiny:

> Dominga:　　Toca, mi Gasipar.
> 　　　　　　(Solo. Cantando van bailando)
> 　　　　　　Juraro tiene Dominga
> 　　　　　　de querer á Gasipar.
> Dominga:　　Y no me pienso mudar
> 　　　　　　aunque ma se me pringa.
> Gaspar:　　　¿Que tanto firme estarás
> 　　　　　　aunque le pese á mi amo?

Dominga:	Hasta que á la igresia vamo con lo créigo detrás.
Gaspar:	Mira lo mexo, Dominga, que te vienen á pringar, y no me pienso mudar, aunque mase me pringa.[104]

[Dominga:	Play, Gaspar, my love!
(*Solo. While singing, they start dancing*):	Dominga has sworn to love Gaspar.
Dominga:	And the threat of being burned with boiling lard will never stop me from loving.
Gaspar:	Will you remain strong, even if it angers my master?
Dominga:	Till the day we enter the church with the cleric behind us.
Gaspar:	Careful now, Dominga; be careful! They're coming to punish you, and I'll never stop loving you; no matter the consequences.]

The wives of the slaveholders then soon arrive, challenge their husbands' threats of torture, and suggest the slaves marry. Rubio and Ruiz, as a result, acquiesce and the play ends with the departure of Dominga and Gaspar (now accompanied by a group of other blacks) toward the residence of the local priest.

As the performance continues, the protagonist Dominga—more beautiful than a bright, shining star ("crara estrella")—takes center stage to avow her agency, legitimacy, and social status as former royalty and a now baptized subject. Through the historical backdrop that overlaps Aguado's *Los negros*, we learn that Dominga and Gaspar come from the Kingdom of Mali—"Tumbucutu," the text says—but were born in the Kingdom of Kongo and later baptized in Seville ("Dominga me yamo, Manicongo nacimo, Sevylla batizamolo").[105] Codified in her agentive voice and subject positioning is her savvy ability to demonstrate her integration into the society of Counter-Reformation Spain. Aguado, as creator and mediator of Dominga's habla de negros language and voice, positions her as a benevolent, baptized Christian woman. And to that end, he challenges and critiques the false notion of Black inferiority. Through Dominga's defense of black Africans, Aguado upholds the idea that blacks are indeed human and virtuous by modifying the biblical Song of Songs message "I am black and/but beautiful" to "toro somo pecandole," or "we are all sinners"—a claim that implicates white people in the religious narrative of holiness, purity, and salvation. Dominga's firm declaration facilitates the playwright's ideological standpoint as collateral, or evidence, for legitimating her marriage to Gaspar.

*

As explained earlier in this chapter, the entremés, as Eugenio Asensio has shown, was not an inherently inferior artistic medium limited to crude burlesques and the depiction of contemporary customs but a complex, protean form that, rooted in folk art and contiguous with the picaresque novel, was capable of considerable nuance and subtlety in its depiction of Spanish social structure and mores.[106] *Los negros* emerged during a period (1600–1620) when the entremés began to use verse, the privileged medium of literature, and to rely heavily on satire and caricature in its depiction of black Africans and other dominant and marginalized groups.[107]

Aguado's use of the entremés, as a theatrical genre and form, lends itself to the image of the black body as a site to examine the black mouth and ideas of orality as they relate to blackface performance's necessity to portray banquet scenes and food thematically. My food studies reading of *Los negros* takes cues from Kyla Wazana Tompkins in *Racial Indigestion*, where she more closely binds food studies to feminist, queer, and gender studies, as well as to critical race theory.[108] In doing so, like Tompkins, I want to argue for the intellectually limited inheritance of the epidermal ontology of race[109]—hence, my decision to title this chapter "Black Skin *Acts*" in relation to blackface performance and the themes of eating, food, and the black mouth it enacts.

Scholarship on *Los negros* has overlooked the skit's ambient food culture. This juncture of my analysis of Aguado's text argues for the triangulation between the recurring themes of food, dancing, and singing. My exploration of these modes of representing Blackness in Spanish early modernity also serves as a more in-depth discussion of my ideas about eating practices and food culture in the subsequent chapter on Rodrigo de Reinosa's poem "Gelofe, Mandinga." To that end, via the trope of feasting on Blackness in Aguado's *Los negros*, this section uncovers the ways in which the play's final banquet scene puts forth a discourse about the culture of eating insofar as the presence of food cannot be detached from our analysis of blackface performance as a technique to dramatize the habla de negros–talking black mouth.

Toward the end of *Los negros*, the play's stage directions call for all the blacks available on stage to fall in formation to dance the zarabanda with tambourines and rattles ("Ven entrando todos los negros que pueden en orden, danzando la zarabanda, con tamboriles y sonajas"):[110]

> TODOS.
> Tu, pu tu tu.
> (*Solo.*)
> En lu desposorio,
> tu, pu tu tu ...
> le daremos á toros,
> tu,
> canelonen gordos,
> tu,
> torta y bicicochos,
> tu,
> rábano y cohombro,
> tu,
> perejil y repoyo,
> tu,
> pasas y mondongo,
> tu,
> calabaza y hongo,
> tu,
> culantriyo de pozo,
> tu,
> y porque los novios,

tu,
duerman con reposo,
tu,
un caldiyo de poyo,
tu,
Tanta vida les dé Dios
cuanta pueden desear.
A la boda de Gasipar
y Dominga de Tumbucutu
toro habemon de bailar.
Toca, negro.
Toca tú.
Tu, pu tu tu.
(*Y bailando y cantando acaban.*)

[EVERYONE.
Tu, pu tu tu.
(*Solo.*)
At your wedding,
tu, pu tu tu . . .
we'll hand out to everyone,
tu,
fat cannoli,
tu,
cakes and cookies,
tu,
radishes and cucumbers,
tu,
parsley and cabbage,
tu,
raisins and mondongo,
tu,
pumpkins and mushrooms,
tu,
culantro from the well,

tu,
because the bride and groom,
tu,
will slumber for a bit,
tu,
some chicken consommé,
tu,
May God grant them the bountiful life
they so much desire.
At the wedding of
Gaspar and Dominga of Timbuctu,
everyone dances and has a good time.
Play black man!
Play!
Tu, pu tu tu.
(*Dancing and singing, they finish.*)]

Although it would be easy for present-day readers to perceive this final dance scene as a minstrel show, it is important to remember that early modern Spanish theatergoers and playwrights interpreted this scene differently. And in particular, given the racial demographics of African-descended populations across Andalusia at the time, it is plausible for black Africans and their descendants to have formed a significant part of the audience and to have negotiated a complex understanding of Aguado's dramatization of African diasporic culture.

The play's numerous references to its black characters' musical abilities have some basis in historical fact, and it illuminates the rich oral literature of habla de negros vernacular expression in its conjoining of dance, music, and the word in Aguado's *Los negros*.[111] The playwright's more sympathetic adaptation and transformative image of sub-Saharan African song and dance also echoes black feminist and postcolonial scholar Sylvia Wynter's insight that "the stereotype of the dancing/singing minstrel *over-saw* an important truth: the black transplanted the dance because it was a central part of the oral/ritual structure of his religious world."[112] Even further, the habla de negros sonic enterprise showcased in *Los negros* demonstrates Alexander G. Weheliye's adroit commentary on "how black cultures have contributed to the very creation and imagination of the modern, interrogating the facticity of Blackness, that is, how certain groups of humans became black through a multitude of material and discursive powers."[113] Aguado's black characters are dissident figures who—like many of the other African-descendant characters studied in this book—challenge us to wrestle with the fact that Blackness is an effect of Western modernity, although not reducible to a colonialist imposition on black people.[114]

The closing lines of *Los negros* show us that eating and feasting are racially performative acts. While habla de negros–speaking mouths are never visible in the play, but obviously assumed and known to exist, the singing and talking black mouths Aguado creates in *Los negros* render food to stimulate biological urges and to promote craving and lust. Again, the text's dizzying, excessive repetition of food is revealing:

> At your wedding,
> tu, pu tu tu . . .
> we'll hand out to everyone,
> tu,
> fat cannoli,
> tu,
> cakes and cookies,
> tu,
> radishes and cucumbers,
> tu,
> parsley and cabbage,
> tu,
> raisins and mondongo,
> tu,
> pumpkins and mushrooms,
> tu,
> culantro from the well,
> tu,
> because the bride and groom,
> tu,
> will slumber for a bit,
> tu,

> a bit of chicken consommé,
> tu,
> May God grant them bountiful life
> they so much deserve.

Aguado's textual repertoire here thus activates most vividly my rendering of a blackface performance that would appear in a habla de negros text's closing baile de negros scene. The passage centers and links the image of food with hospitality, grace, bonding, and celebration. In this ceremonious celebratory scene, the black mouth speaks, laughs, and eats in the face of the violent desires of white supremacy; in fact, speech, laughter, and eating are conjoined as tropes of the black cultural presence and resistance operative in Aguado's *Los negros*. The previous passage illustrates the sonic Blackness and vocalization of the play's conglomeration of black performers' habla de negros speech. Within it, the sonic Blackness operative in this medley evoke a unique black slave culture. In addition to the context of the quote's celebratory space of a wedding banquet, Aguado's food imagery also reprises allegorically the hearth: the site of the home where African-descended persons cooked, prepped, served, and shared food—not only for their masters *but* among themselves. Ultimately, *Los negros* sends a message that there is Black joy in dancing and singing, not just buffoonery and misery at the expense of a White desire and gaze.

I further nuance my analysis of the aforementioned closing verses by connecting and tracing them back to Rodrigo de Reinosa's twenty-six-verse-long poem "Mangana, Mangana," a work meant to be sung and danced to in *guinea* style:

> *Mangana, mangana*
> *no tener vino ni chucaracana.*
>
> Yo me ir a porta de ferro
> con mi esporta y asadón,
> a buscar esterco de perro
> con que comprar camisón:
> mi amo no dar jubón
> si mí trabajas no gana,

Mangana, mangana,
no tener vino ni chucaracana.
Yo me ir a porta de villa,
antes que salir el sol,
con mi pala y esportilla
a coger la caracol,
para mi amo comprar col
que vender en el aduana;
mangana, mangana,
no tener vino ni chucaracana.
Fin.
Yo me iba allá a la horta
para el nabo mercar,
e abrir pasico la porta
y hortelano no fallar;
y los nabos le hurtar,
y una cebolla albarrana;
mangana, mangana,
no tener vino ni chucaracana[115]

[*Mangana, mangana*
I have no wine or goodies to eat.
I'm heading off to the iron door (Puerta de Hierro)
with my sword and pickax.
I'm looking for dog manure,
so that I can buy a night shirt.
My master gives me no soap,
but if I don't work, I make no money.
Mangana, mangana
I have no wine or goodies to eat.
I'm heading off to the city gate (Puerta de Villa),
before nightfall,
with my stick and my dagger
in search of snails
so that my master can buy cabbage
to sell in the town square.

Mangana, mangana
I have no wine or goodies to eat.
End.
I was headed off to the orchard
in search of turnips to sell,
but upon opening the way to the gate
that gardener never fails,
he already stole my turnips
and my delicious country-grown onions.
Mangana, mangana
I have no wine or goodies to eat.]

Like Aguado's *Los negros*, Reinosa's "Mangana, Mangana," written a century prior, reveals and indicts the injustices of slavery. And like Aguado's play, Reinosa's racially performative text bears witness to the slave's voice, complaints, and pleas for food, which lend themselves to the image of eating as central to the performative production of linguistically raced bodies in early modern Spain. Such a mode of performativity behooves us to think about the ways in which food imagery in early modern Castilian depictions of Blackness account for the perceived viscerality of Black difference, but also the way in which food in both Aguado and Reinosa metaphorizes fleshly experience—enslavement, freedom, and marriage as examples—at the threshold of habla de negros linguistic expression.

Hispanic Blackface 2.0: From the Bozal's Black Mouth to *Conguitos*

If blackface performance cannot be separated from habla de negros language, as this chapter has contended, then habla de negros cannot be theorized without a close reading of the term "bozal." As I think about further habla de negros language *outside of* its early modern periodized context, the insights of Gilles Deleuze and Félix Guattari, in their essay "What Is a Minor Literature," remind me that many people today—as well as back then in the early modern period—live in a language that is not their own.[116] "Rich or poor," argue the two philosophers, "each language always implies a deterritorialization of the mouth, the tongue, and the teeth."[117] What the two critics speak of holds true for the Black Experience vis-à-vis habla de negros language. Paradoxically, early modern Spanish constructions of Africanized Castilian fragment and rupture the black body, precisely indicating the "deterritorialization of the mouth, the tongue, and the teeth" to which Deleuze and Guattari refer. The notion of deterritorialization manifests in early modern dictionary definitions that create a visual economy of excessive "big black lips" through the word "bozal." I understand habla de negros speech forms to hyperembody the bozal imaginary alongside the maxillofacial economy the term purports in the racial imagining of *how* illiterate black slaves might enunciate, pronounce, and speak Castilian incorrectly. Hyperbole and the racialized-linguistic constitution of the bozal, for instance, are congruent concepts that establish the rhetorical value of hyperbole as a master trope in literary texts and nonliterary documents to connote and denote Blackness as excessive matter.

Originally, the word "bozal" meant "savage" or "untamed horse," ultimately referring to the Portuguese and Castilian spoken by black African slaves. The "bozal" is also a muzzle: the device employed to censure, silence, and tame humans' words and to also prevent animals from barking and biting. As David Wheat points out, the term is comparable to *chapetón*, a Spanish-American word that referred to rosy-cheeked Iberians newly arrived in the Americas.[118] But Africans labeled as "bozles" were not merely inexperienced greenhorns; they were viewed as newcomers to the Iberian world in general, unacquainted with its social and cultural practices.[119] As the category's use rapidly declined on the Iberian Peninsula, due to shrinking black populations, the term did, however, continue to circulate in the Anglophone slave vernacular and Spanish Caribbean colonies—primarily in Cuba—well into the twentieth century, circulating in Blackface *teatro bufo* performances and private religious celebratory gatherings called *cajón de muerto* from the Congolese-centered Palo Mayombe religious-spiritual traditions.

My reading of bozal embodies a somatic-linguistic relationship. The prolix lexicographer Covarrubias defines "bozal" as "el negro que no sabe otra lengua que la suya; y la lengua, o lenguaje se llama labio, y los labios bezos; de boca, boza, y de allí bozal"[120] (The black who knows no other tongue than his own. The tongue, or language, derives its name from the lips, and big lips come from "boca" to "boza," from which we get "bozal"). Covarrubias's entry reveals Habsburg Spain's somatic and cultural fixation on big African lips. The trope of big (African) lips recurs in countless sixteenth- and seventeenth-century Spanish archival, poetic, prosaic, and theatrical works. Therefore, Covarrubias's etymological treatment of the word "bozal" fixates on bodily excess, the grotesque, the scatological, and the uncanny, each functioning as metadiscourses that further characterize literary authors' renditions of habla de negros linguistic embodiment on the written page.

The *Diccionario de Autoridades*—the first dictionary of the Castilian language published by the Real Academia Española, in six volumes, between 1726 and 1739—reiterates, yet qualifies, Covarrubias's seventeenth-century definition of "bozal." The *Autoridades* categorizes "bozal" as "el inculto y que está por desbastar y pulir. Es epíteto que ordinariamente se da a los negros, en especial cuando están recién venidos de sus tierras: y se aplica también a los rústicos. Es lo contrario de ladino"[121] (illiterate, thus in need of educating and polishing. It is the epithet that is ordinarily given to blacks, especially when they are recent arrivals from their native lands; it also applies to rustic people. It is the opposite of *ladino*). While Covarrubias's conceptualization of bozal hinges on an anatomical taxonomy linked to a definition of habla de negros speech, the entry from the *Diccionario de Autoridades* closely turns to ideological ways of envisioning habla de negros in relation to the black Africans who speak it. Binary oppositions are also furnished: polished versus unpolished; literate versus illiterate. Primeval, the "African" (barbarian) bozal is antithetical to the "Hispanicized" (civilized) ladino. The two dichotomous terms war with each other conceptually and ideologically.[122]

Bozal speech, as a textured, polysemous synonym for habla de negros, cannot be examined without thinking about the ideological implications of ladino as a terminological variable of Whiteness. The bozal's link to habla de negros operates as the coterminous antithesis of the ladino's link to vernacular Latin known as ladino or romance. If an African spoke Castilian "properly," then that individual was deemed "ladino."[123] And when ladino appeared in slave contracts, for example, it classified the slave and implied his/her greater worth.[124] As consistent with dictionary entries from Covarrubias and the *Diccionario de Autoridades*, which sought to animalize the black (bozal) mouth, white performers and playwrights utilized early Spanish stages to fixate on black people's mouths. The categories of bozal and ladino, in sum, are dichotomous categories that salute a larger systematic way of early modern

FIG. 8. "Conguitos" postcard.

Spanish measures to domesticate the so-called *un*domesticated bozal African slave through language. An articulation of cultural and linguistic domestication, where the racialized bodies and speech of African-descended bozal and ladino subjects exists, both reinforce and destabilize imperial Spanish linguistic and racial markings.[125]

*

Moving past the way in which blackface performance and habla de negros language converge and splice on early Spanish stages, I close with a meditation urging Hispanic studies scholars and students to unpack the legacy and the possible connections between the early modern Spanish representations of blackface we have covered in this chapter and the blackface—or, perhaps, "chocolate"—iconography of the long-popular chocolate-and-peanut candies

FIG. 9. Igrexa de San Fiz de Solovio, Santiago de Compostela.

named "Conguitos" (little guys from the Congo), whose logo is a caricature of a black man (or boy) reminiscent of a similarly racialized logo in the United States from an earlier era (fig. 8).[126]

In addition to the racialized image of anthropomorphized chocolate confectioneries for consumption and sale, we can also discuss the visual iconography of the stargazing wise king Balthazar. As I think about the legacy of blackface cosmetic and performative practices in early modern Spain, I am curious as to when and where one begins to trace the racialized performance of blackfacing Balthazar. At what point in time does the racial impersonation of Balthazar begin in Spanish (and Latin American) popular culture? In art history, as well as in the original twelfth-century theatrical work *Auto de los Reyes Magos*, Balthazar is neither blackfaced nor racialized with the same negative connotations of the so-called dark Other we would understand today. To the contrary, figures 9 and 10 communicate a different visual iconography of a black Balthazar. The image from the Igrexa de San Fiz de Solovio was the site of the actual first pilgrimage church in Santiago de Compostela. Figure 10 is a relief of a black Balthazar from an early

FIG. 10. Early fourteenth-century romanesque portico, Catalonia.

fourteenth-century Romanesque portico in Catalonia. These lingering meditations and critical inquiries behoove us to continue creating new scholarly projects on the materiality of Blackness—chromatic and otherwise—in medieval Iberia that cannot be detached so easily from visual iconographies of blackface in present-day Peninsular Spanish and Latin American popular culture and social media.[127]

2

THE BIRTH OF HISPANIC
HABLA DE NEGROS
Signifying for the Black Audience in Rodrigo de Reinosa

In 1490, Fernão da Silveira, court official and poet to King João II, poeticized the voice of an African king from Sierra Leone visiting Évora, Portugal:

> A min rrey de negro estar Serra Lyoa.
> Lonje muyto terra onde viver nos.
> Lodar caytbela Tubao de Lisboa,
> falar muao novas casar pera vos.
> Querer a mym logo ver vos como vay.
> Leyxar molher meu, partyr muyto synha,
> porque sempre nos servyr vosso pay;
> folgar muyto negro estar vos rraynha.
> Aqueste gente meu taybo: terra nossa
> nunca folguar, andar sempre guerra.
> Nam saber quy que balhar terra vossa.
> Balhar que saber como nossa terra.
> Se logo vos quer mandar a mym venha,
> fazer que saber, tomar que achar.
> Mandar fazer taybo lugar, Des mantenha!
> e loguo meu negro, senhora, balhar.[1]

[I am the king of blacks from Sierra Leone.
Our land is very far away.
A *Tubao* vessel from Lisbon arrived
carrying news of your wedding festivities.
I immediately wanted to see what you, the Portuguese, are
    like.
I left my wife's side in a hurry,
for we always serve your Lord,
and we blacks are happy you're the Queen.
The people here are good.
In my Sierra Leone we never rest because we're always at
    war.
I don't know what to dance here in Portugal,
but I'll dance what I know is custom in Sierra Leone.
So, if you insist,
I'll perform for you what I know and will choose the best
    dance.
Let the festivities begin and may God protect us!
And now I, the black man (king), Dear Queen, will dance.]

Silveira's sixteen-verse-long poem was recited on 30 November 1490 in Évora in celebration of the wedding festivities and marriage of Prince Fernando, son of João II and inheritor of the Portuguese Crown, to Isabella, the daughter of the Catholic Monarchs Queen Isabella I of Castile and Ferdinand II of Aragon. Silveira's vocalization of the Sierra Leonean king's voice exemplifies the material and performative expressions of African diasporic dance and music catalogued in Garcia de Resende's *Cancioneiro geral* (compiled ca. 1483; printed in 1516). The *Cancioneiro geral* introduces the theatricalized performance under the following title: "Coudel moor por breve de hūa mourisca rratorta que [man]dou fazer a senhora princeza quando esposou." Resende describes the dance scene, or *mourisca retorta*, as it is called, in his *Vida e feitos del rey Dom João segundo* as follows:

> E ouve ahi hūa muito grande reprsentaçam dhum rey de Guinee em que vinham tres gigantes espantosos que pareciam vivos, de mais de quarenta palmos cada hum, com ricos vestidos todos pintados

d'ouro, que parecia cousa muito rica; e com elles hũa muy grande e rica mourisca retorta em que vinham dozentos manilhas polos braços e pernas douradas que cuidavam que erão d'ouro e cheos de cascavees dourados e muito bem concertados: cousa muy bem feita e de muito custo por serem tantos, e em que se gastou muita seda e ouro; e faziam tamanho roydo com os muytos cascavees que traziam que se nam ouvião com elles.[2]

[Here today marks a grand performance by the king of Guinea, who entered with three frightening lifelike giants, each standing over forty yards tall. They were lavishly adorned in gold, and with them was a dance troupe of two hundred men painted in black, all extraordinary dancers whose arms and legs were covered in thick, heavy gold bangles with bells. For such a large group and large sum of money spent on the copious amounts of silk and gold, it was a performance very well done and in good taste. The dancers made so much noise with all their bells that one didn't know if they were howling among themselves.]

Each of the aforementioned passages from Resende's *Cancioneiro geral* represents not only a mise-en-scène but, more interestingly, a black-en-scène. As a performance of Blackness, where the vernacular and the nontextual carry pertinent meanings, Silveira's textual poeticizing of the Sierra Leonean king's African diasporic language and voice comes to life through dance, mediation, literariness. After all, as we are explicitly told, the scene is a blackface performance represented by two hundred dancers adorned and dressed as black Africans draped in silk and gold. The textual presence of the African king's *fala de preto* speech, as it is enhanced theatrically by the mourisca retorta dance, marshals, on the one hand, and renders legible, on the other hand, Mary Louise Pratt's term "contact zone." I find Pratt's terminology apt for analyzing the *Cancioneiro geral*'s Luso-African references because it illustrates an elite, courtly space in which peoples geographically and historically separated come into contact with each other.[3] To be clear, I do not read Silveira's imagined African king as a powerless slave. Rather, I treat him as a sovereign dignitary. Scholars must be cautious not to immediately assume that all blacks in early modern Iberia were automatically enslaved by the Portuguese and later the Spanish as chattel. Just as it is easy to assume and equate racial Blackness in early modern Iberia with bondage, it is also plausible to assume otherwise. By the late 1400s, for example, Iberians and sub-Saharan Africans on the Upper Guinea coast maintained their interaction and spurred the formation of a creolized Luso-African society. As David Wheat explains, "Iberian clergymen visited the Rivers of Guinea as missionaries and diplomats, and Portuguese and Luso-African traders integrated themselves into commercial networks geared toward regional exchange, rather than large-scale slave production, all along the Upper Guinea coast."[4] "As late as the 1630s," Wheat adds, "Iberian merchants' acquisition of Upper Guinean captives for export remained merely one element in a broader system of trade that included the extensive participation of Luso-Africans and Africans of diverse status and the exchange of European commodities alongside local products such as millet and beeswax."[5] Pratt's "contact zone" theory suitably encapsulates my discussion of Silveira's and Resende's aforementioned quotes insofar as the "contact zone" attempts to invoke spatial and temporal copresence of subjects previously separated by geographic and historical disjunctures, and whose trajectories now intersect.[6] Even the materiality of the dance troupe's clothing and dress—sub-Saharan African gold, bangles, and bells—harmonize with the evocation of "à mourisca," or the Moorishness, of silk fabric, which also vividly characterizes Pratt's "contact zone" paradigm. A "contact" perspective is productive for my analysis of the *Cancioneiro geral*'s image of Africanized Portuguese language and West African dance because it treats the relations among black Africans and Iberians—in this case, the court of João II—in terms of copresence, interaction, and interlocking understandings and practices, often within radically asymmetrical relations of power.[7]

Silveira's lyrics also attest to the voyages of Vasco da Gama to the African continent, where the opening line—"A min rrey de negro estar Serra Lyoa" (I am the king of blacks of Sierra Leone)—captures the language of a king from Sierra Leone. The linguist John Lipski frames the royal figure's Africanized Portuguese in the chronicles of Gaspar Correa and the voyages of Vasco da Gama. Lipski confirms that Silveira "provides a realistic sample of what the first groping linguistic contacts between Africans and Portuguese speakers must have been like."[8] In the context of black Africans—enslaved and free—and the proliferation of the Africanized languages they spoke on Iberian soil, Resende's profound knowledge and thorough study of blacks in early modern Portugal must not go unnoticed. His *Chronica de el-Rei D. João II* informs us that by the end of the fifteenth century, eighteen thousand black and Iberian Muslim slaves constituted 16 percent of the population in Évora—at the time the second largest city of Portugal, capital of the Alentejo, preferred residence of the later kings of the dynasty of Avis, and the location of Silveira's aforementioned poem.[9]

The legacy and ligature of Resende's documentation of Africanized Portuguese in the *Cancioneiro geral* carries over into Renaissance Castilian court poetry. The earliest and most concrete example of Spain's inheritance of African diasporic language from Portugal occurs at the turn of the sixteenth century, thus inaugurating the birth of literary Hispanic habla de negros. Between 1516 and 1524, a *montañés* poet from the highlands of Cantabria by the name of Rodrigo de Reinosa (a contemporary of Garcia de Resende) composed the habla de negros poems "Gelofe, Mandinga" and "Mangana, Mangana."[10] A third poem attributed to him, titled "Canta, Jorgico, Canta" (ca. 1520–24), does not use Africanized Castilian entirely—with the exception of the refrain "no queré cantá"—but is often catalogued in Reinosa's corpus of habla de negros poetry.

Reinosa's poems take place in the metropolis of Seville, the same city I discuss anecdotally in the introduction and reference throughout this book. A pioneer in the cultivation of habla de negros and *germanía* (the language of street thugs), Reinosa was versed in different dialects and languages. He specialized in the literary representation of other speech forms characteristic of Renaissance Spain's urban underworld: that of ruffians (*rufianes*), prostitutes (*rameras*), Celestinesque figures (*alcahuetas* and *comadres*), and shepherds (*pastores*) from the countryside. Textual criticism has viewed the poet as perpetuating racist stereotypes that debase and deride blacks in his poetry.[11] Yet I am not convinced of such claims. In Reinosa's depiction of these various marginal groups and their linguistic variants, he disrupts social and cultural boundaries while arguably reinforcing them. But furthermore, the poet ruptures sociocultural and racial boundaries along the lines of the visual, social class, and space. Conceptually and theoretically germane to the collective argument of this book, this chapter unravels the complex ways in which Rodrigo de Reinosa contests how present-day readers—as well as the established critical reception bestowed on Reinosa's corpus of habla de negros poetry that has guided this readership—would interpret his habla de negros poetry as what I call an early modern form of cultural and literary "Blaxploitation."[12]

"Gelofe, Mandinga" captures vividly the knotty tug-of-war struggle between reconciling the racist stereotyping of black Africans and their empowerment. While at first glance Reinosa's representation of habla de negros is difficult to decipher, his exploration of Africanity and Black subjectivity is nuanced and sophisticated. "Africanity" is a term that I elect in order to manufacture a critical vocabulary for scholars, students, and general readers of Reinosa's "Gelofe, Mandinga."[13] The concept and notion of Africanity in Reinosa makes visible for my audience what has been rendered invisible: characteristics of sub-Saharan African culture and expression. "Gelofe, Mandinga" mediates a larger didactic conversation about the diversity of West African customs and culinary habits, whose virtues illustrative of Africanity will shed light on Reinosa's rich cartographical and material indexing of West African goods and objects that describe foods associated with the quotidian life unique to many West African ethnic grounds and their kingdoms. Reinosa renders his black African characters visible and vocal in his poetry. I firmly contend that he animates their presence through the poem's caption—*pliego suelto*—"Comiençan unas coplas a los negros y negras" (Here begin some couplets to the black men and women [of Seville]), which ultimately recognizes Seville's large black population at the turn of the sixteenth century.

For Reinosa, "Africa" as a geographic space and concept is not an abstraction. In this chapter, I aim to reposition him as an early modern Castilian writer cognizant of West Africa and its diverse cultures, numerous ethnonyms, and ethnolinguistic identities. I argue henceforth that Reinosa exposes his audience to West African customs and foodways through characteristics of black expression such as the verbal art of signifying. The exact definition of signifying is contested because it is used to refer to so many communicative phenomena, from tongue-in-cheek reference to prior speakers and writers to playfully insulting a conversational adversary.[14] For the interests of this chapter, signifying refers to (1) the playful insulting of an adversary and (2) an indirect method of communication whereby the speaker builds meaning intended for a restricted audience using signals that only the intended audience will be able to recognize and decode. Other tactics such as rhyming, mimicry, call-and-response, repetition, teasing, and shouting out (one's name or another phrase) cannot be overlooked in our analysis of the role of signifying in "Gelofe, Mandinga." I will further explore signifying as a hybridized form of cultural politics—as articulated by black Africans in

Spain—that, on the one hand, illustrates an inner dialectical quality of subversive black speech and, on the other hand, complicates the relationship between black spectators (the audience) and the performance of race, gender, and black diasporic identity positioning. In the Spain of Felipe II, one of the earliest examples of signifying manifests as irony and self-defense in Juan Latino's two-book epic poem *Austrias carmen*, which chronicles the Battle of Lepanto and asserts himself as a worthy heir to Virgil.[15]

The effect of signifying is that unfamiliar listeners mistake or fail to grasp the full significance of the communication.[16] Comba and Jorge's signifying speech acts show that the intended audience—"a los negros y negras [de Sevilla]" (to the black men and women [of Seville])—appreciates the artistry of the signifier, is aware of the vernacular game in play, and can decode hidden meanings.[17] By contrast, the unintended audience, which may be victimized through verbal attacks embedded in signifying, is unaware of the game and any artistry or skill employed by the speaker.[18] This is precisely why I urge my readers to imagine Reinosa's audience as black. When, for once, African diasporic people are privileged as predominant audience members of "Gelofe, Mandinga," we as present-day readers then realize that Africanized Castilian has a symbolic power, an expressive force that rebuts the tendentious "racist stereotype." A reiteration of two central inquiries will help guide our outlook on signifying in "Gelofe, Mandinga": (1) how might the black audience of "Gelofe, Mandinga" hear and ingest habla de negros? and (2) how might they internalize this language that is simultaneously spoken and performed by their ethno-racial counterparts? In sum, my goal here is to interrogate the implications that underwrite signifying as a verbal practice, rhetorical mode, and literary device constructed and mediated by Reinosa and expressed by his two black African protagonists, Comba and Jorge.

Can Reinosa Signify? Habla de Negros and Signifying for Reinosa's Black Audience

Before I go on to analyze textual examples of signifying in "Gelofe, Mandinga," it is imperative to clarify that Reinosa is a white writer who constructs the habla de negros language spoken by the poem's protagonists, Comba and Jorge. Secondly, habla de negros exhibits a larger African diasporic paradigm of signifying, cultural and racial ideologies, and African cultural survivals. Third, as a result, we can deduce that habla de negros is not fully controlled nor policed by a White gaze; it, in fact, operates *outside* of a White gaze, albeit paradoxically, since it is produced by a white writer.

Thus, can Reinosa signify? To ask this question is counterproductive and misdirected. If anything, the question is fueled by latent anxieties that, upon leaving their dormant state, reify an essentialist racial discourse—thereby insinuating, on the one hand, that white authors can only produce literary works *about* white people and, on the other hand, that black writers are the only ones who can "realistically" portray an "authentic" account of their people's Black Experience in the world. In *The Signifying Monkey: A Theory of African-American Literary Criticism*, Henry Louis Gates Jr. does not, in fact, say that signifying is exclusive to black writers. "Signifyin(g), of course," Gates asserts, "is a principle of language use and is not in any way the exclusive province of black people, although blacks named the term and invented its rituals."[19] In defining "signifyin(g)" as a cultural and theoretical concept, Gates reiterates, "it is difficult to arrive at a consensus of definitions of Signification."[20] He declares, "This difficulty of definition is a direct result of the fact that Signifying is the black term for what in classical European rhetoric are called figures of signification. Because to Signify is to be figurative, to define it in practice is to define it through any number of its embedded tropes."[21] And because signifying is troping, it encapsulates the figurative difference between the literal and the metaphorical. Consequently, because the term presupposes an "encoded" intention to say one thing but to mean another, I am called to ask: What assumptions and anxieties drive the inquiry behind "can a white author signify?" Signifying and its rhetorical tropes configure the categories of classical Western rhetoric. Gates insightfully explains, "Black language use recalls Montaigne's statement in 'On the Vanity of Words,' that 'When you hear people talk about metonymy, metaphor, and allegory, and other such names in grammar, doesn't it seem that they mean some rare and exotic form of language?' Rather, Montaigne concludes, 'They are terms that apply to the babble of your chambermaid.' We can add that these terms also apply to the rapping of black kids on street corners, who recite and thereby preserve the classical black rhetorical structures."[22] What Gates highlights in this passage conveys no different of a meaning than the rich habla de negros verbal battles between Comba and Jorge in "Gelofe, Mandinga." Thus, if signifying is the figurative difference between literal and figurative meanings, which the European literary and rhetorical traditions have portrayed over time, then Reinosa, through his creation of "Gelofe, Mandinga," transcends the urge to both essentialize and racialize the practice of signifying. As opposed to asking, "Can Reinosa signify?"—also inscribed playfully in Ron Shelton's 1992 movie *White Men Can't Jump*—I propose, instead, to interrogate the implications that foresee signifying as a practice and literary device used by both black and white authors. By "implications," I refer to a set of power relations that, in one sense, sustain a White power structure that ideologically portrays blacks and their habla de negros language negatively and, in another sense, challenge the same power relations buttressed by a systemic White structure therein. As an example of the implications of signifying, Gates emphasizes, "Black writers, like critics of black literature, learn to write by reading literature, especially the canonical texts of the Western tradition."[23] More importantly, he adds, "These black texts employ many of the conventions of literacy form that comprise the Western tradition. Black literature shares much with, far more than it differs from, the Western textual tradition, primarily registered in English, Spanish, Portuguese, and French."[24] What concerns me here is if black authors and their creation of narrative fictions are inherently framed within a Western (White/European) literary and theoretical paradigm, where does one draw the line between a black writing subject and a white author, such as Rodrigo de Reinosa, who uses black characters to signify in habla de negros language? Some skeptical critics would argue that Reinosa *cannot* signify whatsoever—and for that matter cannot "genuinely" write a literary work that "authentically" portrays black people—due to the utterly racist, misogynistic, and violent representations of blacks that are reinforced by Comba and Jorge. In this book, I endeavor to disrupt authenticity and respectability politics that all too often drive our present-day discourses on race about people of African descent. To that end, what I call attention to is the positionality of Reinosa and the reception of his ability to deploy modes of African diasporic signifying practices in "Gelofe, Mandinga." Black authors are just as capable of writing problematic black characters and rejecting nonstandardized forms of Black linguistic expression.[25] For example, black male Harlem Renaissance writers such as Ralph Ellison and Richard Wright rejected Zora Neale Hurston's celebration and exposure of Southern black culture, folklore, and vernacular expression via acts of signifying.[26]

In *The Signifying Monkey*, Gates argues that "black texts Signify upon other black texts . . . by engaging in what Ellison has defined as implicit formal critiques of language use [and] rhetorical strategy."[27] Gates overlooks, however, the problematic ways in which black male writers such as Ralph Ellison and Richard Wright, in the name of "signifyin(g)," deliberately "battle" and upstage other black writers with their harsh criticisms and misogynist undertones. Zora Neale Hurston, a cultural anthropologist and contemporary black woman writer of the Harlem Renaissance, is a prime example of their rivalry. Enacted by signifying, Ellison and Wright "schooled" Hurston for celebrating and privileging African American Vernacular English as a legitimate voice of black people. This is one pitfall of taking for granted the notion that black writers signify with the best of intentions or without gender- and racial prejudice.

A discussion of the historical legacy of African slavery will also better guide our thought processes regarding signifying with respect to the African diaspora and Ibero-Atlantic world history, as well as the politics of *who* gets to signify and *where* signifying takes place. In African American and Africana studies scholarship, there has been the tendentious move to study "signifying," as a critical concept and African cultural survival, only in the geospatial context of the United States. This geographical preference is what I call that of "horizontal migratory patterns," voluntary and involuntary, which privilege the history and historiography of the Middle Passage and the transatlantic triangular trade from the Eastern (West Africa and Western Europe) *to* the Western Hemisphere (the Americas). For the sake of the fields of Black studies and African diaspora studies, respectively, I would like to reframe the limited scope of this geospatial constitution of signifying by emphasizing that the term can, in fact, evolve and operate *outside* of the Americas due to the fluctuation, or "vertical migratory patterns," of black Africans traveling *to and from* the Iberian Peninsula and other Mediterranean European countries from sub-Saharan Africa. Some of the earliest vertical migratory patterns of black Africans occurred during the Roman conquest and occupation of southwestern Europe. Centuries later, at the turn of the medieval period, vertical movements of black Africans took place at the Almoravid trade routes in search of Ghanaian and Mali gold. And during the

Age of Exploration, beginning in the mid-fifteenth century, Prince Henry the Navigator led expeditions off the coast of West Africa, where he, directed by officials of the Portuguese Crown, brought back to Iberia so-called African envoys, who in return were tricked into domestic servitude and bondage. Therefore, just as those black Africans from the Americas—who arrived via a horizontal migratory movement from West to East and vice versa[28]—brought their cultural aesthetics and customs with them, black Africans in Iberia also retained their indigenous beliefs, cultural practices, and epistemologies concerning the world.

*

Who was Reinosa's audience? Why does he write in habla de negros and dedicate his poems to the black population of Seville? In many texts portraying Africanized Castilian, the interaction between performance and audience has gone unexamined. I imagine Reinosa's audience and audiences based on their relationship to the explanatory rubric written for "Gelofe, Mandinga," as I discussed earlier in this chapter. Reinosa's explanatory rubric for this poem represents vestiges of textual production that illustrate the interaction between material and immaterial aspects of textuality. Crucial to the object of this chapter is recognizing how literally we take the concept of the audience itself. I distinguish between Reinosa's "audience" and "audiences" to underscore the dialogic and dialectical interaction the poet has with the public for whom he has composed "Gelofe, Mandinga." I envision Reinosa's "audience" as black, the direct community of people for whom he directs his habla de negros poetry, whereas his "audiences" embody a heterogeneous population whose constitution varied under changing circumstances.[29] The first term implies a collective entity—one that Reinosa might know and appeal to (and even create) as a group; the second emphasizes a variety of experiences and viewing practices that individuals brought to his milieu.[30]

The literary scene to which Reinosa belongs was the royal court. "Gelofe, Mandinga" presents a dimension of Renaissance Spanish culture and society that reflects real-life settings: black African royal courts, a realness that is grounded in the fact that these Africans are, and *were*, real people and not just literary tropes. In *Obra conocida de Rodrigo de Reinosa*, Laura Puerto Moro reassembles a biographical anecdote from Reinosa's life: "Bajo el referente real al fondo de rústicos y personas de color en la nómina de bufones de Palacio, entre paredes cortesanas se mueven, de hecho, los gañanes y esclavos de Reinosa"[31] (Under the royal reference concerning royal funds paid to rustics and people of color—who, in fact, move between the court walls—were Reinosa's farm hands and slaves, who appeared on the payroll for the palace's court jesters). This fascinating information offers more insight into the courtly scene to which Reinosa belonged. Reinosa's royal court setting constructs the poem "Gelofe, Mandinga" as a text to be performed, a performance that both confronts and ruptures, linguistically and visually, courtly speech (*habla palaciega*) and Africanized Castilian (habla de negros). Such a linguistic and visual rupture is predicated on Reinosa not only having black performers but also black addressees and listeners. In the royal setting Puerto Moro recasts, where black Africans are mentioned under the guise of "personas de color," I ask: How might black listeners hear habla de negros? How might they perceive this language that is simultaneously spoken and performed by their fellow ethno-racial counterparts? While the performance history of "Gelofe, Mandinga" is obscure, I argue nonetheless that black Africans were, in fact, active and visible audience members in Reinosa's text. The poem's explanatory rubric emphasizes this important detail when it states: "Comiençan unas coplas a los negros y negras . . . en Sevilla" (Here begin some couplets to the black men and women . . . of Seville). I take this statement as Reinosa's explicit avowal of Seville's large African-descended population, as I have discussed in the introduction. Through this recognition, Reinosa thus *sees* black people and the Africanity of their customs and language. By acknowledging Seville's significant black population in "Gelofe, Mandinga," Reinosa, dialectically, is then able to celebrate and exhibit the existence of African diasporic culture and modes of expression in early modern Spain.

Madam Black Bug-Faced Nigga Wenches and Black Bug-Faced Nigga Dons: An Obscene Philology of Africanity

Reinosa's "Gelofe, Mandinga" constitutes a geometric and rhythmically in-tune poetic structure that clashes with his black characters' grammatically off habla de negros speech. This clash of language relates to the incongruence of habla de negros as an "imperfect" language embedded within the "perfect" poetic form of the copla. The initial problem that Reinosa presents—and one that recurs in a variety of habla de negros poetry of the Spanish Baroque—is the question of *how* to insert habla de negros (as an instance of "imperfection") into a poem's meter and versification (as instances of "perfection"). Reinosa not only achieves this task by using innuendo, perverse double meanings, and scatological effects but, more importantly, through his manipulation of the Castilian high style known as *arte mayor*. Traditionally, arte mayor was held in high esteem for its elite status, reserved for troubadouresque love lyrics found in songbook poetry known as *poesía de cancionero*. Reinosa's insertion of habla de negros language and its subversive inversions of the said elevated court poetic style compels me to refer to Reinosa's use of habla de negros speech forms in "Gelofe, Mandinga" as an obscene philology of Africanity. I manufacture this concept in order to capture Reinosa's versatility at depicting diverse ethnonyms and ethnolinguistic identities associated with peoples from the region of West Africa known to early modern Iberians and Spanish sources as "the Rivers of Guinea."

Written in coplas de arte mayor, "Gelofe, Mandinga" is fourteen stanzas long with lines composed of either eight or twelve syllables. It is a dialogue between a freed African man (Jorge) and an enslaved African woman (Comba) sung in popular tune with elements of the *zajal* form, where usual stress falls as such: 'doñá pŭta négra'. Although "Gelofe, Mandinga" follows the arte mayor style, it sustains and perverts both the arte mayor form and its elevated courtly love content. Arte mayor poetry involves witty wordplay full of paradoxes and puns that are indicative of courtly love. Its language is colloquial and direct, loaded with double meanings of comical, lascivious, and occasionally scatological references. Heavy with stilted declarations of fealty and a scripted set of metaphors, its diction rearranges the structure of medieval society, transforming icons of power and belief (cathedrals, castles, prisons, battlefields) into a sentimental reality of willed male erotic bondage and idolatrous devotion.[32] Reinosa's use of habla de negros exceeds the limits of the late medieval and Renaissance copla through its vulgarity and grotesque imagery.

To illustrate Reinosa's obscene philology of Africanity, I cite "Gelofe, Mandinga" in its entirety:

Comiença ella:	Gelofe, Mandinga te da gran tormento, *don puto negro caravayento.*
Responde él:	Tu terra Guinea a vós dar lo afrenta, *doña puta negra caravayenta.*
Dize ella:	A mí llamar Comba, de terra Guinea, y en la mi terra comer buen cangrejo y allá en Gelofe, do tu terra sea, comer con gran hambre caravaju vejo, cabeça de can, lagartu vermejo, por do tú andar muy muito fambrento, *don puto negro caravayento.*
Responde él:	A mí llamar Jorge, Mandinga es mi terra, comer muito farto taibo alcuzcuz, ¿por qué falar isu, puta negra perra, y aver en tu terra pescado marfuz? Yo te juro a Yos y a éta qu'e cruz que a mí te fazer saltar [sic] la pimenta, *doña puta negra caravayenta.*
Responde ella:	Aver en tu terra muy muita caranga, tener en tu terra muy muito gaul, comer en tu terra muy muito carpanga, deitar muita pulga por ollo do cul. Saber mí cantar el dulce undul, maagana tambén quando me contento, *don puto negro caravayento.*
Responde él.	A mí saber bien bailar el guineo, se querer comigo fazer choque-choque, y con un bezul dos vezes arreo en vostro bezer allá se me troque; si vós querer que a terro vos derroque, yo juro a Yos que no se arrepenta, *doña puta negra caravayenta.*
Dize ella.	¡Jesú, Jesú! ¡Garaos de o demo!

> No tener tú grassa, vós muito falar,
> id muito enbora, que ya me apostemo,
> no verte Grisolmo con vós aquí estar,
> dar a ti fongón, querer a ti matar,
> andar vós de ay, caranga, pioyento,
> *don puto negro caravayento.*

Responde él. Yo ser de Mandinga y estar negro taibo,
y estar garrapata vostro parente,
y vostro lenguaje yo muito ben saibo.
[. . . . .]
Ser terra Guinea de marfuza gente,
no estar taiba, mas muito pioyenta,
doña puta negra caravayenta.

Responde ella. A mí tener yo un otro guardián
que dar a ti, vós, bon fogón barel,
que dar a mí muito pedaso de pan
y bona melcocha y turrón de mel.
Estar vós marfuz y estar taibo él,
y vós estar negro muy gusarapento,
don puto negro caravayento.

Responde él. Estar yo buen negro, de obispo criado,
y ser de Gelofe, a mí andar en Corte,
estar piojo branco vostro cuñado,
tener yo alhoría con que me dé porte,
yo no estar marfuz, estar hombre forte,
fazer choque-choque en vós me contentar,
doña puta negra caravayenta.

Responde ella. ¡Gualá, nunca herrarle, le!
Andar vós y vete, marfuz, ¡achur, chur!
Andar en bon ora vós, bucamandé,
toma para vós, garango, ¡gur, gur!
Vós estar bellaco, muy muito tahur,
Grisolmo me dar fe de casamento,
don puto negro caravayento.

Responde él.	¡Caravajo preto lo corpo te coma,
	caravajo preto te quera comer!
	Si vós tabaniquete querer fazer
	y dexar a Grisolmo, por vuestro me toma,
	aunque tener vós la nariz roma,
	mi amo tener muy muita renta,
	doña puta negra caravayenta.
Ella y concluye.	Comer en tu terra muita moxca assada,
	muito cangreju assar assador,
	cigarra en caçuela con leche quajada,
	assar en parrilla moxquito mayor.
	Yo estar criada del carrajador,
	con mi ama en missa me assento,
	don puto negro caravayento. (vv. 1–80)
[*She begins:*	Jolof Mandinga, it gives you great torment
	Black bug-faced nigga don.
He responds:	Your land of Guinea disgraces you,
	Madam black bug-faced nigga wench.
She says:	My name is Comba, from Guinea I come,
	and in my land we eat tasty crabs.
	But way over there in your Jolof land, or
	from wherever it is you come,
	you all are starving, for there's only bee-
	tles, dogs' heads, and lizards to eat.
	Where you're from everyone is famished,
	Black bug-faced nigga don.
He responds:	My name is Jorge, and Mandinga is my land!
	We eat a lot of good couscous.
	Why even open your mouth to speak, you
	black bitch of a dog?
	Where you come from, your people eat
	rotten fish heads.
	I swear to God on the cross I bear
	I'll make you jump like a black peppercorn!
	Madam black bug-faced nigga wench.

She responds:	There's nothing but tons of fleas over in your land!
	Your land has too many pigeon peas, and you eat nothing but weeds.
	You even pluck fleas from your asshole!
	I, on the other hand, know how to sing the sweet *undul,*
	and even the *maagana* too when it pleases me.
	Black bug-faced nigga don.
He responds:	I'm the master of dancing the guineo!
	Your big juicy lips excite me so much that you'll want me
	to give you two big kisses (on the lips).
	You'll surely want to do the hanky-panky with me.
	We can even do it in the dirt if you like,
	and I swear to God you won't regret it!
	Madam black bug-faced nigga wench.
She says:	Jesus! Jesus! Beware of the Devil!
	You have no manners; you talk too much!
	Now you're pissing me off! Leave my sight!
	Grisolmo won't want to find you here.
	He'll knock you upside the head and want to kill you.
	Get out of here, you scabby louse!
	Black bug-faced nigga don.
He responds:	I'm from Mandinga land, and I'm a classy black man.
	Your people are nothing but mites.
	In fact, I know your language very well.
	[. . . . .]
	People from Guinea are filthy, rotten, and no good!
	Madam black bug-faced nigga wench.

She responds:	I have another guardian who treats me nicely and
gives me pieces of bread, tasty *melcocha*, and honey nougat.
You're bad-looking and he's good-looking, and he'll surely clunk you on the head with a bar!
You black nigga! You black wretch of a maggot!
Black bug-faced nigga don.
He responds:	I'm a refined black man who was raised by a bishop.
Being Jolof, I enter and exit the court.
Your brother-in-law, on the other hand, is a white louse!
I have my freedom and can go about as I please.
I'm a strong man, not a weak one!
Fucking you with my cock will do me good.
Madam black bug-faced nigga wench.
She responds:	God! You'll bear the brand (of a slave)!
Leave! Leave now, you wretch!
Fuck off!
Bucamandé, get on out of here!
Take heed, you lousy-louse, and leave!
Fuck off!
You're a wicked man, a sly weasel.
Grisolmo has given me his word in marriage.
Black bug-faced nigga don.
He responds:	You black-bodied scarab, he'll capture you!
You black scarab, he wants to capture you!
If you want to open a brothel and leave Grisolmo, I'm yours to take.
Even though you have a Roman nose, my Lord has lots of money

| | to compensate you for the fruits of your labor.
Madam black bug-faced nigga wench. |
|---|---|
| *She concludes:* | In your land, you only eat roasted flies, burnt-to-a-crisp crabs, cicadas simmered in condensed milk, and barbequed horseflies! While I sit in mass with my mistress, I serve the chief magistrate (cock). *Black bug-faced nigga don.*] |

The first line of competition between Comba and Jorge is their different ethnic groups, and, as we will come to see later in this chapter, their two distinct faiths. Although the poem's explanatory rubric claims the copla is directed to a larger black audience in Seville, the fact that Comba and Jorge *name* and *identify* their homelands and ethnic backgrounds is significant. In early modern Spanish literature, it was common for many historiographers, theologians, and writers to randomly assign West African ethnic groups—such as "Gelofe," "Mandinga," and "Guineo(a)"—as clichéd African toponyms to refer to black Africans. But it appears that Reinosa, instead, applies these West African ethnic groups quite judiciously. He exacts places of origin for Comba (from Guinea land) and Jorge (from the Islamic Senegambia region); with great verisimilitude, foods and daily customs match each character's respective homeland. "Ethnicities existed in Africa," explains Gwendolyn Midlo Hall, "and interacted widely not only before the colonial period but also long before the Atlantic slave trade began."[33] Just as the great Senegalese scholar Cheikh Anta Diop never denied the existence of African ethnicities, I urge my readers to rethink Reinosa's careful distinction between Comba and Jorge as a historically and socially accurate way of presenting how black Africans might have expressed their cultural differences along ethnic and religious lines.

Comba and Jorge ridicule each other's West African origins by exceeding the limits of social conduct. Emblematic of the burlesque and satirical Galician-Portuguese *Cantigas d'escarnho e de mal dizer*, the two protagonists unleash lethal blows at the oddities of each other's cultural/ethnic difference. (In the preceding section, I liken these so-called lethal blows to signifying.) Benjamin Liu cites the definition of this literary form in the anonymous fourteenth-century poetic treatise that precedes the cantigas in the Cancioneiro da Bibliotheca Nacional: "Cantigas d'escarneo som aquelas que os trobadores fazen querendo dizer mal d'algue e elas, e dize-lho per palavras cubertas que ajā dous etendymentos pera lhe-lo nõ entenderen . . . [sic] ligeyramente. E estas palavras chamā os clerigos hequivocatio"[34] (*Cantigas d'escarnho* are those that the troubadours compose when they mean to speak ill of someone, but they do so with veiled words that have two meanings so that they will not be understood . . . [sic] easily. The learned call these words *equivocatio*).[35] "Mal dizer," explains Liu, "means simply to speak ill of someone without attenuating the language through double meanings, often in the form of direct obscenities."[36] Reinosa echoes the *Cantigas d'escarnho e de mal dizer*'s language of mockery and insult, I would argue, as templates for portraying Comba's and Jorge's signifying speech acts.

"Gelofe, Mandinga" capitalizes on Comba's and Jorge's feuding in order to illustrate the complex interplay between culture, language, and sexuality. Their exchanges of rude wit and scolding epithets exemplify what Liu coins as sexual "misalliances," illicit sexual relations between members of different faiths. Liu argues that sexual misalliances "violate both the properties of sexual behavior and the limits of what is considered to be acceptable interfaith association."[37] "Two kinds of texts," Liu adds, "typically permit themselves to speak of such encounters: legal codes that seek to establish the limits of social conduct, and transgressive texts."[38] A similar gesture that exceeds the limits of what is considered acceptable can be found in the relationship, or lack thereof, between Comba and Jorge. Through the power of speaking, the "relation" between these two characters transgresses the limits of social conduct because they belong to different African ethnic groups and religious backgrounds. But the very transgressive nature of their relationship at once conceals and makes patent the cultural anxieties raised by the presence of Africans in Spain at the time.

Comba's and Jorge's Africanized Castilian—which during Reinosa's time exhibited rich Portuguese lusismos—signals the potential for some Spaniards' cultural anxiety to manifest around habla de negros language due to its perceived illegibility and inaudibility in contrast to "standard" forms of spoken Castilian. Habla de negros represents illegibility because it cannot be deciphered due to its murky phonetic register. Both its illegibility and inaudibility conjure a schizophrenic language that disavows "standard" Castilian as constituted by Antonio Nebrija's 1492 *Grámatica de la lengua castellana*. As one of the first literary examples of habla de negros, the Africanized speech in "Gelofe, Mandinga," on the one hand, excludes whites from understanding it fully and, on the other hand, ironically involves whites due to their familiarity and interaction with blacks in Renaissance Iberian urban centers. This cultural anxiety, predicated on linguistic difference, asserts itself in the desire to control not only sexuality but also language.[39] As the "prólogo" to his *Gramática* famously declares, "Language was always the companion [*compañera*] of empire, and followed it such that together [*junta mente*] they began, grew, and flourished—and, later, together [junta mente] they fell."[40]

Nebrija's concept of history and the companionship between empire and language manifests as a clear push for a coalescing relationship between Castilian as a national language and a theory of empire. For Nebrija, grammar, or language, will facilitate the extension of Spain's growing colonies in the Americas by allowing its foreigners and colonial objects/subjects to learn and learn *how* to read and speak Castilian. The Spanish Empire Nebrija envisions is well mapped out. From tactical assimilation of the invader's contributions, Spain pieced together a language of survival and dominion in both Africa and the New World.[41] The rhetoric of Nebrija's grammar, in tandem with the general underpinnings of language and race, standardizes and upholds the rights and duties of citizens. It is not only Muslims in Africa who will need to learn the Castilian language but also Basques, Navarrese, Frenchmen, and Italians—after all, Christopher Columbus, a recent convert to the Spanish imperial system, communicated in Castilian, Italian, and Latin.

The conception of discourse, for example, plays an important role in Reinosa's construction of Comba's and Jorge's racial difference, gender disputes, and habla de negros language. I am furthermore convinced that Reinosa was aware of Nebrija's *Gramática*. An examination of Foucault's definition of discourse will elucidate the poet's treatment of black Africans in Nebrija's imperialist program of language. In *The History of Sexuality, Vol. 1*, Foucault urges that "we must not imagine a world of discourse divided between accepted discourse and excluded discourse, or between the dominant discourse elements that can come into play, but as a multiplicity of discursive elements that can come into play in various strategies. Discourse transmits and produces power."[42] For Foucault, discourse embodies a set of linguistic and symbolic practices that lays claim to coherence and authority. These linguistic and symbolic codes and practices construct an arrangement of the world: a field of knowledge, a group of privileged subjects who possess that knowledge, a range of objects that can be arranged and distributed with that knowledge, and a set of mechanisms that claims to guarantee the production of "truth" with Foucault's discourse in mind. The theorist helps us nuance the boundaries of our suspicions, misconceptions, and problematic vocabularies that attempt to theorize the critical category of race and Black Spanish in "Gelofe, Mandinga." In that regard, if we focus on Comba's and Jorge's perceived "odd" obscene speech and cultural sensibilities (for white European spectators), we will see how their habla de negros language operates as a performative marker of race that then uncovers not only their inherent subjectivity but also Reinosa's encyclopedic knowledge base of West African culture and culinary traditions.

*

Comba casts her obscene insults at the poem's beginning: "Gelofe Mandinga te da gran tormento, / don puto negro caravayento" (vv. 1–2). She immediately attacks Jorge in the opening phrase "Gelofe Mandinga" and the closing *estribillo* "don puto negro caravayento." The words "Gelofe" and "Mandinga" appear as separate ethnic categories, but Jolof (or Wolof) and Mandinga are two separate ethnic groups with different languages in the Senegambia region. The Portuguese enslaved them during the first phase of their slave trade expeditions in the fifteenth century. Given this historical context, Comba's use of "Gelofe Mandinga" vexes Jorge. He is a free black man, and her play on the word "don" in the line "don puto negro caravayento" is not coincidental. In early modern Spain, "don" was a title reserved only for those belonging to the higher rungs of society. Her use of "don," then, is ironic. From the beginning of the poem, Comba directly and indirectly attacks Jorge's social status and Wolof ethnicity. Her parodic use of "don" is a product of Reinosa's imaginative prerogative. Her verbal strike against Jorge reaches its fullest potential in "puto negro caravayento." In the *Diccionario de Autoridades*, this word means "fag" or "rent-boy." Within a literary register, the Spanish word "puto" can be considered analogous to the English word "catamite." "Catamite," according to the *Oxford English Dictionary*, is a boy kept for unnatural purposes. "Unnatural purposes" almost always implies sodomy at the hands of an older man.

The word "caravayento" also suggests the ugliness in being black. According to Covarrubias, "caravayento" etymologically derives from *escaravajo*. In its derivations of "escravajo," "caravayento" ranges in meaning from (1) the beetle-like insect known as a scaraboid, (2) cockroach-like, (3) scarab, and (4) dung beetle. More explicitly, "caravayento," based on its nominal parent "escravajo" form, refers to "vil animalejo. . . . Para decir que algún hombre o mujer es negro y de ruín talle, decimos que es un escaravajo" (vile animal. . . . In order to say that any man or woman is black and of despicable figure, we say s/he is an "escaravajo").[43]

In response to Comba's verbal blows, Jorge retorts in a similar fashion by saying, "Tu terra Guinea a vós dar lo afrenta, / doña puta negra caravayenta" (vv. 3–4) (Your land of Guinea disgraces you, / Madam black bug-faced nigga wench). Used as an epithet, the ethnonym "Guinea" holds more of a cumbersome and problematic ideation in early modern Spanish history and literature.[44] During the first two hundred years of the Atlantic slave trade, "Guinea" meant what Boubacar Barry defines as Greater Senegambia: the region between the Senegal and the Sierra Leone Rivers. In Arabic, "Guinea" meant "Land of the Blacks." It referred to the Senegal/Sierra Leone regions alone. In early Portuguese and Spanish writings, and especially for Reinosa and his contemporaries, "Guinea" meant Upper Guinea.[45] For Alonso de Sandoval in his *Un tratado sobre la esclavitud* (1627), "Guineans" meant Great Senegambians. In the Iberian context, the earliest information we have about "Guineans" comes from Valencia, Spain. Hall correctly notes that "their 'nation' designations have been interpreted as regional rather than ethnic, cultural, or linguistic. They include 'Guine,' 'Jalof' (Wolof), and, by [the] 1490s, 'Mandega' (Mandingo)."[46] The Mandingo were Mande language group speakers, descendants of the peoples of the Mali Empire, who were prominent conquerors, traders, and interpreters of languages throughout the Greater Senegambia.[47] In line 62, Comba calls Jorge a "bucamandé"—Mandé speaker—a term that convinces me of Reinosa's vast knowledge of West African ethnic groups and tribes. The protagonists' ethnic lineages exist and function as cartographic inscriptions on Reinosa's habla de negros text, thereby illustrating the diverse complexity of habla de negros speakers. Rather than a randomly assigned burlesque deformation, the term "bucamandé," instead, grounds the poem historically and symbolically into a large paradigm of black diasporic culture and identity formation.

These demographic details play a significant role in contextualizing and locating a potential source for the root of the tensions between Comba the "Guinean" and Jorge the "Wolof/Mandingo." When Jorge speaks ill of Comba (as Reinosa mediates his voice), he is not necessarily deploying a stereotypically clichéd corruption of black African culture, language, and geography but rather positions himself as her superior in relation to his ethnic background. In the pages that follow, my textual analysis of Jorge's invectives launched at Comba privilege his formidable Wolof/Mandingo ethnic origins, which will then allow us to nuance our reading of his dialogue with Comba as "doña puta caravayenta," especially as a mode of signifying.

Like its gendered masculine counterpart, the word "puta" not only takes on an entire host of other meanings but, more specifically, reveals Comba as a prostitute. Covarrubias sees the "puta" as "la ramera o ruin mujer" (the prostitute or despicable woman).[48] As the "puta"/"ramera" of Reinosa's text, Comba needs not wear the yellow headdress (or *toca açafranada*, as it was called) stipulated to mark her body as prostitute according to the legal ordinances in effect in early modern Spain.[49] Comba's black skin is enough to render her body legible as prostitute. Jorge's naming of Comba as "puta" is tautological. The text illuminates Comba's status as prostitute when Jorge—offering to do the "choque-choque," or hanky-panky—brags about his sexual prowess as a lover: "en vostro bezer allá se me troque" (v. 29) (to give you two big kisses [on the lips]). As John Beusterien notes in *An Eye on Race*, "The theatrical invention of [habla de negros] helped forge the erotization of the male Black."[50] He adds that "choque-choque" (sex; hanky-panky) was introduced to early Spanish stages by Reinosa's contemporary and interlocutor Juan Pastor in *Farsa o tragedia de la castidad de Lucrecia* (1520/1528).[51] In his essay on the introduction of Africanisms in habla de negros literary texts, Germán de Granda dates the origins of "choque-choque" between 1479 and 1480 to the slave coast of Africa, where he believes the word was first recorded by a Flemish merchant noting that "for the game of love [Africans] say *choque-choque*."[52]

Following Beusterien and de Granda, I read the poem's deployment of choque-choque, in conjunction with the text's repetition of the refrain "doña puta negra caravayenta," as a reinforced misogyny and violent racism against black women. In "Mama's Baby, Papa's Maybe: An American Grammar Book," theorist Hortense J. Spillers describes her existence, as a black woman, as part of a larger system of identification—what she has called "a locus of confounded identities, a meeting ground of investments, and privations in the national treasury of rhetorical wealth."[53] Spillers's terms are suggestive for thinking about Reinosa's "Gelofe, Mandinga" in relation to Comba's black female body. Just as Spillers links herself to the "marked" woman who is called by many names ("Peaches" and "Brown Sugar," "Sapphire" and "Earth Mother," "Aunty," "Granny," God's "Holy Fool," a "Miss Ebony First," or "Black at the Podium"), Comba is triply marginalized as African, slave, and woman. Even her name, "Comba" (stick; twig), functions as the personal pronoun offered in service of a collective function as an enslaved black female prostitute. "Comba" is the registered name often given to black female slaves in the Archivo de Protocolos in Sevilla. In 1495, for example, one archival registry identifies a real-life Comba, who was auctioned off and sold as a slave. The document describes her as a "Negra de Jolof, llamada *Comba*, de sesenta años, vendida en 2000 maravedis" (black woman of Wolof lineage, named Comba, sixty years of age, sold for two thousand maravedis).[54] Outside of the Hispanic archive of slave records, canonical literary texts from Renaissance Spain also evidence "Comba" as a name frequently given to enslaved black women. In Francisco Delicado's *Retrato de la loçana andaluza* (Venice, 1528), the following brief fragment reflects racial assumptions and linguistic code-switching:

> *Loçana.* ¡O qué linda tez de negra! ¿Cómo llamar tú? ¿Conba?
> *Esclava.* No, llamar Penda de xeñora."[55]

> [*Loçana*—Oh what beautiful black skin! What's ya name? Comba?
> *Slave*—No, I'm Penda; I belong to the Lady.]

The undercurrents of racist essentialism are highly sophisticated and marked in this passage. The Loçana thinks she has this black lady with "beautiful black skin" all figured out. Her matter-of-fact tone insinuates that *all* black women are slaves, for the name "Comba" presages bondage, just as the word "negro" for early modern Iberian readers means "esclavo" (slave). The quote also resonates with present-day race relations in the United States. What we as readers witness in this exchange is no different, in its racist essentialism, from a nonblack person who, upon meeting a person of African descent for the first time, addresses that individual in African American Vernacular English (AAVE) and then assumes their name to be "Fa' Nay-Nay" or "Boo-Quanda." Thus, in light of my previous citing of Spillers, the racialized and hypersexualized naming of black women—whether in early modern Iberia or present-day United States—conjures a host of controlling images and fantasies. My gesture to Africana studies scholarship is not anachronistic or irrelevant. The comparative move I make here is crucial, for it allows us to make better sense of the fluid and interrelated social dynamics at work in African diasporic communities located in early modern Iberia.

Along with the various racially gendered ideologies that inform Reinosa's poem, the Comba from "Gelofe, Mandinga" inherits historical significations of her black female body that are wrapped up in notions of labor and property. While she works her body physically and sexually, Comba will always remain owned in some shape or form. As a slave body that prostitutes, Comba transforms from being human into being property. This is the distinction between "flesh" and "body." Flesh, in other words, for Spillers, is not simply raw, human matter; it represents a body that also shows, that reveals, the markings of the symbolic order on its skin.[56] It is a supplement to the black body that merely (re)enacts its symbolic marking and naming by using the skin of race as a covering over/of human flesh.[57] Therefore, in the process of becoming property, Comba is physically and symbolically transformed from "flesh" into "body." But through close readings of the language Reinosa constructs for Comba, we learn that her lot as slave and prostitute is not at all what it seems; on the contrary, it is *not* that grim. Through Reinosa's orchestration, Comba—like Jorge—acquires and asserts her voice through signifying. When Comba and Jorge signify (upon each other), the "Gelofe, Mandinga" then reveals more complicated notions of what it means to be of African descent in early modern Seville. Comba's and Jorge's signifying speech acts ultimately teach us, as present-day readers, that blacks are subjects who assert their subject positions and subvert their lowly lots.

Yo' Mama Eat Rotten Fish Heads and Candied Bugs: Reinosa's Signifying Speech Acts

This section turns to signifying speech acts as a critical mode for analyzing "Gelofe, Mandinga" because it illuminates Reinosa's role as a cultural mediator. In this context, I read him as a go-between and translator—echoing Trotaconventos in Juan Ruiz's *Libro de buen amor* and Celestina in Fernando de Rojas's *La Celestina*—of Seville's black community. As a European-descended writer who represents black African racial difference through habla de negros, his authorial position and his rhetorical and discursive goals can be complicated by turning to the practice of signifying traditionally linked to African American culture and life in the United States.

As mentioned previously, the exact definition of signifying is contested because it is used to refer to so many communicative phenomena, from tongue-in-cheek reference to prior speakers and writers playfully insulting a conversational adversary.[58] Signifying speech acts are indirect methods of communication whereby the speaker builds meaning intended for a restricted audience using signals that only the intended audience will be able to recognize and decode.[59] In the pages ahead, I discuss and provide illustrative examples of signifying speech acts in "Gelofe, Mandinga." And it is through the signifying tropes of rhyming, mimicry, playing the dozens, call-and-response (antiphony), repetition, teasing, shouting out (one's name or another phrase), and phrases that are emblematic of the notorious yo' mama jokes that the efficacy of Reinosa's signifying speech acts unfolds.

Comba signifies first in "Gelofe, Mandinga." She slams Jorge with insults by asserting her name and lineage (race, or *raza*, in Castilian)—*A mí llamar Comba de terra Guinea*—after Jorge calls her "doña puta negra caravayenta" (madam black bug-faced nigga wench). The battle proceeds by displaying the fullest capacity of signifying:

Dize ella: [Y] allá en Gelofe, do tu terra sea,
comer con gran hambre caravaju vejo,
cabeça de can, lagartu vermejo,
por do tú andar muy muito fambrento,
don puto negro caravayento.

Responde él: A mí llamar Jorge, Mandinga es mi terra,
comer muito farto taibo alcuzcuz,
¿por qué falar isu, puta negra perra,
y aver en tu terra pescado marfuz?
Yo te juro a Yos y a éta qu'e cruz

	que a mí te fazer saltar [sic] la pimenta,
	doña puta negra caravayenta. (vv. 7–18)

[*She says*:	But way over there in your Jolof land, or from wherever it is you come,
	you all are starving, for there's only beetles, dogs' heads, and lizards to eat.
	Where you're from everyone is famished,
	Black bug-faced nigga don.
He responds:	My name is Jorge, and Mandinga is my land!
	We eat a lot of good couscous.
	Why even open your mouth to speak, you black bitch of a dog?
	Where you come from, your people eat rotten fish heads.
	I swear to God on the cross I bear
	I'll make you jump like a black peppercorn!
	Madam black bug-faced nigga wench.]

Rhyming is of extraordinary importance to the production of these lines' humorous effect. The passage's rhythm scheme enhances the signifying moment by the poem's musicality and witty delivery. Coupled with rhyming and metric form, insulting throughout these two stanzas shows how Comba and Jorge signify. The wide array of insults tossed between the two characters is astonishing. Comba's attacks—as they are designed and mediated by Reinosa—against Jorge's home of origin, culinary customs, and dietary habits conflate race with nation. All of a sudden, Jorge's status as a citizen of the Senegambia region conjures a host of negative controlling images that sustain his marked (raced) status and role as "black bug-faced nigga don" ("don puto negro caravayento"). Due to supposed starvation, Comba accuses Jorge of eating dung beetles ("caravaju vejo"), the heads of dogs ("cabeça de ca"), and lizards ("lagartu vermejo"). Comba's signifying black language therefore distances her from Jorge's Africanness—or ethnic/racial Blackness—by aligning her with ideological representations of Whiteness (i.e., being baptized, Catholicism, and having a white lover named Grisolmo).

Playing the dozens is another form of signifying that manifests in the aforementioned exchanges between Comba and Jorge. Playing the dozens, unlike other tropes of signifying, has insidious and hurtful ends. In "Gelofe, Mandinga," playing the dozens produces the effect of humor, and the success of its exchanges turns on insults of one's family members, especially one's mother (i.e., "Yo' mama!"). Indirectly, Comba's and Jorge's respective homelands of the Senegambia region represent the "Mother." Each character's emphasis on degrading each other's respective geographical/"national" "Mother"—through taking issue with cultural and culinary differences—exemplifies playing the dozens as an embedded trope of signifying.

There is one instance in the poem where Jorge immediately corrects Comba when she deliberately derides his ethnic background. In response to the subjunctive mood expressed in her language—"y allá en Gelofe do tu terra *sea*" (but way over there in *Gelofe*, or *wherever* it is you're from), Jorge makes it very clear that he, in fact, "comer muito farto taibo alcuzcuz" (eats a lot of good couscous). We first encountered the term "taibo" at the beginning of this chapter in Fernão da Silveira's poem catalogued in Garcia de Resende's *Cancioneiro geral*. A word of Arab origin, "taibo" means "good" or "refined." The word "alcuzcuz," or couscous, confirms that Jorge knows Arabic, if not speaks it to some level of proficiency, thus belonging to one of the major Islamic ethnic groups from the Senegambia region of West Africa. This passage exemplifies signifying through an unstated, yet clearly pointed, rhetorical statement: I'm a black who does *not* eat "Black" foods. On a similar level, this rhetorical remark resonates with literary critic Claudia Mitchell-Kernan's example of a conversation had among three women who are about to dine together:

> One woman asks the other two to join her for dinner, that is, if they are willing to eat "chit'lins." She ends her invitation with a pointed rhetorical question: "Or are you one of those Negroes who don't eat chit'lins?" The third person, the woman not addressed, responds with a long defense of why she prefers "prime rib and T-bone" to "chit'lins," ending with a traditional ultimate appeal to special pleading, a call to unity within the ranks to defeat white racism. Then she leaves. After she has gone, the initial speaker replies to her original addressee in this fashion: "Well, I wasn't signifying at her, but like I always say, if the shoe fits wear it."[60]

Both this exchange at dinner and Jorge's reiteration that he eats only good couscous reveal a triangulation among signifying, nation, and race. Jorge relies on the idea of "good couscous" to signify on Comba's culinary and cultural barbarism. The adjective "marfuz" ("rotten"; "trashy") contrasts with the positive connotation of taibo. As a counterattack against Comba, Jorge emphasizes his knowledge of Arabic language and Islamic heritage— through the dichotomous usage of taibo and *marfuz*—as forms of cultural assimilation and cultural "nationalism." Like the black woman in the aforementioned quote who prefers prime rib and T-bone steaks *over* chit'lins (a traditional US-black American dish customary on slave plantations), Jorge also rejects traditional black cuisine common to most West African countries and ethnic groups: the consumption of (rotten) fish heads. Jorge and the woman who prefers T-bone steak both signify on what they perceive as culinary barbarism—rotten fish heads and chit'lins—to disassociate themselves from a more broadly understood "black" community. And as Mitchell-Kernan notes, this form of signifying is allegorical, for its "significance or meaning of the words must be derived from the known symbolic values."[61]

Jorge's hypermetric denouncement of Comba as a "black bitch of a dog" ("puta negra perra" [v. 14]) then escalates into multiple attacks referencing the rotten fish ("pescado marfuz" [v. 15]) consumed by the people of her Guinean homeland. Jorge continues by swearing in God's name, and on the cross he bears, that he will make Comba jump like a black peppercorn— "Yo te juro a Yos y a éta qu'e cruz / que a mí te fazer saltar [sic] la pimenta, / *doña puta negra caravayenta*" (vv. 16–17). Jorge's verbal threats embody his rejection of an ideological heathenism associated with sub-Saharan Africans from non-Islamic lands, specifically Comba and her kind. In addition, Jorge professes the omnipotent union of Islamic-Christian religiosity and the ultimate power of Christianity as signaled by the crucifix he wears on his body. I underscore this observation because the Wolof/Mandingo were prominent among the many African slaves and their descendants brought to the Iberian Peninsula who were converted to Christianity and spoke Portuguese and/or dialects of Spanish.[62] In this context, Jorge accomplishes signifying through mimicry, repetition, and cursing out Comba. On Reinosa's part, however, this manifestation of signifying purports violence. Through Reinosa's control, Jorge violently mimics and mocks Comba's black African origins and culture. As most Wolof were Islamized, it is likely that Jorge was originally

Muslim (before Christian conversion) and possibly lighter in complexion than Comba, for he repeats emphatically that she is dark-skinned ("puta negra perra" [v. 14] and "la pimenta" [v. 17]), ugly, and animallike. The cross that Jorge bears on his body also functions as a tool of violence. Throughout the text, Jorge figuratively and literally signifies on Comba's heathen body. Accordingly, the cross will make her jump like the black peppercorn she is. To get a rise out of the audience, Reinosa diametrically opposes Jorge's cross against Comba's black body. The ideological conceits of this textual image, portrayed by Reinosa, in sum, works as a violent *pulla*, or cutting remark, against Comba.

In his essay "The Context of Enslavement in West Africa: Ahmad Baba and the Ethics of Slavery," Paul E. Lovejoy clarifies that Muslims from the western Sudan were identified as Mandingo.[63] Slaves ending up in both Spain and its American colonies were labeled as such at the time. There is nothing at all coincidental about Jorge's ethnic and religious position in "Gelofe, Mandinga." Spanish philologist José María Cossío remarks that the poet "distingue perfectamente las distintas procedencias de uno y otro negro, y creo que es tomado del natural el que él presuma de comer *alcuzcuz*, como *mandingo* influenciado aún por costumbres moras, en oposición a la mayor incivilidad de la negra, plenamente caracterizada de Guinea"[64] (distinguishes perfectly between the distinct origins of each black character, and I believe we can naturally assume that Jorge boasts of eating couscous, as a Mandingo influenced still by Moorish customs, in opposition to the greater incivility of Comba, who is completely characterized as being from Guinea). Once we, as readers (and listeners), learn of Jorge's Arabic language and Islamic background, our perception of him changes, and it most certainly would have changed during the period in which Reinosa composed this "Gelofe, Mandinga." Reinosa's ability to not only distinguish between different West African ethnic groups but to actually reference their aesthetic sensibilities and culinary habits illustrates the verisimilitude in the accuracy of how and *what* objects and products Comba and Jorge employ in order to signify on each other. The theme and subject matter of food unites the discussion of race and difference in early modern Iberia. In many respects, you *are* indeed *what* you eat. There is a material ontology at work here. Markers of Catholicism and Hispanic identity index an individual's lineage and racial and religious backgrounds. By drinking wine, for example, one could assert one's

Catholic and Hispanic identity.[65] In this instance, Jorge assertively declares his religious and "national"/ethnic identity in his response to Comba by saying, "Mandinga es mi terra, comer muito farto taibo alcuzcuz" (vv. 12–13) (Mandinga is my land! / We eat a lot of good couscous.). In summation, the motif of food carries a symbolic value. When using food to signify against each other, their shared form of signifying operates at the level of allegory in order to critique each other's cultural and "national" differences.

As cultural mediator, Reinosa is fully aware of the cultural and ethnic differences between black Africans and Iberian Muslims. His role as a mediator allows him to frame a suggestive portrait of the image of Iberian Muslims in Renaissance Spain. To that effect, Reinosa catalyzes a nuanced image of Islamicized black Africans in "Gelofe, Mandinga" through Jorge's Africanness, a cultural and ideological Blackness constructed by signifying and his identification as a Gelofe-Mandinga subject. Discussing the image of the Moor in medieval Portugal, for example, Josiah Blackmore delineates an understanding of the Moor "as a construct that resists easy categorizations as an undifferentiated figure of otherness."[66] Reinosa, as a result, simultaneously elevates "Gelofe, Mandinga" through his position as poet and Jorge's metarole as an Islamicized black African. The Iberian conceptualizations of Moorishness vis-à-vis Africanness in "Gelofe, Mandinga" reflect Blackmore's observation of the advances in recent years of critical work that free the Moor from the strictures of the "self/other" binary.[67] Reinosa thus exalts Jorge's Islamicized Blackness through the linguistic mode of habla de negros and signifying. Due to his knowledge of medieval and Renaissance Portuguese literary works and historiographical tracts (most notably the *Cancioneiro geral* and Gomes Eanes de Zurara's *Crónica da tomada de Ceuta* and *Crónica de Guiné*), I suggest that the Cantabrian poet recapitulates the Portuguese practice of empire in the continent of Africa, which allows for a more holistic understanding of Castilian literary and ideological productions of Iberian Muslims that address a metanarrative of sub-Saharan Africanness.

The metanarrative of Africanness—or, more pointedly, the poetic expression of African diasporic culture—that manifests in "Gelofe, Mandinga" is the signifying speech act of verbal dueling. Dueling is an act of signifying that is humorous in its directness. It illustrates the numerous varieties of epithets uttered between Comba and Jorge. In AAVE, the vulgar appellatives "motherfucker" and "nigger" are rather common terms of address—and in some context, endearment—in such acts of verbal dueling. In the case of "Gelofe, Mandinga," I see the closing estribillo, "doña puta negra caravayenta" and "don puto negro caravayento," operating in a similar fashion. (Hence my English translation of "doña puta negra caravayenta" as "madam black bug-faced *nigga* wench.") Through Reinosa's orchestration, Comba and Jorge use these two lines to signify in violent ways. And without a doubt, these two vulgar phrases exhaustively repeat racist and misogynistic modes of thinking on the behalf of Reinosa and his audience's laughter at them. But these two closing lines are also linguistic codes recognizable to and understood by the black men and women spectators outlined in Reinosa's text. In Spanish, for example, the word "nigger," per se, does not translate directly or smoothly. Instead, a Spanish speaker's attempt to use this word is conveyed through intonation and tone—which also becomes apparent in Reinosa's poem. Because verbal dueling treads a fine line between play and real aggression, it is a kind of linguistic activity that requires strict adherence to sociolinguistic rules. To correctly decode the message, as is the case in "Gelofe, Mandinga," spectators must be tuned in to the correct frequency of the signifying speech act to understand its meaning.

"Gelofe, Mandinga" ends with Comba's tongue-in-cheek remark: "Yo estar criada del carrajador, / con mi ama en missa me assento, / *don puto negro caravayento* (vv. 78–80) (While I sit in mass with my mistress, I serve the chief magistrate [cock]. / *Black bug-faced nigga don*). Her tongue-in-cheek retort encapsulates the powerful effects of signifying so much that she, as Kimberly W. Benston puns, "tropes-a-dope." Tongue-in-cheek signifying operates as an example of a black rhetorical trope Comba utilizes to outsmart Jorge the "dope." While traditionally tongue-in-cheek gestures are slyly humorous and lack literal meaning in intent, I, however, take Reinosa's representation of this subset of signifying as an indicator of Comba's inherent agency and authority. The end of the poem highlights her ability to enter and exit policing institutions of early modern Spanish society: courts, palaces, and the church. While Reinosa inserts the obscene word "carrajador" (echoing the phallic cock, or "carajo"), he disguises it with Africanized Castilian in order to signal the various ways in which black Africans—both enslaved and free—have accessed the state and interacted with its agents (e.g., a chief magistrate, sheriff, or mayor), who at some point in time either disciplined or enjoyed their black bodies.

On the one hand, Comba's grandiose ending nullifies Jorge's misogynist language that seeks to lodge her in the site of the brothel (i.e., "Si vós tabaniquete quere fazer / y dexar a Grisolmo, por vuestro me toma" (vv. 69–70) (If you want to open a brothel and leave Grisolmo, I'm yours to take).[68] On the other hand, Comba's tongue-in-cheek response aligns her with the Catholic Church, piety, and religious obedience. Reinosa's "Gelofe, Mandinga" has rendered visible the presence of African diasporic cultural expression through signifying speech acts in early modern Iberian literature. In sum, Comba and Jorge's signifying speech acts operate dialogically together in a double-voiced, hybridized form of cultural politics. Such a dialogic hybrid form ultimately shows how Reinosa engages the processes of merging and of dialogization of ethnic and cultural differences set critically against each other.

3

BLACK DIVAS, BLACK FEMINISMS

The Black Female Body and *Habla de Negros* in Lope de Rueda

Commonly referred to as "negra" (Black Woman), "negrilla" (Little Black Chick), "puta negra" (Black Bitch; Black Ho), "ébano" (Ebony), "carbón" (Coal-Black), "galguinegra" (Black Doggedy Bitch), and "azabache" (Anodyne Jet) in a variety of early modern Spanish literary texts, black women from early modern Iberia have been aesthetically, culturally, and institutionally robbed of their agency and humanity. Similar to what theorist Hortense J. Spillers articulates in her tour-de-force essay "Mama's Baby, Papa's Maybe: An American Grammar Book," not everybody knows their names (in early modern Spanish cultural and literary studies). Beyond merely uncovering these women's anonymity (at times profanely in literary texts and historically in the early modern Spanish archive), in this chapter I assign an agentive voice to black women literary characters, thereby exploring the possibility of them as authoritative and thinking subjects. In urban centers across Spain, such as the Renaissance metropolis of Seville, which I discuss at length in the introduction, black women strolled the city's labyrinthine streets bearing the names Antonia, Boruga, Catalina, Dominga, Francisca, Guiomar, Lucrecia, Margarita, and Sofía. These black women's names have also been reproduced in the literary repertoire of early modern Spanish figures such as Agustín Moreto, Cervantes, Calderón de la Barca, Diego Sánchez de Badajoz, Góngora, Quevedo, Lope de Rueda, Lope de Vega, María de Zayas y

Sotomayor, and Rodrigo de Reinosa. What is striking about the variety of poetic, prose narrative, and theatrical representations of so-called negra characters—and the white writers, both female and male, who portrayed them—is the rhetorical power and value of paradox. Early modern Spanish negras have always occupied a liminal space and paradoxical status where their agential voices and sartorial style—as expressed through bodily expression and self-fashioning as well as material culture—triumphs present-day critics' belaboring of white (mainly male playwrights' and poets') stereotyping of black women as obscenely hypersexual yet brutishly ugly, intellectually inferior, and helplessly weak.[1]

I read against the dominant body of scholarly criticism in early modern Hispanic studies that has insisted on emphasizing the primacy of the aberrant and abject image of the black female body in early modern Spanish literary history. Echoing Daphne A. Brooks's theorization of the abundance of representation of black women as aberrant, this chapter retrieves "ways to read for the viability of black women making use of their own materiality within narratives in which they are the subjects."[2] What most concerns me in this discussion of black women, specifically Rueda's theatrical representation of Eulalla and Guiomar, is the possibility of Rueda troubling the way in which we, as present-day critics, perceive racial, gender, and corporeal spectacle in Renaissance Spanish culture. Reading across the gaze of the normative spectator, I am most interested in mining what we might call a politics of opacity that illuminates a way to consider the performances of Eulalla and Guiomar in Rueda's *Eufemia* and *Los engañados*. We can think of the politics of opacity in Rueda's construction of these black women as a figurative site for the reconfiguration of their black and female bodies on display that confound and disrupt conventional constructions of the racialized and gendered body.[3] If, as I have already established in chapter 1, habla de negros language cannot be separated from the cosmetic embodiment, theatrical performance, and sonic Blackness located in blackface performance on early Spanish stages, then the subject of the black female body, I argue henceforth, cannot be divorced from the habla de negros language spoken by black women. In other words, the Africanized Castilian frequently linked to early modern Spanish staged performances of black women serves as a proxy for the negra character to mobilize a politics of opacity, as this chapter highlights. I underscore this chief claim in an analysis of two interlude skits—specifically referred to as a paso or an entremés in early modern comedia studies—that showcase the black female characters Eulalla and Guiomar in Lope de Rueda's *Comedia Eufemia* (1542/1554) and *Comedia de los engañados* (1538/1558) (hereafter *Eufemia* and *Los engañados*).

Miguel de Cervantes Saavedra, in his prologue to *Ocho comedias y ocho entremeses* (1615), recalls Rueda having blackfaced and cross-dressed as a black woman in his own theater company. Cervantes's fond account of Rueda emphasizes the actor-author's celebrity and fame—"varón insigne en la representación y del entendimiento" (a man famous for his performances and for his intelligence), "en el tiempo de este célebre español"[4] (in the time of this Spanish celebrity)—and adept representation of the motley crew of characters he created and performed. Cervantes's reiteration of the word "celebrity" in the prologue—"célebre," "famoso," and "insigne"—is useful for my study of Eulalla and Guiomar. Following Cervantes's testimony, Rueda's celebrity status (if not also the celebration of his notoriety and performative prowess of staging roles of black African women) is afforded by and acquired from black women. Just as theater scholars of Rueda's oeuvre have attributed his success to the performances of the *bobo* (simpleton or clownish fool), the *pastor* (rustic shepherd[ess]), the *rufián* (lawless criminal; street thug), or the *vizcaíno* (native of Biscay; Basque countryperson), I situate the theatrical *negra* as a salient contributor to the playwright's fame. By doing so, we can then begin to recognize, on the one hand, the theatrical *negra*'s foundational importance in early modern Spanish theater studies and, on the other hand, position Rueda's theatrical representation of black women in his short-skit plays as radical and spectacular performances of black women's ability to resist and refuse to be reduced to a function of white well-being.[5]

What Rueda's *Eufemia* and *Los engañados* point to in this chapter is that in many of those moments when antiblack racism and misogyny appear to (re)produce their most aberrant and abject representations of the black women characters (Eulalla and Guiomar), these two figures inhabit the limits of *habla de negros* language and aesthetic form, performing moments of spectacular visibility, at times despite and beyond Rueda's intentions.[6] In order to illuminate each of these women's agential authority and subversive speech acts, I am proposing that we read them via the categories of "black divas" (aligned with Eulalla) and "black feminisms" (linked to Guiomar). In the particular case of Eulalla, for example, positioning her as a diva reveals her strategies of self-creation and self-defense to destabilize "Whiteness" as an already-assumed stable cultural, ideological, and racial structure. Empowering the racially gendered quality of each woman's habla de negros speech, my two terms, "black divas" and "black feminisms," resituate Eulalla and Guiomar in an early black feminist theoretical context that allows us to read them radically using their bodies and their Africanized Castilian language as performative instruments of subjectivity rather than existing merely as objects of spectatorial ravishment and domination.

Guiding this study is its close reading of Rueda's intervention in the representation of Eulalla's and Guiomar's black female bodies as sites that enact and exhibit witty wordplay that is corporeally inscribed in material objects (e.g., books and letter writing, clothing, hair and makeup, and foreign exotic animals). Not entirely mutually exclusive from Cervantes's gracious testimony of Rueda's celebrity status (which, again, is predicated on the playwright's *technê* for blackfacing and cross-dressing as a black woman), I contend that the recurring reference to Rueda's celebrity status, posthumously in late sixteenth- and seventeenth-century Spain, also influences the playwright's living relationship to the fame created by his black women characters. To that end, Rueda's portrayal of Eulalla and Guiomar serves as a beacon for today's scholars and students of gender, performance, and race studies to augment their initial critical approach to analyzing black women in Renaissance Spain. Just as Eulalla and Guiomar marveled their sixteenth-century audiences with their claim to power and respect, their spectacular performances in *Eufemia* and *Los engañados* will also legitimate early modern Spanish black women's claims to female authorship for present-day readers.

Making a Case for Black Feminist Theory in Early Modern Hispanism: Ar'n't I a Woman?

Look at me! Look at my arm! I have plowed, and planted, and gathered into barns, and no man could head me—and ar'n't I a woman? I could work as much and eat as much as a man (when I could get it), and bear de lash as well—and ar'n't I a woman? I have borne thirteen chilern and seen 'em mos' all sold off into slavery, and when I cried out with a mother's grief, none but Jesus heard—and ar'n't I a woman?[7]
—Sojourner Truth, 1851

In 1851, nine years before the Civil War, Sojourner Truth delivered these words in a speech at a women's rights convention in Akron, Ohio. Although Truth was addressing a nineteenth-century Victorian, US-American audience, I see a direct correlation between the message articulated in her powerful speech and the habla de negros voices mediated by literary and nonliterary representations of women of African descent in early modern Iberia (and in particular Rueda's theatrical representations of Eulalla and Guiomar). She provides an incisive analysis of the definition of the term "woman." "Sojourner Truth exposes," writes Patricia Hill Collins, "the concept of woman as being culturally constructed by using the contradiction between her life as an African-American woman and qualities ascribed to women."[8] For the intents and purposes of this chapter's multivalent critical intervention in and theoretical contribution to both gender and women's studies *and* race studies in early modern Hispanic studies, I insist that Sojourner Truth's question, "And ar'n't I a woman?" points to the contradictions inherent in the blanket use of the term "woman"—which, in early modern Hispanic studies, has had profound consequences in the scholarly analysis of and critical attention given to black women in early modern Hispanic literary texts and historical documents. Simply put: black African women are undertheorized in early modern Hispanic studies. And as a result, scholarly criticism of black women in early modern Hispanic studies—or as she is known in the field, the negra—has analytically and theoretically erased black women's agency and personhood. My choice to privilege Rueda's theatrical representation of Eulalla's and Guiomar's black female bodies as self-inscribed sites that realize corporeal and linguistic links to materiality—books and letter writing, clothing, cosmetics and hair, and foreign exotic animals—perform black feminist intellectual work: the work of theorizing black women's subjectivity in the early African diaspora. (As established in the introduction, I argue that early modern Iberia *is* part of the African diaspora and that the African diaspora *must* be theorized to encompass Iberia's contribution to and presence in African diasporic studies and thought.) This is the kind of theorizing Barbara Christian has asked us to take seriously when she reminded scholars that "people of color have always theorized.... And I am inclined to say that our theorizing ... is often in narrative forms, in the stories we create, in riddles and in proverbs, in the play with language, since dynamic rather than fixed ideas seem more to our liking."[9]

Concerning the tenability of black feminist theory in my literary analysis of gender, race, and habla de negros, I argue that the various representations of African-descended women in the literary corpus examined in this book at large—and more specifically in Rueda's performative and theatricalized ideations of Eulalla and Guiomar—transcend masculinist and racist images employed by European dramatists, historiographers, theologians, and writers in their own self-representations. My close readings of Eulalla and Guiomar, herein, marshal an explicit directive to ultimately offer a critical intervention across a variety of disciplines. As I have outlined in the introduction, the interdisciplinary scope of this book and its application of black feminist theoretical practices in this present chapter thus underscore the urgent need for specialists, students, and nonspecialists alike to accept black female literary characters from early modern Iberia as salient protagonists in the performative articulation of gender-feminist politics, female sexuality, and racial dissidence that resonates today. A variety of scholarly enterprises ranging from nuns' convent writing to the role of female protagonists in Spanish Golden Age comedia studies often, if not always, turn to twentieth-century (white) feminist theory to deconstruct patriarchy and highlight European women's agency and resistance. A similar theoretical reading practice is necessary in the critical study of black women—both historical and literary—in early modern Iberia. There is also a lot at stake for Hispanism altogether when employing black feminist theoretical practices to catalyze a rigorous mode of studying the presence and role of black women in early modern Spanish literary texts. To this end, black feminist readings are not antithetical to the scholarly exercise of the literary analysis of early modern Spanish texts.

In early modern English literary studies, for example, reading black women vis-à-vis black feminist criticism has been under way since the early 1990s, chiefly in Lynda Boose's article "'The Getting of a Lawful Race': Racial Discourse in Early Modern England and the 'Unrepresentable' Black Woman" and Kim F. Hall's classic *Things of Darkness: Economies of Race and Gender in Early Modern England*. Focusing almost entirely on dramatic texts, Joyce Green MacDonald's 2002 monograph *Women and Race in Early Modern Texts* converses fluidly with my examination of black women in Renaissance Spanish theater in this chapter. As MacDonald affirms, "Black feminist criticism in American literature and the social sciences has done more than any other body of work to restore women of African descent to historical visibility, often building new methodological and theoretical frameworks which can allow such suppressed subjects to be recovered."[10] "But in following the models constructed by such theorists and critics," she adds, "I am also aware of the historical constraints that may keep me from following exactly the same lines of analysis."[11] Like MacDonald, my focus is not the racial and self-representation of black women, for none of the texts I discuss in this chapter were authored by black women. Rather, *Eufemia* and *Los engañados* were written by Lope de Rueda, a white man. But to amend, probe, and provoke the canonical and theoretical bounds that confine both early modern Hispanism and black feminist theory, I argue that the presence of African *characters*—however whitened, decentered, and policed—opens possibilities for tracing some of the kinds of anxieties, hopes, and desires attached to these characters by their (white) authors and audiences, and thus contributing to uncovering some of the suppressed history of the construction of transatlantic imperial Spanish racial identities.[12]

The epigraphical caveat of Sojourner Truth's speech frames my impetus for privileging and utilizing a black feminist theoretical approach, for it transcends the confines of race, class, and gender oppression. I link the voices of early modern black women literary characters to the voices of resistance, of Sojourner Truth and her sisters—not victims but survivors whose actions and ideas suggest that not only does a self-defined, articulated black women's standpoint exist, but its presence has been essential to black women's survival.[13]

Eulalla the Black Blonde and Her Material World: Black Diva

In *Eufemia* (1542/1554), Lope de Rueda showcases Eulalla in the play's seventh act, or *scena séptima*.[14] In an index of a book found by the bookdealer and editor Joan Timoneda, folio 27, García Pavón publishes this paso, or short-skit play, under the title *La novia negra*.[15] Written in prose and divided into eight acts called scenas, *Eufemia* recounts the story and separation of two siblings—Leonardo and Eufemia—and the difficult and tragic journeys each of them endures. Orphans, the noble familiar realm in which Leonardo and Eufemia reside becomes broken when Leonardo decides to leave home, thus embarking on a journey of whose destination he's unsure (or as his sister Eufemia cautions, "sin saber a dó´").¹⁶ Once Leonardo begins his journey, he then enters the world of Valiano, a "señor de baronías" (baron), who ends up accompanying and looking after Leonardo. The entire dramatic representation of *Eufemia* is organized in a sequence of structured binary encounters: characters pertaining to the dominant class are paired up (Leonardo-Eufemia, Leonardo-Paulo, and Eufemia-Paulo), with a secondary parallel found in the characters belonging to the lower rungs of society (Ximena-Melchior, Vallejo-Grimaldo, Cristina-*gitana*, and Polo-Eulalla).

In the seventh act of *Eufemia*, Eulalla speaks with witty verbal puns and exhibits audacious bodily performances representative of Renaissance self-fashioning. These performative gestures and authoritative speech acts, as a result, showcase her subversive female agency through her knowledge of cosmetic alteration and adornment as well as her will to acquire material objects (e.g., clothing articles and foreign exotic animals). Eulalla's costar is the *lacayo* (valet; footman), Polo, who pursues her as his love interest and future wife:

> Acá me quiero andar siguiendo mi planeta, que, si aquesta mi Eulalla se va conmigo como me tiene prometido, yo soy uno de los bienaventurados hombres de todo mi linage. Ya estoy a su puerta. Aquí sobre la calle, en este apossento, sé que duerme. ¿Qué señas haré para que salga? ¡Oh!, bien va, que aquella que canta es.¹⁷

> [Here I want to continue aligning my astral projection with Eulalla, for if she chooses to wed me, as she's promised me, I'll be one of the luckiest men in my entire lineage. Here I wait at her doorstep, but I'm sure she's sleeping in her room here just above the street. How do I let her know that I'm here? Oh, lucky me! She's awake and singing.]

A close reading of Polo's monologue invites us to unpack the thorny subject matter of social class and race—as foreshadowed by the word "linaje"—as coded references to race (in Castilian, raza) that group people together according to filiations and similarities based on bloodlines or lineage. Though not of the same racial lineage bound by sub-Saharan African ancestry, Lope de Rueda, I argue, constructs a semblance between Eulalla and Polo in light of Polo's reference to lineage: textually, in *Eufemia* they interact as binary opposites and belong socially to the lower class. Even more suggestive is the name "Polo" (meaning "pole" or "axis"), which symbolizes Renaissance knowledge of and studies on astrology and astronomy.[18] I read Polo's relation to planets and planetary axes as figuratively symbolic of the amorous relationship he seeks to establish with Eulalla: a heteronormative racial binary where opposites, theoretically speaking, bond. On one end of the axis, we have Eulalla (black and female), and on the other end of that axis, we have Polo (white and male).

Responding to Polo, Eulalla sings a ballad invoking medieval chivalric romances:

> Gila Gonzale
> de la villa yama.
> No sé yo, madres,
> si me l'abriré.
> Gila Go[n]zale
> yama la torre.
> Abríme la voz
> fija Yeonore,
> porque lo cabayo
> mojaba falcone.
> No sé yo, madres,
> si me l'abriré.[19]

> [Gil González
> from the town, calls [knocks].
> I don't know, ladies,
> if I'll let him in(side).
> Gil González
> knocks at the tower door.
> Open your mouth (throat),
> Leonore, my child,
> because horses
> wet falcons.
> I don't know, ladies,
> if I'll let him in(side).]

As Eulalla's sonorous melody travels outside to the street for Polo and the audience to hear, the ballad she sings adduces the chivalric poetic genre by referencing Gil González Dávila, or de Ávila, the Spanish conquistador and first European to arrive to Central America in the early 1500s.[20] Eulalla's sexually explicit song—a text whose sexual innuendo and phallic imagery subverts the very chivalric decorum of courtly love that Eulalla and Polo parody in *Eufemia*—ruptures the planetary bond (particularly the nuptial bond of matrimony and the physical bond of coitus) Polo attempts to forge with her. In that vein, Eulalla's name echoes that of Eulalia from the Hispano-Roman poetic corpus of Prudentius's *Peristephanon* (*Book of Martyrdom*), which contains fourteen lyric poems on Spanish Roman martyrs.[21] Rueda's Eulalla mirrors Prudentius's Eulalia with respect to her sexual charge and refusal to participate in the commodified practice of marriage and rearing children. Moreover, I treat Eulalla as an astute and shrewd woman whose agency and identity positioning are organized and positioned like that of an aristocratic *dama*. Her obsession with makeup and cosmetic alterations—ranging from lightening her skin to bleaching her hair—capture how Eulalla self-asserts and self-defines her authority and subjectivity in *Eufemia* as a diva. Eulalla's performative embodiment of diva-like qualities allows her to resuscitate her agential authority and subversive power.

By reconsidering *Eufemia*'s construction of Eulalla as a diva, I pose a way in which to complicate the parameters of what gets deemed as "political" or "resistant" in early modern Spanish literary depictions of black women. An arguably controversial moniker used to describe (black) women's mutual artistry in early modern Spanish literature, the term "diva" captures black women's agency, power, and subjectivity. The *Oxford English Dictionary* defines the word as follows: "DIVA, *n*. A person, typically a woman, who is self-important, temperamental, and extremely demanding; a successful and glamorous female performer or personality."[22] My familiarity with Rueda's fascinating portrayal of Eulalla leads me to conclude that the category of diva is functional much earlier than scholars have thought. I position Eulalla as a diva based on the strategies of self-creation and self-defense that the term implies. The cosmetic, the performative, the sartorial, and the sonic are constitutive elements of Eulalla's presence in Rueda's sixteenth-century theatrical work just as they are in modern works. As a diva, Eulalla's notoriety and marketability hinge on her savvy self-fashioning and somatic Blackness that is fluid and performative yet deceptive and paradoxical. The interdisciplinary scope of this chapter—and for that matter, the book as a whole—underscores the urgent need for specialists, students, and nonspecialists alike to accept black female historical figures and literary characters from early modern Iberia and its colonial kingdoms as salient protagonists in the performative articulation of gender-feminist politics, female sexuality, and racial dissidence that resonates today.

Stephen Greenblatt, in the introduction to his *Renaissance Self-Fashioning*, identifies "a change in the intellectual, social, psychological, and aesthetic structure that govern the generation of identities [in the early modern period]."[23] Eulalla's racial formation along the lines of her gender and racial performativity best describes Greenblatt's idea that "*fashion* seems to come into wide currency as a way of designating the forming of a self."[24] He adds, "Fashioning may suggest the achievement of a less tangible shape: a distinctive personality, a characteristic address to the world, a consistent mode of perceiving and behaving."[25] Greenblatt's theoretical formulation of Renaissance self-fashioning best characterizes Eulalla as a practitioner of her own bodily fashioning with respect to her "distinctive personality," her "characteristic address to the world," and her "consistent mode of perceiving and behaving" that manifest in Eulalla's coquettishly explicit language from the aforementioned song she sings at the skit's opening. Greenblatt's concept of self-fashioning elucidates Eulalla's diva-like behavior, for it encapsulates her articulation and performance of self-definition in *Eufemia*. Moreover, she displays an indifference toward not only marrying Polo but to marriage as a dominating and restrictive institution and so-called rite of passage for women. To grasp the magnitude of Eulalla's agential voice and diverse illustration of diva-like qualities, I cite in its entirety her dialogue with Polo:

> EULALLA.—Siñor, preséntame la siñora Doñaldoça, un prima mía, una hoja de lexías para rubiarme na cabeyos y, como yo sa tan delicara, despójame na cabeça como nas ponjas. Pienso que tenemos la mala ganas.
> EULALLA.—Pues a buena fe que ha sinco noche que faze oración a siñor Nicolás de Tramentinos.
> POLO.—Sant Nicolás de Tolentino querrás dezir. ¿Y para qué hazes la oración, señora?

EULALLA.—Quiere casar mi amos, y para que me depares mi Dios marido a mí contentos.

POLO.—Anda, señora, ¿y cómo agora hazes aquesso? ¿No me has prometido de salirte conmigo?

EULALLA.—¿Y cómo, siñor, no miras más qu'essos? ¿Paréscete a voz que daba yo bon xemplo y cuenta de mi linages? ¿Qué te dirá cuánta siñoras tengo yo por mi migas en esta tierras?

POLO.—¿Y la palabra, señora, que me has dado?

EULALLA.—Siñor, o na força ne va, nerrechos se pierde. Honra y barbechos no caben la sacos.

POLO.—¿Pues qué deshonras pierdes tú, señora, en casarte conmigo?

EULALLA.—Ya yo lo veo, siñor. Mas quiere voz sacarme na pues perdida na tierra que te conozco.

POLO.—Mi reina, ¿pues aquesso me dizes? No te podría yo dexar, que primero no dexasse la vida.

EULALLA.—¡Ah, traidoraz! Dolor de torsija que rebata to lo rombres. A otro güesso con aquesse perro, que yo ya la tengo rosegadoz.

POLO.—En verdad, señora, que te engañas. Pero dime, señora. ¿Con quién te querían casar?

EULALLA.—Yo quiere con un cagañeroz. Dize mi amo que no, que más quere con unoz potecacarioz. Yo dize que no. Dize mi amo: "Caya, fija, que quien tenga l'oficio tenga la maleficio."

POLO.—¿Pues yo no soy oficial?

EULALLA.—¿Quín oficios, siñor Pollos?

POLO.—Adobar gorras, sacar manchas, hazer ruecas y husos y echar soletas y brocales a calabaças, otros mil oficios que, aunque agora me ves servir de lacayo, yo te sustentaré a toda tu honra. No dexes tú de sacar con que salgamos la primera jornada, que después yo te haré señora de estrado y cama de campo y guadameciles. ¿Qué quieres más, mi señora?

EULALLA.—Agora sí me contenta. Mas, ¿sabe qué querer yo, siñor Pollos?

POLO.—No, hasta que me lo digas.

EULALLA.—Que me compras una monas, un papagayos.

POLO.—¿Para qué, señora?

EULALLA.—La papagayos para qu'enseña a fablar en jaula, y lo mona para que la tengas yo a mi puertas como dueña de algo.[26]

[EULALLA.—Sir [Polo], lady Doñaldoça, a cousin of mine, gave me some bleaching patches to bleach my hair, and since I'm so delicate, they strip my head of its hairs. I think she's trying to hurt me.

EULALLA.—Well in good faith, it has been five nights since I've been praying to Nicholas of Turpentine.

POLO.—Saint Nicholas of Tolentino, you mean to say? And why are you reciting that prayer, my lady?

EULALLA.—My master wants to marry, and so that God himself will provide me with a husband of my own to marry.

POLO.—Come on, my lady. How are you going to do that? Didn't you promise me that you'll marry me?

EULALLA.—What do you mean, sir? Doesn't it seem to you that I'd lead by good example and tell you my lineage? How does it sound that I have a number of friends in these hands?

POLO.—And the word of marriage you gave to me, my lady?

EULALLA.—Sir, not even by force are one's rights lost. I can't lose my honor by going into this blindly.

POLO.—By marrying me, what honor are you to lose, my lady?

EULALLA.—And now I see it, sir: you want to deflower me.

POLO.—My Queen, what're you saying? I could never do such a thing; I'd rather die.

EULALLA.—Oh, you traitor! The pain of twisted lies all you men say. You can't fool me; go tell that to someone else.

POLO.—Sure, my lady, you're fooling yourself. But tell me, my lady, with whom were you going to marry?

EULALLA.—I want to marry a knight. But my master says no; he prefers a pharmacist. I said no, but my master says: "Hush, my dear, for one who has a job is good enough in and of itself."

POLO.—Well, are you implying that I'm not good enough?

EULALLA.—What jobs do you have, Mr. Pollos?

POLO.—I repair hats, remove stains, make distaffs and spindles, and patch stockings and brocades, among a thousand other jobs that, even though you see me now working as a servant, I'll sustain every bit of your honor. Don't stop yourself from letting me take you out [on a date], for afterward I'll make you a lady of the *estrado*; of sedans and fancy tanned coats. What more do you want, my lady?

EULALLA.—Now I like the sound of that! But, you know what else I want, Mr. Pollos?
POLO.—No. Not until you tell me.
EULALLA.—I want you to buy me a monkey and a parrot!
POLO.—What for, my lady?
EULALLA.—The parrot so that I can teach it how to talk in its cage and the monkey so that I can have it on hand, as an owner of something.]

In this rich dialogue, Rueda positions Eulalla as a subject who is not only savvy but also plots her destiny and social position. The power of Eulalla's words, as illustrated by her conversation with Polo, manifests in bell hooks's assertion that "dialogue implies talk between two subjects, not the speech of subject and object. It is a humanizing speech, one that challenges and resists domination."[27] Through dialogue, and its humanizing capacity, Eulalla works out her knowledge and predilection for the fineries of what her world, as far as she knows, can buy her, as she simultaneously disregards and exploits Polo. Once Eulalla ends her exchange with Polo, his so-called *planeta* aligns with nothing of amorous stability but, instead, with financial ruin. Eulalla's authority and power are contingent upon the ways in which she debases and subordinates Polo. Although they both belong to the lower rungs of Renaissance Spanish society, Eulalla—through her back-and-forth demands and rejections—turns Polo into the victim-puppet of her money-driven desires.

Eulalla's performance and sensibility as a diva cannot be detached from her desire to acquire and utilize animals for her subject positioning as a black woman. To illustrate this, I quote the direct passage where Eulalla expresses her desire for foreign animals, such as a female monkey ("una monas") and a parrot ("un papagayos"):

EULALLA.—Agora sí me contenta. Mas, ¿sabe qué querer yo, siñor Pollos?
POLO.—No, hasta que me lo digas.
EULALLA.—Que me compras una monas, un papagayos.
POLO.—¿Para qué, señora?
EULALLA.—La papagayos para qu'enseña a fablar en jaula, y lo mona para que la tengas yo a mi puertas como dueña de algo.[28]

[EULALLA.—Now I like the sound of that! But, you know what else I want, Mr. Pollos?
POLO.—No. Not until you tell me.
EULALLA.—I want you to buy me a monkey and a parrot!
POLO.—What for, my lady?
EULALLA.—The parrot so that I can teach it how to talk in its cage and the monkey so that I can have it on hand, as an owner of something.]

If we are to read Eulalla as a black diva, then her divaness—as it is predicated on her self-identification with European aristocratic aesthetics and fineries—*cannot* be detached from the references she makes to exotic animals such as monkeys and parrots. In *La imagen de los negros en el teatro del Siglo de Oro*, Baltasar Fra-Molinero privileges a racialized simian reading of Eulalla that renders her—as well as many, if not all, black Africans depicted by Europeans in early modern Spanish literature—subhuman.

Covarrubias's pictorial image of the (female) monkey (fig. 11) captures Fra-Molinero's abject reading of Eulalla:

EMBLEMA 98.
Siendo la mona abominable, y fea,
Si acaso ve su rostro en un espejo,
Queda de si pagada, y no desea
otra gracia, beldad, gala, o despejo.
La malcarada, se tendrá por dea;
Del rostro acicalando el vil pellejo,
Y cada qual, de gloria desseoso,
Lo feo le parece ser hermoso.[29]

[Being the abominable, and quite ugly, female monkey—
if she happens to see her face in the mirror—
she is pleased with herself and desires
no other grace, beauty, finery, or gaiety.
A hideous creature, she takes herself for a goddess,
yet she paints her saggy face.
But everyone who desires fame
takes ugliness for beauty.]

Keeping Covarrubias's visual iconography of *la mona* in mind, I read against a body of scholarly criticism that animalizes Eulalla, in simian terms, for the "ridiculousness of [her] pretensions to act 'White.'"[30] Just as there is validity in interpreting Eulalla's aspiration to act "White" (or, perhaps, in simian terms, to mimic cultural forms) as fraudulent and outlandish in the eyes of (white) spectators, I would also contend that her cultural alignment and ideological identification with Renaissance European aesthetics and customs (or, rather, her parodic performance of aristocratic "Whiteness") reveals an ideation of Renaissance self-fashioning that relates back to Eulalla's desire for acquiring exotic animals. Her request for a monkey and a parrot underscores my advocacy for a Renaissance self-fashioning analysis that attends to an animal studies approach. In order to illuminate Eulalla's authorial savvy and subject positioning as a black diva, this section, in the pages ahead, applies an animal studies reading in order to uncover Eulalla's agency and power. To borrow Martha Few and Zeb Tortorici's methodology of "centering animals," as articulated in their groundbreaking edited volume *Centering Animals in Latin American History*, I will rehearse close readings of the monkey and parrot on which Eulalla calls as a means to critically interrogate, and thus situate, her in the category of the "human" and the reconceptualization of the early modern subject. Arguing for the concept of the "human" ("humane" or "humanity") in early modernity, Georgina Dopico ventures that "Spain as a consequence of its imperial appetites and the political-theological hand-wringing that sometimes accompanied it . . . was particularly interested in what lies at the edges of the human: the beast and the sovereign, but also the monster, the machine, the hermaphrodite, the native, the slave, and the divine."[31] Dopico's argument here facilitates my methodological and theoretical approach to dismantling conventional readings of Eulalla as a powerless animal.

If anything, Rueda's construction of Eulalla in *Eufemia* represents a metahistorical narrative of Spain's imperial appetite and voracious investment in exploring the animal-human binary. Eulalla inscribes herself into the cultural history of Renaissance menageries at the Habsburg courts in Iberia. I frame Eulalla's desire for tropical animals historically after 1500, when Habsburg collectors spent a great deal of time, energy, and money in the acquisition of luxury wares from distant points of the world.[32] The *Kunstkammer*, or cabinet of curiosities, reflected the peculiarities and tastes of its princely owners.[33] The

FIG. 11. Sebastián de Covarrubias, *Emblema 98* "La mona," 1610. From *Emblemas morales* (Madrid: Fundación Universitaria Española, 1978).

discovery of direct sea routes to Africa, Asia, the Far East, and the Americas in the sixteenth century opened up a global market and traffic for goods, which afforded discriminating collectors a unique opportunity to buy, commission, and collect an assortment of commodities (spices, medicinal drugs, plants, seeds, herbs), luxury goods, furniture, textiles, all forms of exotic wares, and, above all, animals and birds never before seen in Europe.[34]

The monkey and the parrot in the text underscore the aristocracy's wealth and imperial expansion into North and sub-Saharan Africa, Asia, the Far East, and the Americas. As mediated by Rueda, the articulation of Eulalla's desire for exotic animals further demonstrates her knowledge of Renaissance material cultural and mercantile affairs. Her desire for these animals, I suggest, transcends her supposed poorly executed simian-ascribed mimetic practice and parodic performance of European aristocrats. To Rueda's credit, the animal-human binary he edifies in the skit—in direct relation to Eulalla's desire for tropical animals—destabilizes and shifts the role of Eulalla's personhood and subjectivity: she, as a black woman, transforms into the proprietor and instructor of animals. As a metaphorical extension of the Kunstkammer, Eulalla thus becomes an imagined part of, or participant in, a larger Western and non-Western tradition of collecting in the early modern period.

Referencing a period of Spanish imperial expansion that had transpired some sixty years after Columbus first returned from the Americas and more than twenty-five years after Cortés eradicated most of the Aztec Empire, Eulalla's diva mentality partakes fully in the colonial Spanish-American enterprise when she requests of Polo a monkey and a parrot. Eulalla's parrot signals a larger geographical imaginary that consists of imperial Iberia's vast oceanic expansion across Africa, Asia, the Far East, and the Americas.[35] As shown in figure 12, Covarrubias's visual image of the *papagayo*, in his 1610 *Emblemas morales*, describes the bird with the following exemplary message:

> EMBLEMA 78
> El Papagayo, el Tordo, la Piçaça,
> Perciben lo que oyen, enseñados
> Del ocio maestro, que con traça
> Les tiene sutilmente amaestrados:
> Tal es el charlatan hombre de plaça,
> Que con papeles de otro, bien limados,

Poniendo de su parte la memoria
Sola, pretende ganar fama, y gloria.³⁶

[Taught by their master,
the parrot, the Tordo, and the Piçaça
are experts of leisure and perceive what they hear.
Taught by tracing,
you can subtly train them:
Such is the charlatan, man of the plaza,
well-polished, and who carries the documents of others.
Memorizing everything,
but memory alone is the pretense of winning fame and
    glory.]

A year later, in 1611, Covarrubias, in his *Tesoro*, builds on his moral definition of the bird by highlighting the animal's connection to Iberian imperial expansion. The lexicographer defines "papagayo" as

[una] ave índica conocida, de varias plumas con las colores finísimas, imita la voz humana y percibe todo lo que le enseñan. Díjose papagayo por el papo que tiene gayo, que vale tanto como vario en colores y alegre. Al que habla algunas cosas bien dichas, pero que se conoce no ser suyas sino estudiadas, decimos hablar como papagayo.³⁷

[a bird known from the East Indies, full of plumage of various lengths and lustrous colors. It imitates the human voice and absorbs all that is taught to him. It is called the *papagayo*, for its gay caw, which is to say, both gay of color and of mood. To whomever it speaks, it says nice things, but let it be known that these words are not his own but rather studied; that is why we say talking like a parrot.]

Language occupies an important configuration in the image of the papagayo in relation to Eulalla's habla de negros speech and her desire to teach the bird *how* to speak in its cage. For Rueda's audience, the perceived pretense of Eulalla's attempt to teach a bird how to speak—similar to the way in which Covarrubias constructs a moral judgment against the papagayo for its

FIG. 12. Sebastián de Covarrubias, *Emblema 78* "El papagayo," 1610. From *Emblemas morales* (Madrid: Fundación Universitaria Española, 1978).

loquacious verbosity and semblance of a charlatan—would have been a ridiculous trifle. For some spectators, how could a black woman—who already speaks a racially marked and linguistically profane variation of Castilian—possess the knowledge to instruct an animal to talk? In Renaissance writing, the ridicule of women and other subordinate people overlapped with the textual imagery of parrots. Rueda's insertion of the papagayo serves as a foil to Eulalla's excessive habla de negros speech (as constructed by its grammatical errors, run-on sentences, and wordiness). However, as opposed to treating Eulalla as a ridiculous animal who aims to teach another animal (the parrot) how to speak, it appears to me that her gesture to gift the bird language, or at least the ability to talk, positions her culturally and ideologically into the dominant ruling class' aesthetics and values. As a thinking subject, I argue, Eulalla aspires to reappropriate the parrot for her own empowerment, self-advancement, and ultimate investment in parrot culture.

Eulalla's relationship to the monkey and the parrot must also be analyzed through the methodology of the visual. Her awareness of the capital and symbolic power of monkeys and parrots in her Renaissance milieu operates as a foil to royal portraiture, where black Africans frequently appeared as props framed adjacent to their white aristocratic sitters (as if they were foreign, exotic animals or collectible items).

*

Rueda's *Eufemia* destabilizes a conventional racial logic that reduces Eulalla to a static, voiceless prop. Eulalla is not a prop. Rueda's theatrical representation thus casts her into a position of power, as if she were an aristocratic sitter—let us imagine, for instance, Cristóvao de Morais's *Portrait of Juana de Austria with Her Black Slave Girl* (1553)—who collects, possesses, and trades foreign goods of the Kunstkammer (fig. 13). In the following and closing section, I analyze Eulalla's cosmetic practice of altering her hair and skin color in order to further uncover her agential authority and subversive power through her material acquisition of Whiteness—which ultimately functions as a commodity whose value is directly related to its scarcity and use.

In *Eufemia*, two short passages referencing Eulalla's hair and skin color have stirred up much controversy: (1) "Siñor, preséntame la siñora Doñaldoça,

FIG. 13. Cristóvão de Morais, *Portrait of Juana de Austria with Her Black Slave Girl*, 1553. Oil on canvas, 99 × 81 cm. Musées Royaux des Beaux-Arts de Belgique, Brussels, inv. no. 1296.

un prima mía, una hojetas de lexías para rubiarme na cabeyos y, como yo sa tan delicara, despójame na cabeça como nas ponjas" (Sir [Polo], lady Doñaldoça, a cousin of mine, gave me some bleaching patches to bleach my hair, and since I'm so delicate, they strip my head of its hairs)[38] and (2) "Tráigame para mañana un poquito de moçaça, un poquito de trementinos de la que yaman de puta" (Tomorrow, bring me a bit of mustard and a bit of turpentine from the one known as the whore).[39] Critics have insisted on seeing Eulalla as tragic and devoid of any agency and racial identity. The critical reception bestowed on her bleach-blond hair—as well as other black women who have also colored and straightened their hair—has been regarded as a subordinating act to a white beauty culture.[40] What I glean from Eulalla's obsession with cosmetic recipes for altering her hair and skin color operates at the level of Rueda's meta-appropriation of Blackness and Whiteness. Rueda's racial appropriation of Eulalla is multivalent: on the one hand, it operates as the playwright's white appropriation of her Africanized Castilian and cosmetic adornments, and, on the other hand, her representative appropriation of European medieval and Renaissance standards of female beauty as she inserts herself into the cultural histories of hair and makeup.

I read Eulalla as a repository of knowledge, for she characterizes the lavish, shrewd, and witty characteristics of a diva. As illustrated thus far, she knows what she wants and refuses to defer her dreams to Polo (a white man). Further, I situate her as a well-read and up-to-date connoisseur of the beauty practices and cosmetic trends readily furnished by Fernando de Rojas's *La Celestina* (Burgos, 1499). *Celestina* was translated into all the major European languages and reprinted in some eighty-four separate Castilian editions before 1650.[41] Rojas's *Celestina* was by all accounts one of the most popular, best read, and most influential books of early modernity.[42] Eulalla knows the natural world and its ecological benefits, as expressed specifically by her request for "moçaça" (mustard) and "trementinos" (turpentine) from "la que yaman de puta" (the one known as the whore) to lighten the skin color on her hands.[43] Given the historical context and literary history of *Celestina*, I surmise that the "puta" (whore) of whom Eulalla speaks is a Celestinesque figure—a mirrored iteration of Rojas's Celestina, who employs her rhetorical arts and knowledge of medicine, herbs, astrology, weaving, sewing, and cosmetics.[44] To that end, I urge my readers to frame Eulalla—as well as other historical representations of women of color who lived their lives as go-betweens, healers, and witches in early modern Iberia—as a coterminous metaphor, or representative, of the cultural and literary discourses of Celestina.

As a practitioner of cosmetic alteration and adornment, Eulalla's role in *Eufemia* requires a rethinking of the concept of hegemony. Her beauty politics destabilize the notion that black women's objectification as so-called Others is so complete that they become willing participants in their own oppression. Eulalla's black beauty is multifaceted in its approach and execution. Her racial politics, or, rather, racialized self-awareness and self-perception, resist the norms against which black women are scrutinized and stigmatized. Eulalla challenges Whiteness even though she attempts to cosmetically fashion her body to embody it. Whiteness for Eulalla is *not* the central focus of black beauty norms.

To invoke the words of Frantz Fanon in his essay "The Fact of Blackness," Eulalla captures how Blackness is an object in the midst of other objects.[45] The evidence of visual representation of blacks in the early modern period suggests that long before both Spain and, later, England gained a foothold in the Atlantic slave trade, blacks played an important role in the symbolic economy of elite culture. Black Africans were brought to Spain not only as slaves with the absolute objectification of the state but also as curiosities who represented the riches that could be obtained by European travelers, traders, and collectors in the Atlantic world—a historical fact that Rueda indeed complicates in *Eufemia* through Eulalla's embodied performance and Africanized Castilian. The early modern Spanish archive contains numerous historical records of black women who navigated early modern Portuguese and Spanish societies similarly to Eulalla. Let us consider the embroideress Catalina de Soto of Granada. The jurist and historian Francisco Bermúdez de Pedraza writes about de Soto in his *Historia eclesiástica de Granada* (1639). Known as the "Queen of Black Women" (Reina de negras), Bermúdez de Pedraza describes Catalina as follows: "Yo la conocí en mi puecia y me iba tras ella pareciéndome gran novedad ver una negra muy aseada y compuesta, con dos criadas blancas detrás de ella"[46] (I met her as a young man and used to tag along behind her because I was so amazed by the great novelty of seeing a clean and well-dressed black woman with two white women servants walking behind her). Famous for her embroidery and needlework, Bermúdez de Pedraza records that de Soto also appraised trousseaux for wealthy white women during their engagements. I reject the notion that Catalina de Soto's life story is, was, and therefore must be treated as "exceptional." To do so only empowers and reinforces a reductively pejorative stance on black women's agency, personhood, and worth, as if they can never escape, resist, or supersede the clutches of European colonialism and antiblack racism. To that end, the archival dossier of Catalina de Soto inaugurates a revised critical lens with which to interpret Rueda's literary and theatrical representation of Eulalla's racially gendered performance of the black female body in *Eufemia*.

Visual culture offers a powerful and perplexing sense of possibilities for black women in early modern representation.[47] Each of the following images depicts black women with blonde hair—the Queen of Sheba (fig. 14) and Beyoncé (fig. 15)—whose function here is to assist our visualization of Eulalla's self-inscription of white women's aristocratic fineries. Accordingly, I assign

FIG. 14. Konrad Kyeser, *Bellifortis*, 1405. Niedersächsische Staats- und Universitätsbibliothek Göttingen, 2 Cod. Ms. Philos. 63, Cim., fol. 122r.

FIG. 15. Promotional poster for "The Mrs. Carter Show World Tour," 2013–14.

Eulalla to the category of "black blonde." Rueda's text tells us that she is, in fact, a black blonde when she uses "hojetas de lexías para rubiarme na cabeyos" (bleaching patches to dye [her] hair blonde).[48] I do not aim to reinforce a white iconic "original" but instead to call into question and facilitate the term's location on the black female body. Through the process of Stuart Hall's conception of translation as a process of cultural change in which cultural practice becomes translated, Eulalla's black female body becomes *different* from what it once was because of the impact of new spaces and times. This is particularly plausible for Eulalla's case if we are to imagine her being removed coercively from western sub-Saharan Africa as a slave and then placed in a sixteenth-century Iberian metropolis such as Lisbon or Seville. Black beauty, especially Eulalla's black beauty, can be seen as something that has "evolved" and has become *different* from what it once was. Translation always involves critique, deconstruction, and reconstruction that emerge as beauty is inscribed on the body's *surface* through stylization. Eulalla's stylization operates at the level of appropriation and an inscription onto the surface of her body.

Just as I identify Eulalla as a black blonde, I also channel her as a premodern version of the global pop star Beyoncé, insofar as I recognize Eulalla's ability to translate what are taken to be "white" looks and sensibilities that appear specifically in Beyoncé's "The Mrs. Carter Show World Tour" poster that operate as racially coded signifiers. The two visual representations of Beyoncé that I comparatively trace back to Eulalla weave a narrative that destabilizes the idea of Whiteness as an exclusive category. Both Beyoncé's and Eulalla's self-inscribed performative embodiment of Whiteness encapsulates Susan Gubar's term "racechange," or the "traversing of race boundaries, racial imitation or impersonation, cross-racial mimicry or mutability, white posing as black or black passing as white, pan-racial mutuality."[49] Like Beyoncé's reinscription of early modern European queens such as Elizabeth I and Marie Antoinette (an iconographic image to which she returns in her *Lemonade* album, released 23 April 2016, as the African [Egyptian] queen Nefertiti), Eulalla's cosmetic adornment and self-constructed image as a black blonde in *Eufemia* harness Gubar's insightful "racechange" theory through an act of cross-racial mimicry and mutability with regard to the way in which Lope de Rueda exercises his liberty to alter and render the black female body physically and racially mutable.

Theories of race and racial mutability do not reign supreme in US-American culture and cultural studies. To the contrary, we can talk about race as a serious strategy for analyzing and interrogating presences and representations of Blackness—as well as Whiteness and other ethnic racial formations—in early modern European texts across scholarly disciplines and languages. The bibliography is massive and growing all the time.[50] Let us take, as evidence, Peter Erickson and Kim F. Hall's recent special issue curated in *Shakespeare Quarterly* titled "'A New Scholarly Song': Rereading Early Modern Race." Their collection is a constructive response to the "profound and disillusioning moment of alienation for many people of color" at the 2013 annual meeting of the Shakespeare Association of America.[51] Peterson and Hall explain that the 2013 meeting represented a step back for the Shakespeare Association of America, and that it revealed the recursiveness of early modern race studies, where the importance of race is either ignored altogether or subject to an unhealthy back-and-forth in which scholars focusing on race confront the same questions and pushback from editors, readers, and audience members whose only investment in race seems to be disciplinary.[52] This can be attributed partially to the fact that the vanguard of critical race studies—one primary analytic with which I am in dialogue in this monographic study—takes place elsewhere, and that early modern Hispanic studies interlocutors cannot be expected to be knowledgeable about the extensive body of race theory of the past fifty years.[53] But after more than twenty years of scholarship in early modern studies, I can only conclude—as suggested by Peterson and Hall—that these acts of refusal are also due to a pathological averseness to thinking about race under the guise of protecting historical difference.[54] I concur with their charge that "many scholars genially dismissive of race know little of the extensive scholarship on race—in either its early modern or modern form."[55] And "more alarmingly," they add, "there will be fewer of us doing the vital work of thinking about race then and now if graduate advisors and other mentors continually discourage students from entering early modern race studies."[56]

Ignoring or disparaging race will not make it go away as a question for our time—or during the early modern period. The connection I see and forge between Beyoncé and Eulalla is not a foolish scholarly errand. In the classroom, at the graduate and undergraduate levels, I have taught the twinned image of these women in my "Black Africans in the Hispanic Black Atlantic:

Then and Now" seminar. From this pedagogical experience, I have encouraged my students to advocate for the methodological use of the contemporary as a frame to rethink the so-called old and disconnected early modern period to illuminate new readings that are not at first apparent. Even further, as I develop future book-length projects on African-descended women in imperial Spain and its colonial kingdoms, I find it inspiring and necessary to study black women pop stars—like Beyoncé—and their production teams, who, in fact, have studied and researched the long-standing legacy of African-descended women in ancient, premodern, and early modern history and literature to fashion and to reinvent their brand and iconographic image. (My recent participation in the "Beyoncé's *Lemonade* Lexicon" Feminist Research Seminar, sponsored by the Institute for Research on Women and Gender at the University of Michigan, reflects my scholarly commitment to this approach.) To that end, race scholarship needs to continue to expand beyond the limits of England and its colonies, providing a wider European purview that combines different linguistic and national traditions. Hence, in the case of Hispanic studies, my comparison of Rueda's Eulalla to Beyoncé seeks to challenge how the study of race is often isolated in separate language departments, thus encouraging more active collaborations across disciplines and geographies.

*

Eulalla's obsession with power and sociocultural upward mobility is reflected in José Antonio Maravall's idea that material wealth governs the *pícaro*'s (rogue, swindler) desire for upward social mobility. Eulalla also fits in the literary tradition of the picaresque tradition. As a bad girl, Eulalla relies on cosmetic alteration and adornment to legitimate her cultural capital. Pierre Bourdieu sees "cultural capital" as a set of knowledge, skills, and various forms of cultural acquisitions, such as educational or technical qualifications.[57] Eulalla acquires and negotiates her cultural capital through *hojetas de lexías* (cosmetic hair-bleaching patches) and the application of *afeites*, ranging from *mudas* (cosmetic balms or ointments), *moçaça* (mustard), and *trementinos* (turpentine). For Eulalla, economic capital is constituted by material wealth in the form of money and luxurious objects. So that the self-perception of her honor will not be compromised and forfeited, she demands that her white male suitor, Polo, should he be lucky enough to marry her, gifts her foreign animals: "una monas, un papagayos" (a monkey and a parrot).[58] She also requests of her white female patrons—"la monja Santa Pabla" and "la señora Doña Beatriz" (Saint Pabla the nun and Lady Doña Beatriz)— aristocratic fineries: brocade for her blonde hair and a "ventayos" (*ventalle*, or fan).[59] These objects in return represent a symbolic capital—accumulated prestige or honor—readily associated with aristocracy. As a result, Eulalla is then able to crystallize her own self-awareness through the symbolic power of her expressive Black vernacular culture of habla de negros.

To echo Hazel Carby, black women's bodies must not be policed! Lope de Rueda complicates Eulalla's stylized beauty practices by demonstrating how the categories of race, gender, and social class are not necessarily acquired but are, in fact, *learned* without obvious teaching or conscious learning. Citing Omi and Winant, black feminist critic Patricia Hill Collins notes that "Black women are not simply grafted onto existing social institutions but are so pervasive that even though the images themselves change in the popular imagination, Black women's portrayal as the Other persists. Particular meanings, stereotypes, and myths can change, but the overall ideology of domination itself seems to be an enduring feature of interlocking systems of race, gender, and class oppression."[60]

Collins's remarks capture Eulalla's impetus for using cosmetics to alter her body. I reference this body of critical theory to underscore the complexity of Eulalla's conception of beauty, especially her *black* beauty. Critics have insisted on reading Eulalla as a tragic, pathetic figure who lacks agency.[61] To the contrary, Eulalla is not a dupe of white male patriarchy and racism void of beauty agency, as she can only yearn for Whiteness. Black beauty—Eulalla's *black beauty*, moreover—is multifaceted in its approaches and goals. Her racial politics, or racialized self-awareness and self-perception, speak norms against which black women are judged. Eulalla troubles the fixity and primacy of White aesthetics even though she attempts to cosmetically fashion her body to represent them.

At the skit's closure, Polo rejects Eulalla's commentary on "fazer una muda para la manos" (making a [whitening] balm for my hands). He objects by saying: "Que con essa color me contenta yo, señora. No has menester ponerte nada. A ser más blanca no [me] valías nada" (Your skin color pleases me already, my lady. You don't need to put anything on, for if you were any whiter, you would be worthless to me).⁶² The established canonical reading of this passage positions Polo as a slave trafficker who wants to sell Eulalla into slavery, thereby making her his slave. According to this particular interpretation, Polo's plea—"A ser más blanca no [me] valías nada"—communicates the reason why he begs Eulalla *not* to whiten her skin. Polo's proto-capitalist and slave trader point of view—as suggested by traditional readings of this passage—would find no commercial value in Eulalla's cosmetically altered black female body.

I offer a counternarrative that objects to the proposed canonical reading of the relationship between Eulalla and Polo. Satisfied with Eulalla's so-called natural physical features, I read Polo's position in the skit as coterminous with what Collins deems as "constructing an Afrocentric feminist aesthetic for beauty."⁶³ Because Polo rejects the white skin and blonde hair Eulalla prizes, he proclaims her somatic Blackness as beautiful. He thus challenges Eurocentric masculinist aesthetics that foster an ideology of domination. The message Polo conveys transcends the almost clichéd biblical maxim "Black is Beautiful," as we have seen throughout this book. It is not harmful to take Polo's love for Eulalla at face value, and to think otherwise is to reify an oversimplified treatment of Eulalla and Polo's complex relationship in the entremés.

Eulalla's witty final words allude to a larger discourse about cosmetics. Her understanding of cosmetic adornment originates from a social repository controlled and designed by women:

> EULALLA.—Assí la verdad, que aunque tengo la cara morenicas, la cuerpo tienes como un terciopelo dobles.
> POLO.—A ser más blanca no [me] valías nada. –Adiós, que assí te quiero para hazer reales.
> EULALLA.—Guíate la Celestinas, que guiaba la toro enamorados.⁶⁴

> [EULALLA.—Yes, that is true. But even though I have a black face, your body is as hairy as velvet two times over.
> POLO.—If you were any whiter, you would be worthless to me. Farewell! As you are, I want(ed) you in order to earn some reales.
> EULALLA.—Let (the) Celestina guide you, the one who guided all lovesick men.]

When Eulalla cites the notorious go-between/matchmaker Celestina, I am led to believe that she possesses some kind of educational training or literary knowledge. The likelihood of Eulalla's literacy is buttressed by the fact that she would have been a domestic slave working in an aristocratic household. In sixteenth-century Spain, for example, owners often Hispanicized their domestic slaves by teaching them basic reading and writing skills. Just because Eulalla speaks habla de negros, and *not* "proper" Castilian, in the text does not allow us to assume that she does not know how to read. If we are to explore the possibility of Eulalla's literacy—in cosmetics, material culture, and print culture—via Rueda's construction of her role in the skit, then we must frame her as a sub-Saharan African who has become "Latin." As sub-Saharan Africans gradually attained various levels of Iberian cultural fluency, Iberians measured their transformation on a scale of acculturation ranging from "bozal" to "ladino," with intermediate levels such as "half bozal," "not very ladino," and "between bozal and ladino." In *Eufemia*, Rueda utilizes his black women characters to negotiate varying forms of becoming ladino.

Rueda gives Eulalla the last word in the skit, as she retorts to Polo: "Guíate la Celestinas, que guiaba la tora enamorados" (Let [the] Celestina guide you, the one who guided all lovesick men).[65] I nuance my reading here by illustrating Eulalla's grammatical error in the text: "la toro enamorados." The correction should read as "todos los enamorados," or "all lovesick men." Yet Eulalla's sarcastic pun is predicated on Polo behaving as if he were a "lovesick *bull*," as in "la toro enamorados," or "el toro enamorado." Polo, unfortunately, is denied an opportunity to reply to Eulalla's tongue-in-cheek comeback. Having the last word, Eulalla tropes the dope, Polo, by silencing him into his place. It is Eulalla's hyperbolic and expressive Africanized Castilian—the kind that even her prized parrot would have spoken—that turns the pun on its head!

As a case study, Lope de Rueda's theatrical representation of Eulalla has served to demonstrate the contradictory and paradoxical ways in which the playwright explores the subversive potential articulated in Eulalla's embodiment of the intersecting tropes of hair, skin, and race. Whether codified racially as a wig of braided hair used in blackface performance or in terms of Eulalla's blonde hair, this section closes by reiterating that hair cannot be detached from the racially gendered ideologies that construct it. As a racial signifier, hair and skin communicated and produced political and social power.

As in the case of Eulalla in *Eufemia*, we learn that the racially gendered politics of hair and skin on black women's bodies transcend their seductive roots for authority and power.

Guiomar's Authorial Unmasking: Black Feminism

In the third act of *Los engañados*, Lope de Rueda showcases the domestic house servant Guiomar, who argues with the aggressive white house servant Julieta and reasons with the "open-minded" dama Clavela. In this paso, Rueda plots a two-pronged ideological viewpoint about race relations in Renaissance Spain: (1) antiblack sentiments against black Africans (as demonstrated by Julieta) and (2) an awareness of black humanity and personhood (as demonstrated by Clavela). Throughout the skit, Julieta violently attacks Guiomar because she talks back and refuses to renounce her noble sub-Saharan African lineage. To demonstrate Julieta and Guiomar's point of contention in the text, I cite the crux of the three women's conflicted exchange as follows:

> GUIOMAR.—¡Jesú Jesú! ¿No mira vosa mercé que proguntar quín sa yo? Mira, mira, fija. Ya saber Dios y tora lo mundo que sar yo sabrina na reina Berbasina, cuñados de la marqués de Cucurucú, por an mar y por a tierras.
> JULIETA.—Sí, sí, no le ronquéis.
> CLAVELA.—Calla, rapaza. ¿Reina era tu tía, Guiomar?
> GUIOMAR.—¡Ay, siñora! ¿Pensar vosa mercé que san yo fija de alguno negra de par ahí? Ansí haya bono siglo álima de doña Bialaga, sinora.
> CLAVELA.—¡Gentil nombre tenía para dalle buen siglo!
> GUIOMAR.—Sí, siñora. Doña Bialaga yamar siñora mi madre, y siñor mi padre Eliomor. Cuenta que quiere lesir don Diegoz.
> JULIETA.—Mirá cómo queréis essos bledos. ¡Qué gentiles nombres para un podenco!
> GUIOMAR.—Por esso primer fijo que me nacer en Potugal le yamar Diguito, como siñor saragüelo.
> CLAVELA.—Su agüelo dirás.
> GUIOMAR.—Sí siñora. Su sabuelo.

CLAVELA.—¿Hijos tienes, Guiomar?

GUIOMAR.—¡Ay, siñora! No me lo mientas, que me faze lágrima yorar. Téngolo, siñora, la India le San Joan de Punto Rico. Y agora por un mes la goso m'escribió un carta a que la ringlonsito. ¡Tan fresco como un flor de aquele campo! ¡Ay, entraña la mía, fijo mío!

JULIETA.—Tan desatinada y tan borracha me venga el bien.

GUIOMAR.—¿Quín sa borracha, Chuchuleta? ¡Ay, mandaria, mandaria! ¡Plégata Dios que mala putería te corra y no veas carralasolendas!

CLAVELA.—¡Ay, amarga, que carnestoliendas y qué mal pronunciadas!

JULIETA.—¡Mal corrimiento venga por ti, amen!

GUIOMAR.—Andá, patiñas medrosas, no es mi honras tomame contigos.

JULIETA.—¡Mire qué fantasia! Pues callá, doña negra, que agora ha mandado su Alteza que a todos los negros y negras hagan pólvora.

GUIOMAR.—Cagajón paral merda, tomá pala vos y a mandamento.

CLAVELA.—Y déxala, Guiomar, que es una loca. Si no, dime. ¿Qué es lo que tu hijo te envió a dezir?

GUIOMAR.—Aquella mochacho, aquella mi fijo, métemelo a prinsipio de carta diziendo: "Lutríssima madre mía Guiomar, la carta que yo te cribo no e para besamano, sino que sa bono. Bendito sea Rios, loado sea Rios, amén." ¡Ay! ¡Dios te la preste, fijo de la coraçon y de l'antrañas!

CLAVELA.—No llores, Guiomar, no llores.

GUIOMAR.—No podemo fazer otro, porque tenemo la trógramo toro, toro, yeno de fatriqueras.[66]

[GUIOMAR.—Jesus, Jesus! Doesn't Your Grace think to ask who I am? God knows, and the entire world knows, that I'm the niece of Queen Berbasina, in-laws of the Marquis of Cucurucú, across the seas and lands.

JULIETA.—Sure, sure. I won't bark at her.

CLAVELA.—Hush, you thievish raptor! And so, Guiomar, your aunt was a queen?

GUIOMAR.—Oh, my lady! Your Grace thinks that I'm a daughter of some black wretch in these parts? It has been a good century since Lady Bialaga has been dead.

CLAVELA.—What a respectable name she had to last her a century!

GUIOMAR.—Yes, my lady. Madam Bialaga was my mother's name, and my father's name was Eliomor. But he prefers the name Don Diego.

JULIETA.—Look how you just run your mouth. What respectable names for a dog!

GUIOMAR.—That's why my first son, who was born in Portugal, is called Dieguito, like his *saragüelo*.

CLAVELA.—His *agüelo* [grandfather], you mean to say.

GUIOMAR.—Yes, my lady, his *sabuelo* [grandfather].

CLAVELA.—Do you have any children, Guiomar?

GUIOMAR.—Oh my lady! Don't bring that up, for it makes me cry. I have a son, my lady, who's in the Indies of San Juan, Puerto Rico. This August he wrote me a letter from that distant corner of the world. He's as fresh as a countryside flower over there! Oh, how I miss my son so much!

JULIETA.—How foolish and drunk!

GUIOMAR.—Who's drunk, you fresh bitch? Oh, get me a hammer! I swear to God I hope bad whoring falls on you, such that you never see the sight of meat or get laid!

CLAVELA.—Oh, you bitter woman. You mean to say "carnestoliendas"; you're a horrible speaker!

JULIETA.—I hope you get syphilis! How about that!

GUIOMAR.—Go on, you cowardly crud; my dignity won't be wasted on you.

JULIETA.—Oh, what a fantasy! Hush then, Queen Black Bitch, since Your Highness has now sent all of her blacks to make gunpowder.

GUIOMAR.—Diarrhea mouth! You and your shit-filled mouth! Take this stick here and go fuck yourself.

CLAVELA.—Enough, let her be, Guiomar. She's crazy. If not, then tell me: what is it that your son wrote in the letter?

GUIOMAR.—I've memorized what my son said: "Most illustrious mother of mine, Guiomar! The letter I write to you here is not intended as a farewell but rather a polite gesture of saying I'm fine and all is well. Blessed be God. Praised be God. Amen." Oh! May God give him life. My son is my heart; he came from this belly here!

CLAVELA.—Don't cry, Guiomar, don't cry.

GUIOMAR.—I have no other choice, because we've gone through it all, as deep as pockets run.]

This passage rehearses a critical standpoint of Guiomar's articulation of a black feminism that is linked directly to her sub-Saharan African agency in the following two ways: (1) her noble lineage and familial bonds traceable to West Africa and (2) the larger history of Luso-African diplomacy and letter writing. For skeptics of Guiomar's humanity, intelligence, and power in this scene, I underscore her embodiment as a savvy black woman who puts on notice the racist ideology and logic that deems enslaved black women as illiterate and inept.

The names of women Guiomar shares in the previous quote—her aunt, Reina Berbasina (Queen Berbasina), and her mother, Doña Bialaga (Lady Bialaga)—signal her affiliation with and genealogical connection to West African aristocracy. What I observe here in Rueda's portrayal of historically rooted references to Spanish sociocultural exchanges with West-Central Africa is not far-fetched. In fifteenth-century Iberia, for instance, the first black Africans arriving in major urban centers such as Lisbon and Seville were free emissaries and royal sovereigns. Although a traditional reading may dismiss words such as "Berbasina," "Bialaga," and "Cucurucú" (cock-a-doodle-doo) as the immediate comic-induced effects of habla de negros language, I historicize the etymology of "Berbasina"—as it relates to Guiomar's reference to her aunt as Queen Berbasina—in late sixteenth-century Iberian terms as "an ethnonym derived from the Wolof political title *Bur ba Siin*, meaning the 'ruler of Siin.' Like its neighbor Saloum, Siin was a Serer homeland that had been incorporated into the former Jolof empire. Serers from both Siin and Saloum were known to Iberians as 'Berbersí,' 'Berbecín,' or 'Berbacins.'"[67] Borrowing from David Wheat's brilliant *Atlantic Africa and the Spanish Caribbean, 1570–1640*, I frame Guiomar's connection to Berbasina historically in order to center these proper nouns as real sites that once existed and facilitated sub-Saharan African and Iberian trade. Even more, the word "Bialaga" gestures a relationship to the Bight of Biafra. While Guiomar's aunt (Queen Berbasina) and mother (Lady Bialaga) could have been hypothetical royal sovereigns, the fact that she positions them as "cuñados de la marqués de Cucurucú, por an mar y por a tierras"[68] (the sisters-in-law [or coinage; money], bound by sea and land, of the Marquis of Cucurucú) is highly erudite and suggestive on Rueda's part. The playwright's *cuñados* wordplay aligns Guiomar's maternal elders with African nobility, the minting of coins and other metal objects, *and* the monetization of black bodies (especially the offspring of royal African sovereigns sent to the Iberian Peninsula, and in this case Guiomar). In the context of cuñados, Rueda foregrounds—as mediated by Guiomar's habla de negros language—a familial bond and genealogical logic that is then overlaid with the economic subtext of slave trading. Guiomar's agentive voice, as Rueda designs it in the text, highlights the (re)production of people like that of a *cuño* (stamp; seal) that also (re)produces the proto-capitalist modernity of an effigy minted by the stamp itself. Guiomar's insightful commentary positions her as a thinking subject who, in one sense, inverts race relations and, in another sense, subverts the power invested in Julieta's antiblack racism. The rhetorical value of Guiomar's autobiographical mode in the skit, as she relates it back to her royal African lineage and the sinister legacy of African slave trading, both animates and captivates Clavela's protection and sympathy. Once Guiomar finishes recounting her story, Clavela abruptly silences Julieta with the quip: "Calla rapaza. ¿Y reina era tu tía, Guiomar?" (Hush, you thievish raptor! And so, Guiomar, your aunt was a queen?).

If Guiomar articulates a black feminist subject position by underscoring her royal sub-Saharan African lineage of African women, then let us acquire another ideation of how Rueda's *Los engañados* anchors her black feminism: the letter she reads from her son Dieguito: "'Lutríssima madre mía Guiomar, la carta que yo te cribo no e para besamano, sino que sa bono. Bendito sea Rios, loado sea Rios, amén'"[69] (Most illustrious mother of mine, Guiomar! The letter I write to you here is not intended as a farewell, but rather a polite gesture of saying I'm fine and all is well. Blessed be God. Praised be God. Amen). Via the correspondence, Guiomar reveals the letter's origins when she shares Dieguito's post in "la India le San Joan de Punto Rico" (the Indies of San Juan, Puerto Rico).[70] While the letter does not reveal any (auto)biographical information about Dieguito (although we are told he was born in Portugal and named after Guiomar's father, Eliomar, or Don Diego[z]), it does inform us, however, that enslaved and free black Africans were literate, thinking subjects who received authorization to travel from Seville to the Spanish Americas.[71] Further, I also treat Rueda's repetitive instantiation of global Spanish imperialism—that is, Eulalla's obsession with exotic and foreign animals and Dieguito's letter from Puerto Rico—as a concerted technique for cohering the geographic circulation of commodities, knowledge, and merchandise in imperial Spain. Through the performative act and textual insertion of Dieguito's letter, again read aloud by his mother, Guiomar, Rueda then imbues *Los engañados* with an intertextual quality. To advocate for black women's agency, I reiterate Guiomar's personhood as a literate subject, for she enacts the ceremonious gesture of reading her son's letter. As a performance, the letter she reads aloud to Clavela, Julieta, *and* the audience at large has an affective appeal: the audience can identify with the nostalgia Guiomar expresses for her son, who was sent off to the Americas.

Rueda's theatrical representation of the remittance of letters, letter writing, and the event of African mariners and migrants settling in the Spanish Caribbean does much more than parody the historical imagination of imperial Spain's participation in the transatlantic and transpacific colonial enterprises. Instead, it inculcates in the most profound way the verisimilitude of black Africans' roles as de facto and de jure agents in early colonial Spanish territories across the globe. What I am signaling here is that Rueda's geographical reference to San Juan, Puerto Rico, dialogues with a larger sixteenth-century transatlantic imperial Spanish discourse. And for Rueda's audience, I would insist that black Africans of Dieguito's ilk are not a foreign concept. "The Spanish empire's reliance on Africans to populate and sustain its Caribbean colonies," explains Wheat, "stands in stark contrast to other European powers' use of voluntary or indentured European migrants for these purposes."[72] "Although western European expansion in the Americas might be imagined as a series of interactions between native Americans, white settlers, and black slaves," he adds, "these ostensibly primordial categories cannot adequately explain the development of Spanish Caribbean sites in which racial descriptors often failed to correspond to fixed legal, social, or economic status."[73] Wheat's population estimates confirm and render plausible Rueda's literary account of Dieguito's life overseas in early colonial Puerto Rico: "Nearly forty thousand African and Africa-descended workers inhabited Spanish Caribbean seaports and rural areas by the first decade of the seventeenth century, revealing that in the early modern Iberian worlds, settlers—or more accurately, *pobladores*, those who peopled Iberian colonies overseas—were often anything but white or European."[74]

My reading of Dieguito's role as de facto "colonist" or migrant—as gleaned from how I historicize the perceived literary fiction of his letter to Guiomar—is predicated on his mother's agency and subjectivity as an

African woman who (re)traces her royal African lineage. Just as Dieguito's narrative undercuts the primacy of white settlers as the dominant figures presented in historical narratives and complicates the very notion of European colonization of the Americas,[75] Guiomar's role in *Los engañados* is anything but marginal or passive. As a mother, the black feminist silhouettes of Guiomar's habla de negros language corroborate her "Berbasina" "Biafra" genealogies—ethnonyms we can thread historically to the Rivers of Guinea and the Bight of Biafra. The categories of mothers and motherhood also cannot be overlooked in my black feminist reading of Guiomar. She heralds her self-definition and subject position by recounting *her* sub-Saharan African matriarchs: Queen Berbasina (her aunt) and Lady Bialaga (her mother). Guiomar's memory of them, as created by Rueda, weaves a narrative of matrilineal authority and power captured by those textual moments where she talks back to Julieta and self-defines her role as a nonpassive subject in the play. As the skit closes, Rueda leaves us with the following exemplary message: unlike Guiomar's costar Julieta, whom Rueda, I suggest, constructs as a divisive force in the *Los engañados*, Guiomar *unites* women. Clavela shows sympathy for Guiomar by telling her not to cry about Dieguito's transatlantic absence ("No llores, Guiomar, no llores") and reassures his well-being overseas ("Bien está," she says).

In this chapter, I have examined Lope de Rueda's black women characters'—Eulalla and Guiomar—agentive voices via their contestatory habla de negros speech acts. Utilizing the critical categories of "diva" and "black feminisms" as new strategies for analyzing their racially gendered and highly provocative theatricalized performances in *Eufemia* and *Los engañados*, I have proposed that black feminist theoretical approaches not only serve to redirect critical attention on black women literary characters but also elevate the theoretical apparatus employed in Hispanic studies. Black women characters—or the "negra," as she is commonly called in early modern comedia studies—also fight to protect their womanhood and social standing in early modern Spanish society. Just as their white female counterparts represented in theatrical works written by men (let us consider, for example, Gil Vicente's *Auto de la síbila Casandra*, Calderón's *La vida es sueño*, or Lope de Vega's numerous plays) or plays written by women about women (I am thinking of Ana Caro de Mallén, María de Zayas y Sotomayor, and Sor Juana Inés de la Cruz), black women also offer us complex and multivalent roles to examine. Rueda's characters Eulalla and Guiomar are indeed forces with which to be reckoned and which should be taken seriously in our scholarly criticism.

To that end, Eulalla and Guiomar are not the only black women characters who speak assertively and subvert power dynamics in their scenes with white actors. In Diego Sánchez de Badajoz's *Farsa teologal*, for example, the work closes with a black woman who defends herself from a shepherd's countless vicious attacks. The Aragonese dramaturg Jaime de Güete, in *Tesorina*, showcases the slave Margarita, who fights against male chauvinism and misogyny. Margarita's role in *Tesorina* ought to capture more widespread critical attention, for she safeguards not just her black womanhood but the womanhood of *all* women. When Margarita refuses to tell her master, Timbreo, and his shepherd, Giliracho, the whereabouts of the women who have disappeared on set, she angrily replies: "Tú Xaber y digir no" (v. 2369) (You know where they are, and aren't saying anything), which, as a result, provokes Timbreo's wrathful retort: "¡Valgaos el diablo, morruda!" (v. 2370) (Go to hell, you smashed-in-faced bitch!). The heated exchange then escalates with back-and-forth expletives, to which Margarita exclaims to Giliracho: "Patanax, viyaca, borde" (v. 2414) (Boor, scoundrel, scumbag), "Viyaco" (v. 2532) (Villain), and "Don boraxo" (v. 2547) (Mr. Drunkard). What angers her is Giliracho's devious neglect to reveal where he has seen the missing women. She shouts, "Dale, xux, / te yuro esta crux / qui yo te quibraré el dente" (vv. 2542–44) (Come here, you! I swear on this cross that I'll break your teeth). Recycling lines from the heated exchange between Jorge and Comba in Reinosa's "Gelofe, Mandinga," Güete also positions Margarita in a nonpassive role. The work ends with Sircelo, Giliracho's lackey, intervening with an attempt to make peace between Giliracho and Margarita.

The variety of textual examples showcasing the presence of black women in the theater of Lope de Rueda allows us to affirm that early modern Spanish theatrical representations of them did not solely position these women as inferior to whites. If anything, these depictions in drama treat them as subjects knowledgeable and proud of their presence and skills, their royal origins and wealth of lands, and their previously acquired education and decorum. Are they not women? Eulalla, Guiomar, or otherwise, these black women know they are gifted with wisdom and the resolve to subvert a variety of circumstances that others could not—however white they might be.

AFTERWORD

B(l)ack to the Future: The Postmodern Legacy
of *Habla de Negros*, or Talking in Tongues

But as a serious theme in Spanish literature, the negro slave naturally disappeared from literature when, during the seventeenth century, he began to disappear as a significant social element in Spanish life. He reappeared in poetry in Spanish in the 1920s and 1930s in the *poesía negra* associated particularly with the Afro-Cuban writers of that period. To the student of Reinosa's poems on negro themes this modern *poesía negra* makes, *mutatis mutandis*, a curious impression of *déjà vu*.
   —Peter E. Russell, "Rodrigo de Reinosa's 'poesía negra,'" 1973

Racism—a true "total social phenomenon"—inscribes itself in practices (forms of violence, contempt, intolerance, humiliation and exploitation), in discourses and representations which are so many intellectual elaborations of the phantasm of prophylaxis or segregation (the need to purify the social body, to preserve "one's own" or "our" identity from all forms of mixing, interbreeding or invasion) and which are articulated around stigmata of otherness (name, skin colour, religious practices). It therefore organizes affects (the psychological study of these has concentrated upon describing their obsessive character and also their "irrational" ambivalence) by conferring upon them a stereotyped form, as regards both their "objects" and their "subjects."
   —Étienne Balibar, *Race, Nation, Class: Ambiguous Identities*, 1991

In its reexamination of the past, *Staging* Habla de Negros: *Radical Performances of the African Diaspora in Early Modern Spain* has concerned itself with the present, the future, and the inscription of "the past" within the future. The present, furthermore, as it looks to the future, is shaped by the past. This book has analyzed a rich diversity of early modern Spanish literary production since the turn of the fifteenth century to the late seventeenth century. The early modern period has an important effect on the literary life and quotidian experiences of black persons who have regularly fueled the literary creativity and performative excitement of early modern Castilian writings. And the epigraph from Peter E. Russell's essay on Rodrigo de Reinosa's poesía negra (Black poetry) attests to this reality.

As I reach a conclusion about early modern Spanish representations of habla de negros, I cannot help but define and historicize these texts as examples of a nascent poesía negra that uncannily echo the poesía negra tradition from nineteenth- and twentieth-century Latin American literature. Moreover, I cannot help but acknowledge prefigurations of lexicon, rhythmic intentions, and salient African-sounding innovations that resurface in Latin America's *negrista* movement of the 1920s and 1930s. Early modern poesía negra provides some of our earliest examples of European authors who execute a corpus of writing that represents Africanized Castilian via "African"-sounding words, phrases, and voices. The twentieth-century resurgence of this literary crossover in Spain's former colonies in Cuba and Puerto Rico, for example, would also turn out to be fundamental to national self-definition, albeit with important differences.

The second epigraph, citing Étienne Balibar, also reimagines the variable of race in early modern Spanish literary and cultural studies. In its attempt to place the analytic of critical race studies in conversation with early modern Hispanic studies, this book still asks the following questions: What importance does race have as a meaningful category in the cultural, literary, and performative imaginaries of early modern Spain? What value does race possess in the shaping of critical theory during both the early modern and (post)modern periods? In this book, I attempt to address these knotty questions through considering the movement of time: past, present, and future. My critical move to place race and language in conversation with each other supports this book's comprehensive argument that the two categories are not at all mutually exclusive. I call into question the treatment of race as an anachronistic term by suggesting that during the early modern period there were, in fact, a variety of artists, chroniclers, historians, and writers alike who portrayed race and one's racial otherness through a host of inflected meanings that involved skin color, food and culinary habits, clothing and bodily adornments, bondage (i.e., captivity, domestic servitude, chattel slavery), mathematics (specifically when discussing racial hierarchies, miscegenation, and statutes on blood cleanliness/purity), effeminacy, sodomy, religion, and language. By ultimately situating language at the forefront of examining and thinking about race, I suggest that acknowledging the power of what I call destructive language and its material effects is a good place to address issues of race and to do antiracist work.

Is the final racial-linguistic imprint of staging habla de negros speech events solely a marker of the poverty of a language? I think not. A premise on which I stake significant theoretical claims is the belief that, like any "standard" language, the staging of habla de negros represents a transmission of orders, an exercise of power, and resistance to larger hegemonic power structures. As a linguistic mode to represent linguistic Blackness, habla de negros symbolizes a tetralinguistic model that encompasses the vernacular, the material, and that which is territorial. Coming out of the mouths of slaves, habla de negros is the language variant from the Castilian "norm" that fills a certain function for one material that cannot be filled by that "normal" Castilian standard.

Before I close, I wish to address one last question: What were the aural effects of early modern habla de negros? How did it sound? Because there are no extant audio recordings of this language, an immediate answer would then suggest that there is no way to *know* how habla de negros actually sounded. But to challenge and complicate this claim, I situate these two aforementioned questions in the religious and spiritual rites of Afro-Atlantic religions in the Spanish Caribbean, namely La Regla de Osha (colloquially known as "Santería") and the Reglas Congas (collectively referred to as Palo Mayombe).[1] In each of these religious-spiritual traditions, black slave voices from the colonial slave era are, and can be, heard. Africanness permeates syncretically each of these religions through Central and West African—the Arará, the Bantu, the Carabalí, the Efik, the Fon, the Mina, and the Yoruba, among others—lexicons, expressions, and speech forms.

In the Afro-Cuban religions La Regla de Osha and Palo Mayombe, the *orisha* (Yoruba-based deities) and the nkisi (an earthbound spirit or an object that a spirit inhabits) possess, or "mount," the priests initiated to them. In the case of La Regla de Osha, possession will occur in either initiatory ceremonies of newly ordained priests or drumming celebrations known as a *bembé* or *wemilere*. Drumming ceremonies honoring one's ancestors and other earthbound spirits, known as the *cajón al muerto*, also provide instances where humans undergo trance possession of either an ancestor of theirs or a spirit who speaks in bozal habla de negros. Mediumship, or *espiritismo*—widely practiced across the Caribbean and Latin America—serves as another example where an enslaved African spirit may possess a medium, or *espiritista*, working the *mesa blanca* at a session called a *misa espiritual*. The misa espiritual is akin to the séances of American-styled Spiritualism of the nineteenth century to the present. In moments where an espirtista undergoes trance possession by an African spirit (or any spirit, for that matter, who speaks in a creolized or pidgin tongue), the spirit will "bajar a la tierra," or come down through a (human) vessel, speaking in bozal habla de negros. Drawing on years of fieldwork that I have undertaken in Cuba, Spain, and the United States, espiritistas and priests of the various Afro-Cuban religions mentioned here call Africanized Spanish "lengua," or speaking in tongues. A term often used by older generations of practitioners born in the 1950s and prior, "lengua" refers not only to bozal habla de negros but also to the antiquated Yoruba spoken at the turn of the nineteenth century. This so-called lengua is also still used in divination, Ifá ceremonies, and rituals performed by *babalawos* as well as those directed by the Obá-Oriaté (king who brings the head [Orí] down to the mat), who leads Osha-specific ceremonies. Over the years, I have heard and seen priests, while in trance, communicating with an uncanny resemblance to the habla de negros speech forms, phrases, and lexicon covered in this book. In other words, trance possession *cannot* be separated from our approach to and analysis of the habla de negros language spoken by bozal slaves. For future studies on Africanized diasporic languages and Black Atlantic religions, I am confident that the analytic of trance possession will serve as a compelling heuristic for scholars and students.

In her groundbreaking essay "African Accents, Speaking Child Spirits and the Brazilian Popular Imaginary: Permutations of Africanness in Candomblé," cultural anthropologist Elina Hartikainen provides illustrative examples that offer an alternative epistemological perspective on knowing how African diasporic slave dialects sounded in their primal bozal form. Brazilian

Candomblé, for example, also embodies similar kinds of trance possession. But instead of focusing on the orisha (*orixa*, Portuguese) and nkisi (*inquice*, Portuguese) of Brazilian worship, I direct our attention to the religion's lesser-discussed African child spirits known as *êres* to broaden my example. On possessing their "mounts," the êres arrive to the world speaking African languages while also actively learning the language of their Brazilian followers. Like other foreigners, the child spirits never achieve native, nor near-native, language competency. "Instead," as Hartikainen explains from her interview with the Candomblé priest Tatá Mutá, "they come to communicate in a broken version of Portuguese that displays the influence of their native African tongues":

> [The êres] don't speak Kikongo, Kimbundo, Umbundo or Portuguese. Instead [their speech] is a mixture. . . . It is a bit like an American who in trying to learn Portuguese ends up speaking differently. . . . The *êres* speak African, but they have to communicate in the New World. And so, they have to change their linguistic conduct [*comportamento linguístico*] to be able to communicate with the people of the New World. And then they also speak like children and a bit like the person they are talking to and a bit like the medium they are incorporating. . . . And so they end up speaking a mixture that sometimes even we don't understand.[2]

The ways in which the êres articulate hybridized African speech varieties occur through the modification of their linguistic conduct, which parallels the ways in which black Africans had to learn Spanish and Portuguese in the Old and New Worlds. During trance possession, the orisha, nkisi, and êres alike adjust and reevaluate their African language with Spanish and Portuguese words like those black Africans who learned how to speak Castilian and Portuguese upon arriving to the Iberian Peninsula and the Americas.

*

The powerful linguistic and religious intersections between Africanized Portuguese and Castilian and Black Atlantic religions ultimately reveal larger cultural and psychic connections from deceased African slaves and their present-day followers. And without the prevalence of these religions and spiritualities across the circum-Atlantic world, the aural effects of habla de negros would remain unknown. I am firmly convinced that the sacred practices I have been at great pains to elucidate for my readers speak to a cultural vitality that scholars and the public are quite keen on moving beyond rather quickly. But uncomfortably so; this book's cultural and literary explorations of the descendants of the enslaved and free remind us how Blackness is conceptually, experientially, and linguistically fluid and performative yet deceptive and paradoxical.

Notes

Preface

1. Miller, *Slaves to Fashion*, 5.
2. Ibid., 5.
3. Tompkins, *Racial Indigestion*, 8.

Translating Blackness

1. Wheat, *Atlantic Africa and the Spanish Caribbean*, xviii.
2. Ibid., xix.
3. Lorde, "Burst of Light," 67.
4. Hall, *Things of Darkness*, 8.
5. Wheat, *Atlantic Africa and the Spanish Caribbean*, xix.

Introduction

1. The Arenal reached the outskirts of Seville between the Puerta de Triana and the Torre de Oro. See Caballero Bonald's *Sevilla en tiempos de Cervantes* for additional demographic and historical information about the Arenal of Seville. For a cultural history of the Arenal, see Nash's *Seville, Córdoba, and Granada*, 88–94.
2. A major thoroughfare in the city center of Seville, the Avenida de la Constitución, in present times, is home to the Gothic Roman Catholic Cathedral of Santa María de la Sede. Nestled within this area is the Royal Alcázar of Seville (a royal fortress and palace constructed by Muslim rulers in the eleventh century) and the Archivo General de Indias (one of imperial Spain's most important documentary repositories), which stands inside the sixteenth-century Casa de Lonja de Mercaderes, the old merchants' exchange and market.
3. Black Africans entered the Iberian Peninsula as part of imperial Berber Muslim occupation forces from the Sudan and Ethiopia, as well as during the Almoravid dynasty (1049–1146)

and its trans-Sahara trade caravans that would later furnish Christian Portugal and Spain with gold, slaves, and foreign tropical products. Arab caliphs and monarchs of al-Andalus, such as Abd al-Rahman I, possessed large numbers of black slaves who served as royal bodyguards to emirs or were frequently offered as gifts to dignitaries. As early as 1248, following the Reconquest of Seville, Christian Spaniards acquired black slaves formerly owned by Muslims. By the end of the thirteenth century, Italo-Iberian connections brought black slaves to the Balearic Islands and Valencia. By the monumental year 1492, black Africans—enslaved and free—lived in all major cities and provinces on the Iberian Peninsula: Aragon and Castile, the Algarve, Barcelona, Cadiz, Coimbra, Cordoba, Extremadura, Lisbon, Madrid, Salamanca, Seville, Valladolid, and Zaragoza, and remained in those places well into the early eighteenth century. See Diego Ortiz de Zúñiga's *Annales Eclesiásticos y Seculares de la muy Noble y muy Leal Ciudad de Sevilla, Metrópoli de Andalucía*, a work that collects the most important events that took place in Seville from 1246 to 1671, commenting on the lives of black Africans under the reign of Enrique III of Castile between 1390 and 1406.

4. See Pike, *Aristocrats and Traders*.
5. Castro, *Varias obras inéditas de Cervantes*, 29–30.
6. Many thanks to my dear colleague Steve Dolph for reminding me of Erich Auerbach's 1958 masterwork *Literary Language and Its Public in Late Latin Antiquity and in the Middle Ages*. I also acknowledge Dolph for bringing to my attention the incommensurability of linguistic codes, of the proliferation of "babble" and barbarian garblings of the imperial tongue. For further reading on this topic, see Apter, *Translation Zone*, and Newman and Tylus, *Early Modern Cultures of Translation*.
7. The bibliography on sub-Saharan African slavery in Seville abounds in approach and scope. By no means a definitive list, also consult the following studies: Chaves and García, "Redes de la trata negrera"; Domínguez Ortiz, *Esclavitud en Castilla en la Edad*; Franco Silva, *Esclavitud en Andalucía*; Gil, "De Sevilla a Lisboa"; Cortés López, *Esclavitud negra en la España*; Franco Silva, *Esclavitud en Sevilla y su tierra*.
8. See Chaves and García, "Redes de la trata negrera." Refer also to Lipski, *History of Afro-Hispanic Language*, esp. 14–50.
9. See Francisco Morales Padrón, ed., *Historia de Sevilla de Luis de Peraza*, http://institucional.us.es/revistas/rasbl/6/art_6.pdf.
10. Starting around the timestamp 6:53, we are shown an auction block where sub-Saharan Africans of different ethnic groups are sold on the steps of the Cathedral of Seville. What remains fascinating to me—and clearly indicative of African diasporic artistic, cultural, religious, and spiritual retentions—are the necklaces of bone, minerals, and roots worn by the newly arrived blacks in the scene. The black confraternity known as Los negros (or Los Negritos for others)—considered by many as the first black confraternity in Western Europe under the official patronage of Our Lady of Angels—is also important to my analysis here, for the scene in which it appears shows black men rehearsing for a procession while a wooden statue of West-Central African origin is lit by a candle and elevated high in a corner as if it were a Catholic saint. The character Nubla, an active member of the confraternity in the show, represents a repository of a situated knowledge of West-Central African cosmologies and religious traditions. His house, located on the banks of the Guadalquivir River, further embodies and preserves an overlooked archive and history that reveals a sector of sub-Saharan African

life in early modern Spain. The Los negros confraternity still exists today, but since the eighteenth century, the brotherhood consists of men of European descent. A similar history also belongs to the confraternity of Los mulatos in Seville, of which I have family members. For further reading, see Moreno, *Antigua hermandad de "Los negros" de Sevilla*, and http://www.hermandadlosnegritos.org/hermandad/historia/otras-cofradias/.

11. Lipski, "Español *bozal*," 305. For scholarly criticism on habla de negros, in addition to Lipski's body of work, also consult: Weber de Kurlat, "Tipo cómico del negro"; Weber de Kurlat, "Sobre el negro como tipo cómico"; Weber de Kurlat, "Tipo del negro en el teatro"; Baranda Leturio, "Hablas de negros"; Beusterien, "Talking Black in Spanish"; Beusterien, *Eye on Race*; Fra-Molinero, *Imagen de los negros*; Santos Morillo, "Caracterización del negro en la literatura"; Santos Morillo, "Expresión lingüística de los esclavos negros"; and Belo, "Language as Second Skin."

12. The original Spanish states: "posibilidades estéticas y dramáticas . . . puramente cómico-burlescas," from her essay "Tipo cómico del negro," 139. Echoing Weber de Kurlat's position on habla de negros, Baranda Leturio, in her essay "Hablas de negros," defines Africanized Castilian according to its "finalidad cómica" (315).

13. Lipski, *Latin American Spanish*, 97.

14. Belo, "Language as Second Skin," 4–5.

15. See Jones, "Nuptials Gone Awry, Empire in Decay."

16. For scholarship on race and gender studies in early modern England and the early British Atlantic world, see Erickson and Hulse, *Early Modern Visual Culture*; MacDonald, *Women and Race*; Grier, "Staging the Cherokee *Othello*"; Grier, "Inkface"; Hall, *Things of Darkness*; Little, "Re-historicizing Race, White Melancholia"; Loomba, *Shakespeare, Race, and Colonialism*; Smith, *Black Africans in the British Imagination*; Smith, *Race and Rhetoric in the Renaissance*. Another important reading is Erickson and Hall's introduction in their recent special issue "'New Scholarly Song.'"

17. DeFrantz and Gonzalez, "Introduction," 2–3. For the complete text of Zora Neale Hurston's "Characteristics of Negro Expression," see *Zora Neale Hurston*, 830–46.

18. DeFrantz and Gonzalez, "Introduction," 3.

19. Ibid.

20. Moten, *In the Break*, 1.

21. Ibid.

22. Lorde, "Transformation of Silence into Language."

23. Quevedo, *Prosa festiva completa*, 430. This treatise also outlines maxims and quasi-"scientific" explanations for not only speaking but also acting and behaving like the Basque, Dutch, French, Germans, Italians, and Iberian Muslims. Alchemists and scientists also fall under the humorist's scrutiny, whereby he satirizes contradictions and fallacies of bullfighters, *hidalgos*, intellectuals, knights, and lawyers, to name several.

24. Lipski, *History of Afro-Hispanic Language*, 66. See also Schuchardt, "Kreolischen Studien VII"; Vila, *Elementos de la gramática ambú*; Barrena, *Gramática annobonesa*; Valkhoff, *Miscelânea Luso-Africana*, 166; Günther, *Portugiesische Kreloisch der Jlha do Príncipe*; Ferraz, *Creole of São Tomé*; Ferraz, "Substrate of Annobonese"; Bartens, *Die iberoromanische-basierten Kreolsprachen*, 113–27; Post, "Fa d'Ambu."

25. Lipski, *History of Afro-Hispanic Language*, 220.

26. For a recent study on genre theory and genre studies, refer to Jonathan Culler, *Theory of the Lyric*, esp. 39–90.

27. To access this appendix, consult the publisher's website at: https://www.cambridge.org/core/books/history-of-afrohispanic-language/8AA6476796 57617F16B2348859D0682D.

28. Weiss, "Renaissance Poetry," 159. See original passage in López de Mendoza, *Obras completas*, 442.
29. Weiss, "Renaissance Poetry," 159.
30. Ibid.
31. For additional definitions and a historical contextualization of the villancico, see Juan Díaz Rengifo's *Arte poética española* (1592), Sebastián de Covarrubias's *Tesoro de la lengua castellana o española* (1611), and the *Diccionario de Autoridades* (1737). Refer also to Robert Jammes's edition of *Letrillas*, whose introduction situates the letrilla in its appropriate historical evolution in Spanish poetry.
32. Páez Granados, "Villancico de negro y su pertinente," 183. See also Frenk, "Sobre los cantares populares del Cancionero," and Labrador Herraiz and Di Franco, "Villancicos de negros y otros testimonios."
33. Gaylord, "Making of Baroque Poetry," 229. For recent theorizations of the Baroque and the neo-Baroque as a mode, see Braun and Pérez-Magallón, *Transatlantic Hispanic Baroque*; Levy and Mills, *Lexikon on the Hispanic Baroque*; Egginton, *Theater of Truth*; Suárez and Olid-Peña, "Hispanic Baroque"; Spadaccini and Martín-Estudillo, *Hispanic Baroques*. Refer also to Friedman, "Afterword."
34. AHN, legajo 1953, expediente 66, 19, 1621. For additional reading on the ritual abuse of the body of Christ, a common accusation against *conversos* and *moriscos*, refer to Amelang, *Parallel Histories*, and Pulido Serrano, *Injurias a Cristo*.
35. For additional material on Moriscas sentenced by the Inquisition for witchcraft and sorcery, see Martín Casares, "Hechicería en la Andalucía Moderna." Refer also to Gracia Boix's *Brujas y hechiceras de Andalucía*, and García Ivars, *Represión en el tribunal de Granada*. The Inquisition section of the Archivo Histórico Nacional (AHN) in Madrid houses a handful of cases of Morisca slaves sentenced by Inquisition tribunals across Andalusia. For example, there is the dossier of María from Almería who was brought to the Inquisition for having telekinetic abilities and being the devil's "lover" (AHN, Inq., legajo 2.022, expediente no. 37, causa no. 8, fol. 25v.
36. Sweet, *Recreating Africa*, 6–7.
37. See ibid., 13–30.
38. See ibid., 1, and Sweet, "Teaching the Modern African Diaspora." Also refer to Lovejoy, "African Diaspora"; Palmer, "Defining and Studying the Modern African Diaspora"; and Gomez, "African Identity and Slavery in the Americas."
39. Sweet, *Recreating Africa*, 2.
40. For a rich cultural and historical study on black African slavery in Spain and Europe, refer to Domínguez Ortiz's *Golden Age of Spain*; Earle and Lowe's *Black Africans in Renaissance Europe*; Martín Casares and García Barranco's *Esclavitud negroafricana en la historia*; and Spicer's edited volume *Revealing the African Presence*. While DeCosta-Willis's anthology *Blacks in Hispanic Literature* stands alone as one of the first critical studies that both chronologically and systematically examines the roles of black Africans in medieval and early modern Spanish literature, Johnson's *Devil, the Gargoyle, and the Buffoon*, and Cobb's essay "Afro-Arabs, Blackamoors, and Blacks" (and also in *Blacks in Hispanic Literature*, 20–27) have provided rich bibliographical information, as well as a critical lexicon and framework, for entering the study of black Africans in medieval and early modern Spain. Following DeCosta-Willis comes Fra-Molinero's *Imagen de los negros*. Fra-Molinero's important book shines as a comprehensive study that closely examines the representations of blacks in theater during the Spanish Golden Age. Beusterien's *Eye on Race* provides a subaltern studies analysis to address the ways in which early modern Spanish audiences and readers alike "see" the racial codification and racial difference of Jews and blacks on imperial Spanish

stages. Branche, for instance, in *Colonialism and Race in Luso-Hispanic Literature* presents a critical approach to literary representations of blacks by incorporating critical race studies and postcolonial studies. For a recent study of racial stereotypes commonly associated with black Africans, see Santos Morillo's essay "Caracterización del negro en la literatura."

41. I acknowledge provisionally Barbara Fuchs's aim in *Exotic Nation* to "provide the early modern background for [Dumas's] famous gesture of exclusion . . . by showing how Spain, as a space marked by Moorishness, has long been considered somehow beyond Europe" (4). She adds, and justifiably so, that the rendering of Spain as "African," "[reinforces] the Black Legend with profound consequences for the marginalization of Spain within Europe" (4). Fuchs's astute critique against "the disciplinary marginalization of [Spain] as somehow less European, in historical and literary studies, particularly in the Anglo-American academy" (4), also accounts for the ways in which foreign intellectuals have ridiculed the suggestion of Spain as a "modern" nation-state. See Dufour de Pradt's allegation in *Mémoires historiques sur la revolution d'Espagne*, where he likens Spain to "Africa" in its manners, language, and way of life (1:385–90). Refer also to British travel writer Richard Ford's 1878 *Handbook for Travellers in Spain*, where he too marginalizes Spain as "scarcely European" and "Oriental." Ford reflects this pejorative attitude throughout the entirety of his *Handbook*.

42. Abd al-Rahman I's palace guard was comprised of black soldiers. Hitti notes in *History of the Arabs* occasions on which Muslim residents of Córdoba complained about the predominance of black bodyguards who did not speak Arabic. For the earliest and most extensive discussion of race and color, especially pertaining to Blackness, across the medieval Islamic world, refer to Lewis, *Race and Slavery in the Middle East*. See also Sweet, "Iberian Roots of American Racist Thought."

43. See Fletcher, *Quest for El Cid*.

44. Lipski, *History of Afro-Hispanic Language*, 18. Here, Lipski explains that "most of this early slave trade was carried out through contact with powerful African city-states, including the kingdoms of Mali (centered around Timbuktu), Takrur (along the Senegal River), Ghana (at the southern edge of the Sahara), Oyo (in northern Nigeria), Benin (closer to the Niger Delta), Kanem (near Lake Chad), and the Songhai (at the northern bend of the Niger River). Arab traders from North Africa utilized camel caravans, which went from oasis to oasis, establishing a flourishing bilateral trade with sub-Saharan regions. Commodities exchanged included gold, textiles, dates, kola nuts, pepper, hides, and, to a lesser extent, slaves" (18).

45. For a fascinating study of Timbuktu in the early modern period, see Stafford, "Tarik É Soudan." See also Diadié and Pimentel, *Tombuctú*.

46. In *Exotic Nation*, Fuchs problematizes the Western imaginary's (mis)reading of Spain as the romantic and colorful culture of "Moorish" al-Andalus (1). For a fuller discussion of the construction of and thinking about race and Africa in early modern Spain, refer to *Exotic Nation*, 115–38.

47. Palmié, "Introduction," 13.

48. Ibid., 14.

49. Ibid. See also Gilroy, *Against Race*.

50. Palmié, "Introduction," 14.

51. Foucault, *Archaeology of Knowledge*, 217.

52. Fuchs, *Exotic Nation*, 11–30.

53. Bourdieu, *Language and Symbolic Power*, 54.

54. Beusterien, "Talking Black in Spanish," 84–85.

55. For further discussion of race and language, see Pym's *Gypsies of Early Modern Spain*, and Irigoyen-García's *Spanish Arcadia* and *Moors Dressed as Moors*.

56. Watkin, *Literary Agamben*, 6.
57. Agamben, *Infancy and History*, 59.
58. Ibid.
59. Ibid.
60. Ibid.
61. Frantz Fanon, *Black Skin, White Masks*, 141–55.
62. Bourdieu, *Language and Symbolic Power*, 14.
63. For an approach that somewhat resembles this dynamic through the lens of Bourdieu, refer to Jiménez Belmonte, *Obras en verso del Príncipe de Esquilache*. On economics and economic rationalism in Lope de Vega's *Arte nuevo de hacer comedias*, see Gilbert, "Playing to the Masses."
64. Gilbert, "Playing to the Masses," 122. See also Díez Borque, *Teoría y realidad en el teatro*.
65. Jammes, *Sonetos completos*, 264. For a more conventional interpretation of this poem, see Kelley, "Reading Góngora's *Habla de negros*."
66. Gilbert, "Playing to the Masses," 121–22. See also Fernández Nieto, "Falso humanismo de Lope de Vega," 322.
67. For more on the intersection between value and Blackness, see Barrett, *Blackness and Value*.
68. Bourdieu, *Language and Symbolic Power*, 14.
69. Ibid.
70. Morgan, "'Nuthin' but a G Thang.'" Also, by Morgan, consult *Language, Discourse, and Power* and *Real Hip Hop*.
71. Angel Díaz, "Hip-Hop Is the Most Listened to Genre in the World and There's a Study to Prove It," Complex, July 14, 2015, http://www.complex.com/music/2015/07/hip-hop-most-listened-genre-on-spotify-study.
72. Jeffries, *Thug Life*, 7.
73. Bourdieu, *Language and Symbolic Power*, 12.
74. See Lihani, *Lenguaje de Lucas Fernández*. For literary representations of Basque speech forms, see Penas Ibáñez, "Habla vizcaína en el teatro."
75. Tejerizo Robles, *Villancicos barrocos en la Capilla Real*.
76. For further scholarship on *aljamiado*-Morisco narrative texts and the theatrical representation of Morisco language, see Barletta, *Covert Gestures*; Barranco, "Correlaciones y divergencias," offers an important comparative study of presences of black Africans and Iberian Muslims, and literary representations of their marked speech, in early modern Spanish theater. See specifically the section "Los lenguajes teatrales," 168–71. Other pertinent studies are: Granda, *Estudios lingüísticos hispánicos, afrohispánicos y criollos*; Ynduraín, *Moriscos en el teatro en Aragón*; Santos Domínguez, "Lenguaje teatral del morisco"; and Álvaro Galmés de Fuentes, "La lengua española de la literatura aljamiado-morisca como expresión de una minoría religiosa," conference paper, n.d.

Chapter 1

1. Early modern Spain produced some of the greatest dramatic corpora of world literature, whose bibliography is bountiful and copious. As explained by Bass and Greer: "The *comedia*—the term generally applied to comic, tragicomic, and tragic words alike—was the most popular art form from the latter decades of the sixteenth century through the first half of the seventeenth." They add, "For the considerable segment of the audience that was illiterate, the *comedia* supplied a vision of national history, of religious obligation, and of the political order, as well as models of social deportment. Its ideological power was thus formidable." Quoted from the preface to Bass and Greer, *Approaches to Teaching Early Modern Spanish Drama*, xi–xii. There are many excellent companions and edited volumes on early modern Spanish drama and theater history, including Kallendorf's *Companion to Early Modern Hispanic*

Theater; Mujica's *Shakespeare and the Spanish* Comedia; Thacker's *Companion to Golden Age Theatre*, and Bass and Greer's *Approaches to Teaching Early Modern Spanish Drama*.
2. Thacker, *Companion to Golden Age Theatre*, 152–54.
3. Trambaioli, "Apuntes sobre el guineo o baile."
4. See specifically vv. 680–721 of Act III.
5. Thacker, *Companion to Golden Age Theatre*, 155. Differentiating these forms, see Asensio's *Itinerario del entremés*. On the in-betweenness and subversiveness of an actor's role in the entremés, most notably the actor Cosme Pérez, alias Juan Rana, consult Thompson, *Outrageous Juan Rana Entremeses*.
6. Stephens, *Skin Acts*, 1.
7. See specifically Fanon's *Black Skin, White Masks* and Gilroy's *Against Race*.
8. Ruano de la Haza, *Puesta en escena en los teatros*, 88.
9. Ibid.
10. Willamsen, "Women and Blacks Have Brains Too," 42.
11. Originally, the festivities were planned for April 8, Felipe IV's birthday, but plans were postponed. See *Villamediana*, 357–74.
12. Ibid., 373. Additional recent studies on *La Gloria de Niquea* include: Vélez-Sainz, "Mitología, caballería y espejo de príncipes"; Borrego Gutiérrez, "Libros de caballería y estas cortesanas"; Hernández Araico, "Inverosimilitudes imaginativa de Calderón"; Gutiérrez Arranz, "Mitología en *La Gloria de Niquea*"; Armas, "Play's the Thing"; and Miñana, "Márgenes del poder."
13. Hurtado de Mendoza, *Obras líricas y cómicas*, 152. Refer also to Ferrer Valls, *Nobleza y espectáculo teatral (1535–1622)*, 289.
14. Hurtado de Mendoza, *Obras líricas y cómicas*, 153.
15. Beusterien, *Eye on Race*, 102.
16. Ibid. Beusterien cites Lott's classic *Love and Theft* and Callaghan's *Shakespeare Without Women*.
17. Orr, *Empire on the English Stage*. Miller, *Slaves to Fashion*, 43. On white melancholia and blackface performance, see Little, "Re-historicizing Race, White Melancholia," 90–93. For additional studies on blackface performance in early modern studies, refer to Hornback, "'Extravagant and Wheeling Strangers'"; Mahar, "Black English in Early Blackface Minstrelsy"; Smith, "White Skin, Black Masks"; and Stevens, *Inventions of the Skin*.
18. Brooks citing Saidiya Hartman in *Bodies in Dissent*, 25; Hartman, *Scenes of Subjection*.
19. Brooks, *Bodies in Dissent*, 25.
20. Miller, *Slaves to Fashion*, 43.
21. Mason Vaughan, *Performing Blackness on English Stages*, 4.
22. Miller, *Slaves to Fashion*, 43.
23. Forbes, "Shakespeare, Other Shakespeares," 51–52; Mason Vaughan, *Performing Blackness on English Stages*, 4.
24. Hartman, *Scenes of Subjection*, 30–31.
25. Brooks, *Bodies in Dissent*, 26.
26. See Toll, *Blacking Up*, 38–40 and 67, for a discussion of how minstrel performers occasionally mounted productions that featured onstage progressions of whiteface to blackface.
27. Cortés de Tolosa, *Lazarillo de Manzanares*, 15.
28. Lope de Rueda, a playwright whom we study more closely in chapter 3, wrote plays with Italianate themes. His *Comedia Medora*, for example, was produced and performed by *commedia dell'arte* companies but differs drastically from the Italian form in that the dialogue was composed beforehand and not improvised. In addition, it does not include the familiar Italian characters of the Harlequin, Pantalone, Soldier, and Doctor. A notable parallel, however, does, in fact, carry over into Rueda's black women characters' habla de negros speech, gitano (Iberian Romani) dialect, and the Bergamask *zanni*.
29. Real Academia Española, http://dle.rae.es/?id=ZUmuSQv.
30. Beusterien, *Eye on Race*, 103.

31. Vélez de Guevara, *Virtudes vencen señales*, 85; ibid. On early Spanish stages, explicit instructions were given to blackface the roles of black characters. For example, when necessary, most of Lope de Vega's comedias instructed actors to both blackface and whiteface. In addition, in the 1965 Profeti Italian edition of Vélez de Guevara's *Virtudes vencen señales*, the play's stage directions call for one actor to come out on stage with "teñida la cara de negro" ("the face darkened in black") (86). On this play, see also Fra-Molinero, "Play of Race and Gender."
32. Beusterien, *Eye on Race*, 103–23. Rebelo, *De dos alcaldes y el engaño*.
33. See Jones, "Nuptials Gone Awry, Empire in Decay."
34. Covarrubias, *Tesoro*, 1471.
35. For additional archival sources and historical documentation on the various kinds of jobs held by black slaves, see chapter 7 of Cortés López's *Esclavitud negra en la España*. Also refer to Griffin's *Crombergers of Seville* for thorough archival and historical information about the family and its printing empire.
36. Grier, "Inkface," 195.
37. Ibid.
38. See Jones, "Cosmetic Ontologies, Cosmetic Subversions."
39. Covarrubias, *Tesoro*, 96.
40. Ibid.
41. The use of "alcoholar" also means to "improve," or to paint over, the face (i.e., "cleaning" or "whitening"). In Bartolomé de las Casas's *Brevísima relación de la destrucción de África*—a prelude to his 1552 *Brevísima relación de la destrucción de las Indias*—the friar envisions "alcoholar" in terms of how a historian improves his/her text by cleaning it: "la enjabona o alcohola con la misericordia y bondad de Dios" (one scrubs it or beautifies it with the goodness and mercy of God), refer to p. 38 of web version: http://www.biblioteca.org.ar/libros/3064.pdf. Góngora in *Las firmezas de Isabela* (1610) uses "alcoholar" to refer to painting oneself red with blood—"mal hace quien la acrisola, / y peor quien se alcohola / con una navaja aguda" (she does wrong who purifies herself, / and worse, she who colors herself / with a sharp knife) (vv. 979–81, Act I). Each of these two examples enriches my interpretation of Juana's line "Alcoholemo la cara / e lavémono la vista," as she may be also referring to cleaning up (i.e., whitening) her body and chastising her sight.
42. Navarrete, *Orphans of Petrarch*, 191.
43. Fra-Molinero notes that black women in sixteenth- and seventeenth-century Spanish literature are "characterized by [their] bad temper, 'Black' speech, illusions of grandeur, and 'loose' sexual morals" ("Condition of Black Women," 171). "These stereotypical *negras*," he believes, "nevertheless revealed the other side of any stereotype: difficult relations between the free population and the slave communities in big cities, along with the constant threat to the stability and 'honor' of the families that owned them" (171–72).
44. Vives, *Instrucción de la mujer cristiana*, 73–74.
45. León, *Obras completas castellanas*, 286–87.
46. Quoted from Dopico Black, *Perfect Wives, Other Women*, 252 n. 74.
47. Martín Casares, *Esclavitud en la Granada del siglo XVI*, 146. In this work, Martín Casares explains that "la palabra 'negro' es la que presupone un mayor carácter de estabilidad de la condición personal, puesto que su referente es la naturaleza. El término 'negro' establece un vínculo indeleble con la biología (la piel negra) y, en consecuencia, remite a la naturaleza. Para los pensadores de la España de los tiempos modernos, la naturaleza representaba la inmutabilidad y el estatismo; existía un estado 'natural' de las cosas y de las personas (de ahí el 'derecho natural,' *ius gentium*) considerado inalterable y perdurable en el tiempo, situado por encima de lo humano (social) y relacionado con la divinidad" (146). (The word "black" is one that presupposes a stability of

personal condition, since its referent is nature [human nature]. The term "black" establishes an indelible connection to biology [black skin] and, as a result, refers to nature. According to Spanish philosophers from modern times, nature represented immutability and statism; there existed a "natural" order of things and of persons (hence "natural right," *ius gentium*) deemed inalterable and everlasting in time, situated above that which is human (social) and related to the Divine.)

48. Cotarelo y Mori, *Colección de entremeses, loas, bailes, jácaras*, 1:clxxi.
49. Rodríguez Cuadros, "Hato de la risa."
50. Miller, *Slaves to Fashion*, 43.
51. Tranberg Hansen and Soyini Madison, introduction, 3.
52. Quevedo, *Prosa festiva completa*, 216.
53. Ibid., 430. This treatise also outlines maxims and quasi-"scientific" explanations for not only speaking but also acting and behaving like the Basque, Dutch, French, Germans, Italians, and Moriscos. Alchemists and scientists also fall under the humorist's scrutiny, whereby he satirizes contradictions and fallacies of bullfighters, hidalgos, intellectuals, knights, and lawyers, to name several.
54. Navarro García, *Historia del baile flamenco*, 62.
55. Archivo Municipal de Sevilla, Cuaderno de Actas Capitulares, 27 June 1497. See Gestoso y Pérez, *Curiosidades antiguas de Sevilla II*, 101. The original Castilian states: "que deuian salir al dho. recibimiento todos los negros que ouiese en esta çibdad."
56. Folio 118 from the book chapter dated 1464 under the heading "Esclavos fandangueros."
57. Martín Casares and García Barranco, "Musical Legacy of Black Africans," 52, 56.
58. Beusterien, *Eye on Race*, 153.
59. Quoted from Budasz, "Black Guitar-Players," 5. See also Kubik, "O intercâmbio cultural entre Angola e Portugal," 381–405.
60. Budasz, "Black Guitar-Players," 5.
61. Ibid.
62. Ibid. On Lingua Franca and early Africanized Castilian, see Lipski, *History of Afro-Hispanic Language*, 80–81, 198, 274.
63. Davis, *Blues Legacies and Black Feminism*; Chireau, *Black Magic*; Martin, *Conjuring Moments in African American Literature*; and Brooks, *Searching for Sycorax*.
64. Pérez de Montoro, "Letras de los villancicos de nuestro."
65. See Childs, "Gendering the African Diaspora."
66. Reid, "Yoruba in Cuba." For more historical data on the social organization of black Africans and their descendants in premodern and early modern Spain, see Ortiz, "Cabildos afro-cubanos," 9–15.
67. Reid, "Yoruba in Cuba," 117.
68. Ibid.
69. Quoted in Martin, *Conjuring Moments in African American Literature*, 127.
70. Navarro García, *Historia del baile flamenco*, 59–61; emphasis added.
71. The original Spanish states: "Desde el siglo XV, no dejaron de llegar a nuestros puertos. Primero, los trajeron los esclavos que venían directamente del continente africano. Sevilla era entonces, junto a Lisboa, uno de los centros más importantes en el mercado de esclavos. Luego continuaron llegando, en sucesivas oleadas, procedentes de las islas caribeñas, especialmente, de Cuba. En su origen, en tierras africanas, habían sido danzas rituales hechas en honor de los dioses y diosas de la fertilidad y, por eso, en sus movimientos parodiaban el acto sexual. Todavía se conservan en Cuba algunos de los conjuros que acompañaban la ejecución de estos bailes y no se han olvidado los altares que se solían levantar para honrar a esas deidades" (Since the fifteenth century, they did not stop arriving at our ports. First, they brought slaves who came directly from the African continent. Seville was then, like Lisbon, one of the most important urban centers in the trafficking of slaves. Slaves continued

arriving, in successive waves, from the Caribbean islands, especially Cuba. In their origin, in African lands, there had been ritual dances performed in honor of their gods and goddesses of fertility, and, therefore, in their movements they parodied the sexual act. In Cuba, some of the conjurings that accompanied the execution of these dances are still preserved. Not even the altars used to honor those deities have been forgotten).

72. See Navarro García, *Historia del baile flamenco*, 77. Performers dance the retambo in Sebastián de Villaviciosa's *Entremés de la vida holgana* (1657). The only mentioning of the cachumba—in Cuba known as the cachumba or *cachumbambé*, as explained by Fernando Ortiz in *Glosario de afronegrismos*—appears in a 1603 text from Cuenca titled *Relación muy graciosa, que trata de la vida y muerte que hizo la Zarabanda, mujer que fue de Antón Pintado, y las mandas que hizo a todos aquellos de su jaez y camarada, y cómo salió desterrada de la corte, y de aquella pesadumbre murió*; see Ébora, *Orígenes de la música cubana*, 129. In seventeenth-century Spain, the gayumba shows up in the *Baile de la gayumba*, in which the coplas of dance, in call-and-response, references its so-called moreno (dark), indiano roots:

> Lo que cantan en Indias
> cantarte quiero
> Díseme mi moreno,
> ¡gayumba!
> Que mi ha de vender.
> ¡Cuántos compradores,
> ¡gayumba!
> Tengo de tener.
>
> [What they sing in the Indies
> I want to sing to you.
> Tell me something, my *moreno*:
> Gayumba!
> I might be sold.
> So many buyers,
> I'm going to have!
> Gayumba!]

73. See the chapter "Afro-Cuban Religious Traditions of Regla" in Fernández Olmos and Paravisini-Gebert, *Creole Religions of the Caribbean*, 88–115. In early modern Portugal and colonial Brazil, recorded primarily in witness testimonies and trial records from the Inquisition of Lisbon, ngangas and other kinds of vessels used to house and to communicate with spirits of the dead were incorrectly labeled "fetiços" (fetishes). For more information on fetiços in relation to the Afro-Portuguese world, refer to Sweet, *Domingos Álvares, African Healing*, and *Recreating Africa*.

74. See Banerjee, "Necrocapitalism," and Mbembe, "Necropolitics."

75. See the online version of the *Oxford English Dictionary*.

76. See Nicholas R. Jones, "Legacy and Representation of Blacks in Spain," *Black Perspectives*, 1 June 2018, https://www.aaihs.org/the-legacy-and-representation-of-blacks-in-spain/.

77. See footnotes in Navarro García, *Historia del baile flamenco*, 62–65.

78. Becco, *Negros y morenos en el cancionero rioplatense*, 23.

79. Cervantes, *Celoso extremeño*, in Sieber, *Novelas ejemplares II*, 99–135.

80. For additional commentary on this dance during the reign of Felipe II, see Pellicer y Pilares, *Trabajos de Persiles y Sigismunda*, lxix.

81. Vélez de Guevara, *Diablo Cojuelo*, 74–75.

82. See http://fondosdigitales.us.es/fondos/libros/765/1399/tesoro-de-la-lengua-castellana-o-espanola/.

83. Lope de Vega, *Isla del sol*.

84. Beusterien, *Eye on Race*, 152–53. In *La ilustre fregona*, Cervantes also describes the chacona's emblematic energy of *la bona vida* in the following medley:

> Bulle la risa en el pecho
> de quien baila y de quien toca,
> del que mira y del que escucha
>
> [Laughter rumbles in the chest
> of whoever dances it and plays it;

of the one who watches it and listens to it.]

Cervantes, *Ilustre fregona*, in Sieber, *Novelas ejemplares II*, 169–70.
85. See http://web.frl.es/DA.html.
86. See http://www.cervantesvirtual.com/obra-visor/rasgos-del-ocio-en-diferentes-bayles-entremeses-y-loas-de-diversos-avtores--0/html/021fc47c-82b2-11df-acc7-002185ce6064_57.html.
87. For Solís's *Las amazonas*, see http://www.cervantesvirtual.com/obra/de-las-amazonas-2/, and for his *El niño caballero*, see http://www.cervantesvirtual.com/obra-visor/el-nino-caballero-entremes-inc-no-me-detengais-amigas-h-1-exp-que-nos-mandas-que-nos-quieres-h-2v/html/80c48a9a-728d-4e6e-b035-0ce14f38c8f2.html.
88. See Swiadon Martínez, "Villancicos de negro."
89. In *Historia del baile flamenco*, Navarro García's writes: "Tanto el habla que emplean los personajes que lo interpretan, como las formas dancísticas y los cantos que lo acompañaban, reflejan un profundo conocimiento de la cultura de este grupo y de sus bailes, así como una preocupación para llevarlos a escena con la máxima fidelidad posible" (72) (Like the speech employed by the characters who interpret it, just as much as the dance forms and the songs that accompanied them, black dances reflect a deep knowledge of culture, as well as a concern for bringing them to the performative scene with the utmost exactness possible). The famous *zarambequero*, actor Cosme Pérez (Juan Rana), was well known for his zarambeque performance in Lanini y Sagredo's *El parto de Juan Rana* (1653–58). For more further reading on Juan Rana, see Thompson, *Triumphant Juan Rana*, and *Outrageous Juan Rana* Entremeses.
90. Russell, *Santiago de Murcia's Códice Saldívar IV*, 72. For more information about this dance, see also Ortiz's *Glosario de afronegrismos*.
91. See García Valdés, "'Regidor.'"
92. Ibid., 238.
93. Buezo, *Prácticas festivas*, 268.
94. This convention also overlaps with Calderón's *La muerte*, a mojiganga that presents the devil in a similar manner. The short-skit plays *La casa de los linajes* and *Las Carnestolendas*, also by Calderón, feature black characters who speak in habla de negros.
95. Refer specifically to Irigoyen-García, "'Música ha sido hereje'"; and Irigoyen-García, *Moors Dressed as Moors*.
96. See Larrea, "Sobre el posible origen americano."
97. Stone, "'Quiero llorar,'" 499–500.
98. I invite my readers to listen to Hespèrion XXI's recording of "San Sabeya Gugurumbé" on YouTube: https://youtu.be/c9-ljfm9Lok. The sub-Saharan African rhythms and sounds to which I refer begin at the timestamp 2:52. Under the directorship of Jordi Savall, the ensemble's album *Villancicos y danzas criollas de la Iberia antigua al Nuevo Mundo, 1550–1750* can also be located on iTunes, where other habla de negros villancicos are recorded. The album also features period recordings of the other black dances analyzed in this chapter, such as the chacona and a *moresca* (not necessarily to be confused with moriscos).
99. Jones, "Nuptials Gone Awry, Empire in Decay," 10–11.
100. ACG legajo 1582. For more information on this trial, see Martín Casares, "Comba y Dominga," 185–86.
101. Jones, "Nuptials Gone Awry, Empire in Decay," 10–11.
102. As noted by Mullen in "Simón Aguado's *Entremés de los negros*": "The appearance of Aguado's entremés at the beginning of the seventeenth century seems to stand in sharp contrast to the vicious racism of Francisco de Quevedo's 'Boda de negros' and appears to have anticipated the more sympathetic treatment of blacks found in such works as the anonymous short-skit play *Los mirones* (1623?), which was

attributed to Cervantes by Antonio de Castro" (2).
103. Mullen, "Simón Aguado's *Entremés de los negros*," 239.
104. Cotarelo y Mori, *Colección de entremeses, loas, bailes, jácaras*, 232.
105. Ibid.
106. Mullen, "Simón Aguado's *Entremés de los negros*," 238. For the Spanish original, refer to Asensio's second edition of *Itinerario del entremés*.
107. Mullen, "Simón Aguado's *Entremés de los negros*," 238.
108. Tompkins, *Racial Indigestion*, 3.
109. Ibid.
110. Cotarelo y Mori, *Colección de entremeses, loas, bailes, jácaras*, 234.
111. Mullen frames historically these noteworthy facts about the representation of blacks in Aguado's play: "Not only were black slaves noted as particularly accomplished performers, but on the authority of Emilio Cotarelo y Mori, we learn that [many] popular dances of the day—the *Guineo, Ye-ye*, and *Zarambeque*—were probably of African origin. One must not forget the economic implications implicit in the restraints imposed upon blacks. Music appears to provide one of the few ways open to blacks both in early modern Spain and later in the colonies. We learn from Cervantes in *El celoso extremeño* that black slaves [earned] money by singing at taverns and performing at dances. Alejo Carpentier points out that in nineteenth-century Cuba that number of black musicians was disproportionate to the number of white musicians—a fact he attributed to the fluctuating demand for musicians, which discouraged whites who had other economic avenues open to them" (243); ibid., ccxxxiii–cclxxiii. See also Carpentier's *La música en Cuba*, 108–19.
112. Wynter, "Eye of the Other," 18–19.
113. Weheliye, "Engendering Phonographies," 181.
114. Ibid., 181–82.
115. *Obra conocida de Rodrigo de Reinosa*, 178.
116. Deleuze and Guattari, *Kafka*, 19.
117. Ibid.
118. Wheat, *Atlantic Africa and the Spanish Caribbean*, 216.
119. Ibid.
120. Covarrubias, *Tesoro*, 350.
121. *Diccionario de Autoridades*, http://web.frl.es/DA.html.
122. John Beusterien presents an insightful and thorough reading of the term "ladino" in *Eye on Race*. While tracing its racial-linguistic evolution through his analysis of the figure of the Moor in Diego Ximénez de Enciso's play *Juan Latino*, Beusterien explains that the play presents a roughly parallel series of events that correspond to biographical depictions of this sixteenth-century Latin grammarian and poet from Granada from contemporary histories (106–7). "Jiménez de Enciso's erudite protagonist," he continues, "would be a model for the stock comic figure of the Black university professor found in Cuban theater beginning in the eighteenth century, such as in the character of Aniceto in Pedro N. Pequeño and Francisco Fernández's *El negro cheche o veinte años después* (1868)" (107). For more on the term "ladino," see Wheat, *Atlantic Africa and the Spanish Caribbean*, 216–52.
123. Beusterien, *Eye on Race*, 108.
124. Ibid. The notion of establishing a financial value, or set bill of sale, for slaves based on their linguistic abilities also reached the English slave market. Beusterien tells us that "one English merchant indicated a lower price for the *bozal* in a commentary from 1569: 'For if a negro be a Bossel (*bozal*) that is to say ignorant of the spanishe or Portugale tonge then he or she is commonlye sould for [450] pesos'" (108). See also Martín Casares's *Esclavitud en la Granada del siglo XVI*, where she confirms Beusterien's research on the ladino's appearance in slave contracts. She explains that seventeenth-century Spanish documents show how the terms "bozal" and "ladino" were elusive and slippery.

125. But moving beyond the antithesis between bozal and ladino terminologies vis-à-vis habla de negros language, sub-Saharan Africans identified as ladinos are superb examples of diasporic Africans who created niches for themselves in their new environments, adapting to Spanish rule rather than resisting it. Latinized Africans such as Juan and Francisco Biafara and the farmer Bartolomé Arará, who constructed a church on his ranch, are only a few of the many black African migrants who were adept at negotiating between African and Iberian worlds. For more concrete analysis and data, see Wheat, *Atlantic Africa and the Spanish Caribbean*, 216–81.
126. Lane, "Becoming Chocolate," 385. On blackface in Cuba, see Lane's *Blackface Cuba*.
127. Refer to: Rowe, "After Death, Her Face Turned White"; Ireton, "'They Are Blacks of the Caste'"; Fracchia, "Esclavo negroafricano en las imágenes españolas," 127–49; and Méndez Rodríguez, "Visiones iconográficas de la esclavitud."

Chapter 2

1. Resende, *Cancioneiro geral de Garcia de Resende*, 1:204–5.
2. Teyssier, *Língua de Gil Vicente*, 277. In note 15, Teyssier adds that Carolina Michaëlis de Vasconcelos, *RL*, XI (1908), suggests that Fernão de Silveira wrote this short poem for the wedding festivities of Princess Dona Joana and Henrique IV de Castela in 1455.
3. Pratt, *Imperial Eyes*, 6.
4. Wheat, *Atlantic Africa and the Spanish Caribbean*, 23–24.
5. Ibid., 24.
6. Pratt, *Imperial Eyes*, 7.
7. Ibid.
8. Lipski, *History of Afro-Hispanic Language*, 53.
9. Resende, *Chronica de el-Rei D. João II*, ccii. For additional information about census reports of blacks living in fifteenth-century Portugal, see Saunders, *Social History of Black Slaves*, 47–61. Resende's 1554 *Miscellanea*, stanza lix, "on black slaves," also describes the great number of black slaves entering Portugal and adjacent islands off the Western coast of Africa: "Vẽ grã somma a portugal cadaño tābẽ aas ilhas, he cousa que sempre val, & tres dobra ho cabedal em castella, & nas antilhas" (Every year a great number come to Portugal and the adjacent islands; they are something which is always valuable and will triple your investment if sold in Castile and the Antilles) (Saunders, *Social History of Black Slaves*, 4).
10. Unless otherwise noted, the edition I use for citing Rodrigo de Reinosa's textual corpus comes from Puerto Moro's *Obra conocida de Rodrigo de Reinosa*. Also, unless otherwise noted, all English translations of "Gelofe, Mandinga" are mine. In subsequent sections, there will be offensive, highly racially charged language used and translated from habla de negros to English. Instead of employing literal translations of certain phrases and words, I opt for symbolic translations that capture, on the one hand, the descriptive spirit and vulgarity of the signifying mode commonly expressed in AAVE and, on the other hand, to illuminate Reinosa's obscene language, which enables black subject formation to manifest. For additional commentary on the delicate complexities and difficulties in translating race, Blackness, and marked language, please refer to my prefatory chapter "Translating Blackness."

It is difficult to determine a precise date as to when Rodrigo de Reinosa composed these poems. For more discussion about the problem of dating Reinosa's poetry featuring black characters, see Russell's study "Rodrigo de Reinosa's 'poesía negra.'" Russell suggests that these coplas may have been written in the last decades of the fifteenth century. Refer also to Weber de Kurlat's essays "Sobre el negro como tipo cómico" and "Tipo cómico del negro." She surmises that the "Africanized" coplas were written after the publication of Resende's *Cancioneiro Geral*. See Kaplan's article "Rodrigo de Reinosa's Sympathetic Attitude," where he notes that Reinosa was active from the last decades of the 1400s through the early sixteenth century. In the same essay, Kaplan's evidence for this claim appears in Reinosa's various allusions to the death of King Enrique IV and the ascension to the throne of the Catholic Monarch (events that occurred in 1476).

11. Baltasar Fra-Molinero critiques the cultural and historical formation of stereotyping black Africans in Renaissance Spanish literature in the early 1990s. For further commentary on the stereotyping of blacks during this period, see especially his essay "Formación del estereotipo del negro" and his book *Imagen de los negros*. For recent studies focusing on the stereotyping of black Africans in early modern Spain, also consult Martín Casares and García Barranco's *Esclavitud negroafricana en la historia* and Santos Morillo's "Caracterización del negro en la literatura." On Comba, see Martín Casares's chapter, "Comba y Dominga."

12. The 1970s film genre blaxploitation was originally made for inner-city US black American audiences. Mainly set in poor black neighborhoods, the defining characteristics of Blaxploitation films explore themes of race relations, crime and vice, and violence.

13. The concept and notion of "Africanity" has acquired a wide array of meanings depending on the geographical location where one lives as well as the school of scholarly thought to which one belongs. The term goes back to the early days of Pan-Africanism and negritude movements, as well as "Afrocentricism" and the ideologies that accompany it. From both within and outside the continent of Africa, for instance, see Appiah's *In My Father's House*; Mudimbe's *Invention of Africa*; and "Identity and Beyond: Rethinking Africanity," a collection of discussion papers published in 2001 by Souleymane Bachir Diagne, Amina Mama, Henning Melber, and Francis B. Nyamnjoh.

14. Jeffries, *Thug Life*, 18.
15. For recent studies on Juan Latino, see Martín Casares, *Juan Latino*; Wright, *Epic of Juan Latino*; and Fra-Molinero, "Juan Latino and His Racial Difference." To my knowledge, Henry Louis Gates Jr. is the first literary critic to align Juan Latino with signifying in the African diaspora. For more commentary, see Gates, *Signifying Monkey*, 89–91. On signifying, see also Morgan, *Language, Discourse, and Power*, and *Real Hip Hop*; Yancy, "Geneva Smitherman"; and Williams-Farrier, "Signifying, Narrativizing, and Repetition."
16. Jeffries, *Thug Life*, 18.
17. Ibid.
18. Ibid.
19. Gates, *Signifying Monkey*, 90.
20. Ibid., 81.
21. Ibid.
22. Ibid., 88.
23. Ibid., xxii.
24. Ibid.
25. Lanehart, *Sociocultural and Historical Contexts*, see esp. chapters 2–3.
26. This can also be read as an example of misogynoir, a form of misogyny directed at black women that also involves intraracism that black male patriarchy unleashes against black women. Queer black feminist Moya Bailey coined the term, while Brittney Cooper has also served as a key cultural critic who engages this concept in her black feminist thought. For more information, see the Crunk Feminist Collective blog, http://www.crunkfeministcollective.com.
27. Gates, *Signifying Monkey*, xxvii.

28. Black Africans and their descendants also left the Western Hemisphere for the so-called Old World. Olaudah Equiano is a prime example. In the Hispanic literary tradition, playwright Félix Lope de Vega y Carpio uses the term "indiano" to reference his "mulata" character, Elvira, in the play *Servir a señor discreto* (1610/1618). In this work, Elvira is referred to as an indiana from the Spanish Indies. As an indiana, Lope uncovers the various cultural aesthetics, sensibilities, and linguistic code-switching that Elvira has brought to Spain from the Spanish Caribbean.
29. Low and Myhill, "Introduction," 2.
30. Ibid.
31. Puerto Moro, *Obra conocida de Rodrigo de Reinosa*, 25.
32. Gaylord, "How to Do Things with Polimetría," 81.
33. Hall, *Slavery and Ethnicity in the Americas*, 52. See also Wheat's *Atlantic Africa and the Spanish Caribbean*.
34. Liu, "'Affined to Love the Moor,'" 52. In this essay, Liu cites Jean Marie D'Heur's "*Art de trouver du chansonnier* Colocci-Brancuti," 102–3.
35. Liu's translation.
36. Liu, "'Affined to Love the Moor,'" 52. The *mal dizer* tradition, as well as double-meaning obscenities found in Reinosa's "Gelofe, Mandinga," also embodies the theoretical constitution of jokes found in Freud's *Jokes and Their Relation to the Unconscious* (1905). For Freud, double meaning is a technique of jokes and arises from the literal and metaphorical meaning of words. In Freud's *Jokes and Their Relation to the Unconscious*, consult "The Technique of Jokes" (14–105), "The Motives of Jokes—Jokes as a Social Process" (171–96), and "Jokes and the Species of the Comic" (224–94).
37. Liu, "'Affined to Love the Moor,'" 48.
38. Ibid.
39. Ibid.
40. Translation and introduction by Armillas-Tiseyra, "On Language and Empire."
41. Piedra, "Literary Whiteness," 304.
42. Foucault, *History of Sexuality*, 1:100–101.
43. Covarrubias, *Tesoro*, 807–9.
44. The Portuguese were the first major traffickers of black Africans. They followed a standardized policy of naming these slaves based on the region from which they were taken *or* the port from which they were shipped. In Reinosa's coplas—as also identifiable in other early modern Iberian literary works—the terms *Gelofes* and *Mandingas*, as well as *Biafras* (or *Biafaras*) often served as subcategories taken from the *Castas de ríos de Guinea* (nations from the Rivers of Guinea). Another shipping term used at the time was *Cabos verdes*, because this group of slaves was shipped from the slave port of Santiago in the Cape Verde Islands. See Wheat's *Atlantic Africa and the Spanish Caribbean*, esp. chapter 1.
45. See Hall, *Slavery and African Ethnicities in the Americas*, 80–100, for additional insights and empirical data on this region. For a more geographically and historically contextualized breakdown, I provide a delineation of the major groups from which Europeans tended to obtain sub-Saharan African slaves: (1) "Upper Guinea": now known as the countries Senegal, Guinea, Guinea Bissau, Sierra Leone, western Mali, and Liberia; (2) "Lower Guinea": the leeward coast of the Gulf of Guinea, including the Bights of Benin and Biafra, and the territory including the republics of Ghana, Togo, Benin, Nigeria, and northern Cameroon; (3) "Congo River and Angola": This area encompassed the region around the mouth of the Congo River, known as present-day Gabon, Equatorial Guinea, and the Democratic Republic of the Congo, as well as Portugal's former colony Angola; and (4) Mozambique, also a former colony of Portugal.
46. Hall, *Slavery and African Ethnicities in the Americas*, 82.
47. Ibid.
48. Covarrubias, *Tesoro*, 1384.
49. See Perry's *Gender and Disorder in Early Modern Seville* for a thorough account

of archival and legal records concerning prostitutes and prostitution. Barbeito's *Cárceles de mujeres en el siglo XVII* is also an excellent source. On clothes and garments as social texts of prostitution and disease, see Berco's essay "Textiles as Social Texts," and chapter 1, "Prostitution and Power," of Martín, *Erotic Philology of Golden Age Spain*, 1–42.
50. Beusterien, *Eye on Race*, 108–9.
51. Ibid., 109.
52. Granda, "Posibles vías directas de introducción," 467. Quoted in Beusterien, *Eye on Race*, 109.
53. Spillers, "Mama's Baby, Papa's Maybe," 203.
54. Año de 1495, fol. 258. Consult note 4 in Puerto Moro's *Obra conocida de Rodrigo de Reinosa*, 168–77.
55. Delicado, *Retrato de la loçana andaluza*, 21.
56. Stephens, *Skin Acts*, 3.
57. Ibid.
58. Jeffries, *Thug Life*, 18.
59. Ibid.
60. Quoted in Gates, *Signifying Monkey*, 82.
61. Mitchell-Kernan, "Signifying, Loud-Talking and Marking."
62. Hall, *Slavery and African Ethnicities in the Americas*, 82. Black Africans who were either Christianized, Hispanicized, and/or Latinized were called ladinos. On ladino, Hall explains that "after the conquest and colonization of the Americas began, enslaved Africans continued to be introduced into the Iberian Peninsula. They and their descendants were among the first Africans and peoples of African descent brought to the Americas as 'Ladinos.' The comparatively rapid voyages from Greater Senegambia to the Caribbean encouraged populating early Spanish America with Africans from the Greater Senegambia" (82). Beusterien, in *Eye on Race*, 107–9, also provides excellent information on the racialization of ladinos.
63. Lovejoy's article is a great contribution to both early modern Spanish historical studies and literary studies. His chapter appears in Landers and Robinson, *Slaves, Subjects, and Subversives*, 9–38.
64. Cossío, *Rodrigo de Reinosa*, lxxvii.
65. For more on the discourse of food in early modern Spain, see Nadeau's *Food Matters*.
66. Blackmore, "Imagining the Moor in Portugal," 27.
67. Ibid., 28. See especially Bartels, "Making More of the Moor," and Fuchs, *Mimesis and Empire*. See also Blackmore, *Moorings*.
68. An alternative translation of *tabaniquete*, derived from *tabique* and *tabanque*, suggests Comba would have a threesome with Grisolmo and Jorge. The word "tabanque" involves more physical sexual play—defined as "a potter's wheel"—where she would turn and pass from Grisolmo to Jorge. To aid my translation, I borrow from and follow Lawrance's idea that tabaniquete relates to the germanía word *tabanco* (*burdel* [Spanish]; brothel [English]). For additional philological analysis of tabaniquete, see Lawrance's essay "Black Africans in Renaissance Spanish Literature," and note 1 from Puerto Moro's *Obra conocida de Rodrigo de Reinosa*, 177.

Chapter 3

1. See Fra-Molinero, *Imagen de los negros* and his essay "Condition of Black Women in Spain"; García Sierra, "Sociedad y personajes"; Santos Morillo, "Caracterización del negro en la literatura"; Martín Casares and Periáñez Gómez, *Mujeres esclavas y abolicionistas*; and King de Ramírez, "(Mis)Representation of Female Slaves."
2. Brooks, *Bodies in Dissent*, 7.
3. Ibid., 8
4. Castillo, "Horror (Vacui)," 91.
5. I am enthralled and inspired by, as well as indebted to, Kyla Wazana Tompkins's

and Daphne A. Brooks's language and theorization of black women's agency and resistance. The elegantly written prose in their brilliant works has consistently given voice to the many complex ideas in my head that have been, at many times, difficult for me to put into words.

6. Tompkins, *Racial Indigestion*, 9; Brooks, *Bodies in Dissent*, 7–9.
7. Truth, *Narrative of Sojourner Truth*, 131–33. Truth's 1851 speech is widely quoted. Usually, however, the word "ain't" is substituted for "ar'n't," but I have elected to keep the original "ar'n't" to empower Truth's vernacular speech—just as I do with Eulalla and Guiomar's Africanized Castilian speech—by using the word as it appeared in Truth's 1878 original. Historian Nell Painter examines the accuracy of this speech's attribution to Sojourner Truth in *Sojourner Truth*.
8. Collins, *Black Feminist Thought*, 14.
9. Tinsley, "To Transcender Transgender," 133.
10. MacDonald, *Women and Race*, 15.
11. Ibid.
12. Ibid., 13.
13. Collins, *Black Feminist Thought*, 93.
14. Unless otherwise noted, all textual references and quotations citing Lope de Rueda's *Comedia Eufemia* and *Comedia de los engañados* originate from Alfredo Hermenegildo's Cátedra edition of *Cuatro comedias*.
15. For a complete study of Lope de Rueda's short-skit plays, see introduction and notes from González Ollé and Tusón, *Pasos*, 9–86.
16. Rueda, *Cuatro comedias*, 79.
17. Ibid., 117.
18. See García Santo-Tomás, *Refracted Muse*.
19. Rueda, *Cuatro comedias*, 118. Lope de Rueda in the play *Tymbria* features the black woman Fulgencia, who resembles Eulalla and sings the well-known song "Los Comendadores":

> La Comendadores
> por mi mal me vi,
> amarga te veas
> cuitara de mi.
> La Comendadoras
> de Casalava
> salí de Sevilla
> enora mala
> para la vosotros
> quien no la daba
> y a lo pajesicos
> que van pos de ti
> La Comendadoras.

> [*Comendadores*:
> for my sake, I saw myself,
> you look wounded;
> oh the pain.
> *Comendadores*
> from Casalava [Calatrava]:
> I departed from Seville.
> Good riddance
> to those of you
> who don't fuck
> and to those wankers
> who chase after you
> *Comendadores*.]

For additional commentary, see *Colloquio de Gila* in Cátedra, *Tres colloquios pastoriles*, 462–64. Fra-Molinero also mentions this work in *Imagen de los negros*, 29–30. Also refer to Lope de Vega's play *Los comendadores de Córdoba*.

20. Gil González Dávila is known to be the first European soldier to set foot in Central America, specifically the country we now call Nicaragua.
21. See esp. Jill Ross, *Figuring the Feminine*, 50–80.
22. *Oxford English Dictionary*. Refer to "diva" entry at: http://www.oed.com/.
23. Greenblatt, *Renaissance Self-Fashioning*, 1.
24. Ibid.
25. Ibid., 2.
26. Rueda, *Cuatro comedias*, 119–20.
27. bell hooks, *Talking Back*, 131.
28. Rueda, *Cuatro comedias*, 119–20.
29. Covarrubias, *Emblemas morales*, centuria I, emblema 98.
30. Fra-Molinero, "Condition of Black Women in Spain," 159–78.

31. Dopico Black, "Ban and the Bull," 237.
32. Pérez de Tudela and Gschwend, "Renaissance Menageries."
33. Ibid., 420.
34. Ibid.
35. More specifically, Covarrubias, in *Tesoro*, 1342, defines the geographical origins of the papagayo by referring to it as "ave índica conocida" (well-known bird from the Indies). And "índica," as the *Royal Academia Española* dictionary confirms, refers to the Eastern Indies ("las Indias Orientales"). For additional literary references about papagayos and *monos*, consult Morínigo, *América en el teatro*, 64–82.
36. Covarrubias, *Emblemas morales*, centuria I, emblema 78.
37. Covarrubias, *Tesoro*, 1342, emphasis added.
38. Rueda, *Cuatro comedias*, 118.
39. Ibid., 121.
40. In *Imagen de los negros*, Fra-Molinero describes Eulalla as: "La negra enamorada adquiere mayor refinamiento en el personaje de Eulalla, en la comedia *Eufemia* de Lope de Rueda. De lo cómico se pasa a lo patético, ya que el galán de esta esclava, Polo, es un rufián de cuidado que quiere seducirla y venderla a las primeras de cambio. En Eulalla aparece plenamente desarrollada la ridiculización de las pretensiones de ascenso social de una esclava negra. En su lengua de negro explica sus esfuerzos por aclarar su cara y cabellos—'¿no tengo yo cabeyo como la otro?'—, haciendo suya la fíbula de Esopo representada en los *Emblemata* de Alciato" (The easily infatuated black woman acquires the utmost refinement in the character of Eulalla in Lope de Rueda's *Comedia Eufemia*. Her comical nature overruns with pathetic behavior, for this slave's *galán*, Polo, is a ruffian par excellence who from the start wants to seduce her and sell her for anything possible. Developed in Eulalla's role is the ridiculing of a black female slave's pretensions at social climbing. In her Black language, she explains her efforts by lightening her face and hair—"I don't have hair like the other [white] woman?"—making her own Aesop's fable represented in the Alciato's *Book of Emblems*) (30–31).
41. Gerli, *Celestina and the Ends of Desire*, 13.
42. Ibid.
43. Rueda, *Cuatro comedias*, 121. Referencing current studies on women, recipes, and science in Spain, see work by Cabré, particularly "Women or Healers?." Also on women, recipes, and science, see Leong, "Collecting Knowledge for the Family." On women, science, and cosmetic recipes, see Snook, *Women, Beauty, and Power*, 19–62.
44. Ibid., 48.
45. Fanon, *Black Skin, White Masks*.
46. Bermúdez de Pedraza, *Historia eclesiástica de Granada*. The modern edition, from which I cite, was published in 1989. In this 1989 edition, see page 260 for documentation of Catalina de Soto.
47. Hall, "Object into Object?"
48. Rueda, *Cuatro comedias*, 118.
49. Gubar, *Racechanges*, 5.
50. As a starting point, refer to Smith, *Black Africans in the British Imagination*; Heng, "Invention of Race"; Heng's recent monograph, *Invention of Race*; Greer, Mignolo, and Quilligan, *Rereading the Black Legend*; Mariscal, "Role of Spain in Contemporary Race Theory"; and Sweet, "Iberian Roots of American Racist Thought." For an even more extensive bibliography of race studies over the past fifty years, see Erickson and Hall, "'New Scholarly Song.'"
51. Erickson and Hall, "'New Scholarly Song,'" 1–2.
52. Ibid., 2–3.
53. Ibid., 2.
54. Quoted from ibid., 2 n. 5: "The refusal to see race has been an ongoing issue in race studies"; see, for example, Frankenberg, *White Women, Race Matters*, 137–39; and Morrison, *Playing in the Dark*, 17. It was addressed in early modern race studies scholarship early on; see Hall, *Things of Darkness*, 254–68, and Royster,

"'End of Race.'" On postracial ideology, particularly in the wake of Barack Obama's 2008 election, see Grady's dissertation: "Moors, Mulattos, and Post-Racial Problems." See also Haney, "Is the Post in Post-Racial?," and Bonilla-Silva and Dietrich, "Sweet Enchantment of Color-Blind Racism."
55. Erickson and Hall, "'New Scholarly Song,'" 3.
56. Ibid.
57. Bourdieu, *Language and Symbolic Power*.
58. Rueda, *Cuatro comedias*, 120.
59. Ibid., 119–29.
60. Collins, *Black Feminist Thought*, 78.
61. See Beusterien's *Eye on Race* and Fra-Molinero's *Imagen de los negros*.
62. Rueda, *Cuatro comedias*, 121.
63. Collins, *Black Feminist Thought*, 88.
64. Rueda, *Cuatro comedias*, 121.
65. Ibid.
66. Ibid., 182–83.
67. Wheat, *Atlantic Africa and the Spanish Caribbean*, 34. For additional archival records on this subject, see footnote 15.
68. Rueda, *Cuatro comedias*, 182.
69. Ibid., 183.
70. Ibid., 182.
71. See Bennett, *Colonial Blackness*; McKnight and Garofalo, *Afro-Latino Voices*; and Wheat, *Atlantic Africa and the Spanish Caribbean*.
72. Wheat, *Atlantic Africa and the Spanish Caribbean*, 7.
73. Ibid.
74. Ibid. Refer specifically to the book's introduction, 5–19, and chapter 1, "The Rivers of Guinea," 20–67.
75. Ibid., 8.

Afterword

1. See Fernández Olmos and Paravisini-Gebert, *Creole Religions of the Caribbean*. For a linguistic study of Palo Mayombe, refer to Fuentes Guerra and Schwegler, *Lenguas y ritos del Palo Monte Mayombe*.
2. Hartikeinen, "African Accents, Speaking Child Spirits," 327.

Bibliography

Archival Sources

ACG (Archivo de la Curia Episcopal de Granada), legajo 1582
Aguado, Simón. *Los negros.* MS 17434, Biblioteca Nacional de España, 1602
AHN (Archivo Histórico Nacional), Inquisición
  Legajo 1.829, causa no. 3, fol. 71r
  Legajo 2.022, expediente no. 37, causa no. 8, fol. 25v
  Legajo 524 #11
  Legajo 861, fol. 212r, 1623
  Legajo 862, fol. 34r, 1625
  Legajo 1953, expediente 66, 19, 1621

Libro 916, fols. 106v, 641r–v
Libro 937, fol. 100v
Libro 938, fol. 170v
Avellaneda, Francisco de. *Entremés de los negros.* MS 15143, Biblioteca Nacional de España. 1622.
Lope de Vega. *La isla del sol.* MS S/14809. Biblioteca Nacional de España. 1622.
Rebelo, Manuel Coelho. *De dos alcaldes y el engaño de una negra: Musa entretenida de varios entremeses.* Coimbra: Manuel Dias MS R/12086. Biblioteca Nacional de España. 1658.

Primary Sources

Aguado, Simón. *Entremés de los negros.* Edited by Emilio Cotarelo y Morí. In *Colección de entremeses, loas, bailes, jácaras y mojigangas desde fines del siglo XVI a mediados del XVIII*, vol. 1. Madrid: Bailly-Bailliére, 1911.
Alfonso X (El Sabio). *Cantigas de Santa Maria.* Edited by Jesús Montoya. Madrid: Cátedra, 1997.

Alonso, Dámaso, ed. *Luis de Góngora, Soledades.* Madrid: Ediciones de Árbol, 1935.
Álvar, Carlos, ed. *Gran enciclopedia cervantina*, vol. 2. Madrid: Castalia, 2005.
Barrantes, D. V., ed. *Recopilación en metro del bachiller Diego Sánchez de Badajoz*, vols. 1–2. Madrid: Librería de los Bibliófilos, 1882.

Bergman, Hannah, ed. *Luis Quiñones de Benavente y sus entremeses.* Madrid: Castalia, 1965.

Bermúdez de Pedraza, Francisco. *Historia eclesiástica de Granada.* Granada, 1989 (1639).

Calderón de la Barca, Pedro. *Entremeses, jácaras y mojigangas.* Edited by Evangelina Rodríguez and Antonio Tordera. Madrid: Cátedra, 1982.

———. *Teatro cómico breve.* Edited by María-Luisa Lobato. Kassel: Reichenberger, 1989.

Carpentier, Alejo. *La música en Cuba.* Mexico City: Fondo de cultura económica, 1946.

Castro, Don Adolfo de, ed. *Varias obras inéditas de Cervantes.* Madrid: A. de Carlos é Hijo, 1874.

Cátedra, Pedro. *Tres colloquios pastoriles de Juan de Vergara y Lope de Rueda (Valencia, 1567).* San Millán de la Cogolla: Cilengua, 2006.

Cervantes, Miguel de. *Entremeses.* Edited by Nicholas Spadaccini. Madrid: Cátedra, 2005.

———. *El ingenioso hidalgo don Quijote de la Mancha I y II.* Edited by John Jay Allen. Madrid: Cátedra, 2003.

———. *Novelas ejemplares I y II.* Edited by Harry Sieber. Madrid: Cátedra, 2003.

Ciplijauskaité, Biruté, ed. *Luis de Góngora: Sonetos.* Madison: University of Wisconsin Press, 1981.

———, ed. *Sonetos completes de Góngora.* Madrid: Castalia, 1976.

Correas, Gonzalo. *Vocabulario de refranes y frases proverbiales.* Edited by Louis Combet. Bordeaux, 1627.

Cortés de Tolosa, José. *El Lazarillo de Manzanares.* 1620. http://www.cervantesvirtual.com/obra-visor/el-lazarillo-de-manzanares--0/html/

Cotarelo y Mori, Emilio. *Colección de entremeses, loas, bailes, jácaras y mojigangas desde fines del siglo XVI a mediados del XVIII.* Madrid: Bailly-Bailliére, 1911.

———. "Prologue and Vocabulary." In *Obras de Lope de Rueda,* vol. 1. Madrid: Librería de los Suc. de Hernando, edición de la Real Academia, 1908.

Covarrubias, Sebastián de. *Emblemas morales.* Madrid: Fundación Universitaria Española, 1978.

———. *Obras completas.* Edited by Francisco Monterde. Mexico City: Porrúa, 2001.

———. *Tesoro de la lengua castellana o española.* Edited by Ignacio Arellano y Rafael Zafra. Pamplona: Universidad de Navarra, 2006.

Delicado, Francisco. *Retrato de la loçana andaluza.* Edited by Bruno Damiani and Giovanni Allegra. Madrid: Ediciones José Porrúa Turanzas, 1975.

Diccionario de autoridades. Vols. 1–6. Madrid: Real Academia Española, 1726–39.

Du Bois, W. E. B. *The Souls of Black Folk.* New York: Penguin, 1996.

The English Standard Version Bible: Containing the Old and New Testaments with Apocrypha. Oxford: Oxford University Press, 2009.

Fanon, Frantz. *Black Skin, White Masks.* Translated by Charles Lam Markmann. New York: Grove Press, 1967.

———. *The Wretched of the Earth.* Translated by Richard Philcox. Commentary by Homi K. Bhabha and Jean-Paul Sartre. New York: Grove Press, 1963.

Freud, Sigmund. *Jokes and Their Relation to the Unconscious.* Edited and translated by James Strachey. New York: Norton, 1960.

Gómez de Toledo, Gaspar. *Tercera parte de la tragicomedia de Celestina.* Edited by Mac Barrick. Philadelphia: University of Pennsylvania Press, 1973.

Góngora y Argote, Luis de. *Las firmezas de Isabela.* Edited by Robert Jammes. Madrid: Castalia, 1984.

———. *Letrillas.* Edited by Robert Jammes. Madrid: Castalia, 1980.

———. *Sonetos completos: Luis de Góngora y Argote.* Edited by Robert Jammes. Madrid: Castalia, 1989.

Güete, Jaime de. "Comedia intitulada Tesorina." In *Teatro español del siglo XVI,* vol. 1, 81–170. Madrid: Sociedad de Bibliófilos, 1913.

Herskovits, Meville J. *The Myth of the Negro Past*. Boston: Beacon Press, 1990.

Hurston, Zora Neale. *Zora Neale Hurston: Folklore, Memoirs, and Other Writings*. New York: Library of America, 1995.

Hurtado de Mendoza, Antonio. *Obras líricas y cómicas*. Edited by Francisco Medel del Castillo. 1728.

Jonson, Ben. *The Complete Masques*. Edited by Stephen Orgel. New Haven, CT: Yale University Press, 1969.

Las Casas, Bartolomé de. *Brevísima relación de la destrucción de África*. ElAleph, 2000. http://190.186.233.212/filebiblioteca/Ciencias%20Sociales/Bartolome%20de%20las%20Casas%20-%20Brevisima%20Relacion%20de%20la%20Destruccion%20de%20Africa.pdf.

———. *Brevísima relación de la destrucción de las Indias*. Edited by André Saint-Lu. Madrid: Cátedra, 2003.

Lazarillo de Tormes. Edited by Francisco Rico. Madrid: Cátedra, 2003.

León, Fray Luis de. *Obras completas castellanas*, vol. 1. Edited by O. S. A. Félix García. Madrid: Editorial Católica, 1977.

———. *La perfecta casada*. Edited by Joaquín Antonio Peñalosa. Mexico City: Porrúa, 1999.

———. *Poesías originales*. Edited by Joaquín Antonio Peñalosa. Mexico City: Porrúa, 1999.

López de Mendoza, Íñigo, marqués de Santillana. *Obras completas*. Edited by Ángel Gómez Moreno and M. P. A. M. Kerkhof. Barcelona: Planeta, 1988.

López Pinciano, Alonso. *Obras completas I, Philosophía Antigua Poética*. Edited and prologue by José Rico Verdú. Madrid: Biblioteca Castro, 1998.

López Prudencio, José. *Diego Sánchez de Badajoz: Estudio crítico, biográfico y bibliográfico*. Madrid: Tipografía de la Revista de Archivos, 1915.

———, ed. *Recopilación en metro de Diego Sánchez de Badajoz*. Badajoz: Tipografía de Antonio Arqueros, 1910.

Nebrija, Antonio de. *Gramática de la lengua castellana*. Barcelona: Linkgua ediciones S. L., 2006.

Ortiz, Fernando. *Los bailes y el teatro de los negros en el folklore de Cuba*. Havana: Cardenas y Cia, 1951. Reprint, Havana: Letras Cubanas, 1981.

———. "Los cabildos afro-cubanos." *Revista Bimestre Cubana* 16 (January-February 1921): 5–29. Reprint, Havana: Editorial de Ciencias Sociales, 1992.

———. *Los cabildos afrocubanos del Día de Reyes*. 1921. Reprint, Havana: Editorial de Ciencias Sociales, 1992.

———. *Glosario de afronegrismos*. Prologue by Juan Dihigo. Havana: El Siglo XX, 1924.

———. *Negros brujos*. Madrid: Librería de Fernando Fé, 1906. Reprint, Havana: Editorial de Ciencias Sociales, 1995.

———. *Los negros esclavos*. Havana: Revista bimestre cubana, 1916. Reprint, Havana: Editorial de Ciencias Sociales, 1975.

Painter, Nell Irvin. *Sojourner Truth: A Life, a Symbol*. New York: Norton, 2007.

Pellicer y Pilares, Juan Antonio, ed. *Trabajos de Persiles y Sigismunda: Historia setentrional, tomo 1*. New York: Casa de Lanuza, 1827.

Pérez de Montoro, José. "Letras de los villancicos de nuestro señor Jesu Christo, año de 1693." In *Obras pósthumas líricas sagradas*, 369–72. Madrid, 1736.

Quevedo, Francisco de. *La hora de todos*. Edited by Luisa López-Grigera. Madrid: Editorial Castalia, 1975.

———. *Poesía varia*. Edited by James O. Crosby. Madrid: Cátedra, 2007.

———. *Prosa festiva completa*. Edited by Carmen Celsa García-Valdés. Madrid: Cátedra, 2007.

Quiñones de Benavente, Luis. "El borracho." In *Colección de entremeses, loas, bailes y mojigangas desde fines del siglo SVI a mediados del XVIII*, vol. 2, edited by Emilio Cortarelo y Morí, 562–66. Madrid: Nueva Biblioteca de Autores Españoles, 1911.

———. *Luis Quiñones de Benavente, Entremeses completos*. Vol. 1. Edited by Ignacio Arellano, J. M. Escudero, and

A. Madroñal. Madrid: Iberoamericana, 2001.

———. "El negrito hablador y sin color anda la niña." In *Colección de entremeses, loas, bailes y mojigangas desde fines del siglo SVI a mediados del XVIII*, vol. 2, edited by Emilio Cotarelo y Morí, 605–7. Madrid: Nueva Biblioteca de Autores Españoles, 1911.

Reinosa, Rodrigo de. *Antología de escritores artistas motañeses: Critical Edition by José María de Cossío*. Santander: Librería Moderna, 1950.

———. *Obra conocida de Rodrigo de Reinosa*. Edited by Laura Puerto Moro. San Millán de Cogolla: Cilengua, 2010.

Resende, Garcia de. *Cancioneiro Geral* (1516). *Chronica de el-Rei D. João II*. 3 vols. Coimbra: Imprensa da Universidade, 1798.

———. *Cancioneiro geral de Garcia de Resende*. Edited by A. J. Gonçalves Guimarãis. 5 vols. Coimbra: Imprensa da Universidade, 1909–17.

———. *Miscellanea* (1554). Edited by Mendes de Remedios. Coimbra: Imprensa da Universidade, 1917.

Rojas, Fernando de. *La Celestina*. Edited by Dorothy Severin. Madrid: Alianza, 1999.

Rueda, Lope de. *Las cuatro comedias*. Edited by Alfredo Hermenegildo. Madrid: Cátedra, 2001.

Sánchez de Badajoz, Diego. *Farsas*. Edited by José María Díez Borque. Madrid, Cátedra, 1978.

Sandoval, Alonso de. *Treatise on Slavery: Selections from "De Instauranda Aethiopum Salute."* Edited and translated, with an introduction, by Nicole von Germeten. Indianapolis, Ind.: Hackett, 2008.

Solís, Antonio de. *Entremés del niño cavallero*. In *Comedias de Don Antonio de Solís*. Madrid: Melchor Alvarez, 1681.

Suárez de Figueroa, Cristóbal. *Plaza universal de todas ciencias y artes* (1615). Edited by Enrique Suárez Figaredo. http://users.ipfw.edu/jehle/CERVANTE/othertxts/Suarez_Figaredo_PlazaUniversal.pdf.

Topsell, Edward. *The Historie of Four-Footed Beastes*. London, 1607.

Truth, Sojourner. *Narrative of Sojourner Truth: A Bondwoman of Olden Time*. Compiled by Olive Gilbert. New York: Arno, 1968 [1878].

Unamuno, Miguel de. *La raza vasca y el vascuence, en torno a la lengua española*. Madrid: Espasa-Calpe, 1968.

Valdés, Juan de. *Diálogo de la lengua*. Edited by Cristina Barbolani. Madrid: Cátedra, 1982.

Vega y Carpio, Lope Félix de. *Arte nuevo de hacer comedias*. Edited by Enrique García Santo-Tomás. Madrid: Cátedra, 2009.

———. *Obras*. Edited by Marcelino Menéndez y Pelayo. 15 vols. Madrid: Real Academia Española, 1894–1913.

———. *La victoria de la honra*. *Obras*, vol. 10. Edited by Marcelino Menéndez y Pelayo. Madrid: Real Academia Española, 1894–1913.

Vélez de Guevara, Luis. *El Diablo Cojuelo*. Edited by Enrique Rodríguez Cepeda. Madrid: Cátedra, 2007.

———. *Virtudes vencen señales*. Edited by M. G. Profeti. Pisa: Universitá di Pisa, Istituto di Leteratura Spagnola e Ispano-Americana, 1965.

Villamediana: Obras. Edited with introduction and notes by Juan Manuel Rozas. Madrid: Castalia, 1969.

Vives, Juan Luis. *Instrucción de la mujer cristiana*. Buenos Aires: Espasa-Calpe, 1940.

Whitney, Geoffrey. *A Choice of Emblems*. 1586.

Zanelli, Agostino. *Le schiave orientali a Firenze nei secoli XIV e XV*. Florence: Arnaldo Forni Editore, 1885.

Zayas y Sotomayor, María de. *Desengaños amorosos*. Edited by Alicia Yllera. Madrid: Cátedra, 2006.

———. *Novelas amorosas y ejemplares compuestas por Doña María de Zayas y Sotomayor*. Edited by Julián Olivares. Madrid: Cátedra, 2007.

Secondary Sources

Adams, Jenny. *Power Play: The Literature and Politics of Chess in the Late Middle Ages*. Philadelphia: University of Pennsylvania Press, 2006.

Agamben, Giorgio. *Infancy and History: On the Destruction of Experience*. London: Verso, 1993 [1978].

Aguilar, Ignacio, Luis Gómez Canseco, and Adrián J. Sáez, eds. *El teatro de Miguel de Cervantes*. Madrid: Visor, 2016.

Alexander, Catherine M. S., and Stanley Wells, eds. *Shakespeare and Race*. Cambridge: Cambridge University Press, 2000.

Althusser, Louis. *On Ideology*. London: Verso, 2008.

Althusser, Louis, and Étienne Balibar. *Reading Capital*. Translated by Ben Brewster. London: Verso, 2009.

Amelang, James S. *Parallel Histories: Muslims and Jews in Inquisitorial Spain*. Baton Rouge: Louisiana State University Press, 2013.

Anderson Imbert, Enrique. *Historia de la literatura hispanoamericana*, vol. 1, *La colonia: Cien años de República*. Mexico City: Fondo de Cultura Económica, 1951.

Appiah, Kwame Anthony. *In My Father's House: Africa in the Philosophy of Culture*. Oxford: Oxford University Press, 1992.

Apter, Emily. *The Translation Zone: A New Comparative Literature*. Princeton: Princeton University Press, 2006.

Aranda Doncel, Juan. "Las danzas del Corpus en la diócesis cordobesa durante los siglos XVI y XVII." In *Festivas demostraciones: Estudios sobre las cofradías del Santísimo y la fiesta del Corpus Christi*, edited by Fermín Labarga-García, 321–49. Logroño: Instituto de Estudios Riojanos, 2010.

Arellano, Ignacio, and José Antonio Rodríguez Garrido, eds. *El teatro en la Hispanoamérica colonial*. Madrid: Iberoamericana, 2008.

Arellano, Ignacio, Christoph Strosetski, and Edwin Williamson, eds. *Autoridad y poder en el Siglo de Oro*. Madrid: Iberoamericana, 2009.

Arenal, Electa, and Amanda Powell. *The Answer/La respuesta*. New York: Feminist Press, 1994.

Armas, Frederick A. de. "The Play's the Thing": Clues to a Murder in Villamediana's *La Gloria de Niquea*." *Bulletin of Hispanic Studies* 78 (2001): 439–54.

Armillas-Tiseyra, Magalí. "On Language and Empire: The Prologue to *Grammar of the Castilian Language* (1492)." *PMLA* 131, no. 1 (January 2016): 197–208.

Asante, Molefi Kete. "African Elements in African-American English." In *Africanisms in American Culture*, edited by Joseph E. Holloway, 19–33. Bloomington: Indiana University Press, 1990.

Asensio, Eugenio. *Itinerario del entremés: Desde Lope de Rueda a Quiñones de Benavente*. Segunda edición revisada. Madrid: Gredos, 1971.

Back, Les, and John Solomos, eds. *Theories of Race and Racism: A Reader*. New York: Routledge, 2000.

Bacon, Wallace A., ed. *Essays on the Theory, Practice, and Criticism of Performance: Festschrift for Isabel Crouch*. Las Cruces: New Mexico State University Press, 1988.

Baker, Houston A., Jr. *Blues, Ideology, and Afro-American Literature: A Vernacular Theory*. Chicago: University of Chicago Press, 1984.

Bakhtin, M. M. *The Dialogic Imagination: Four Essays by M. M. Bakhtin*. Edited by Michael Holquist. Translated by Caryl Emerson and Michael Holquist. Austin: University of Texas Press, 1981.

———. *Rabelais and His World*. Translated by Hélène Iswolsky. Bloomington: Indiana University Press, 1984.

———. *Speech Genres and Other Late Essays*. Edited by Caryl Emerson and Michael Holquist. Translated by Vern W. McGee. Austin: University of Texas Press, 1986.

Baldwin, James. *Collected Essays*. New York: Library of America, 1998.

Balibar, Étienne, and Immanuel Wallerstein. *Race, Nation, Class: Ambiguous Identities*. Translation by Chris Turner. London: Verso, 1991.

Banerjee, Subhabrata Bobby. "Necrocapitalism." *Organization Studies* 29, no. 12 (2008): 1541–563.

Baranda Leturio, Consolación. "Las hablas de negros: Orígenes de un personaje literario." *Revista de filología española* 69 (1989): 311–33.

Barbeito, Isabel. *Cárceles de mujeres en el siglo XVII*. Madrid: Castalia, 2000.

Bardsley, Sandy. *Venomous Tongues: Speech and Gender in Late Medieval England*. Philadelphia: University of Pennsylvania Press, 2006.

Barletta, Vincent. *Covert Gestures: Crypto-Islamic Literature as Cultural Practice in Early Modern Spain*. Minneapolis: University of Minnesota Press, 2005.

Barnard, Mary E., and Frederick A. de Armas, eds. *Objects of Culture in the Literature of Imperial Spain*. Toronto: University of Toronto Press, 2013.

Barranco, García. "Correlaciones y divergencias en la representación de dos minorías: Negroafricanos y moriscos en la literatura del Siglo de Oro." In *La esclavitud negroafricana en la historia de España, siglos XVI y XVII*, edited by Aurelia Martín Casares and Margarita García Barranco, 151–71. Granada: Comares, 2010.

Barrena, Natalio. *Gramática annobonesa*. Madrid: Instituto de Estudios Africanos, 1957.

Barrett, Lindon. *Blackness and Value: Seeing Double*. Cambridge: Cambridge University Press, 1999.

Bartels, Emily C. "Making More of the Moor: Aaron, Othello, and Renaissance Refashionings of Race." *Shakespeare Quarterly* 41, no. 4 (1990): 433–54.

Bartens, Angela. *Die iberoromanische-basierten Kreolsprachen*. Frankfurt am Main: Peter Lang, 1995.

Bass, Laura. *The Drama of the Portrait: Theater and Visual Culture in Early Modern Spain*. University Park: Pennsylvania State University Press, 2008.

Bass, Laura, and Margaret R. Greer. *Approaches to Teaching Early Modern Spanish Drama*. New York: Modern Language Association of America, 2006.

Baugh, John. *Out of the Mouths of Slaves*. Foreword by William Labov. Austin: University of Texas Press, 1999.

Bauman, Richard. *Story, Performance, and Event: Contextual Studies of Oral Narrative*. Cambridge: Cambridge University Press, 1986.

Becco, Horacio Jorge. *Negros y morenos en el cancionero rioplatense*. Buenos Aires: Sociedad Argentina de Americanistas, n.d.

Beidler, Philip, and Gary Taylor, eds. *Writing Race Across the Atlantic World: Medieval to Modern*. New York: Palgrave Macmillan, 2005.

bell hooks (Gloria Watkins). *Ain't I a Woman? Black Women and Feminism*. Boston: South End Press, 1981.

———. *Black Looks: Race and Representation*. Boston: South End Press, 1992.

———. *Talking Back: Thinking Feminist, Thinking Black*. Boston: South End Press, 1989.

Belo, André. "Language as a Second Skin: The Representation of Black Africans in Portuguese Theatre (Fifteenth to Early-Seventeenth Centuries)." *Renaissance and Reformation/Renaissance et Réforme* 36, no. 1 (Winter 2013): 3–29.

Bennett, Herman, L. *Africans in Colonial Mexico: Absolutism, Christianity, and Afro-Creole Consciousness, 1570–1640*. Bloomington: Indiana University Press, 2003.

———. *Colonial Blackness: A History of Afro-Mexico*. Bloomington: Indiana University Press, 2009.

———. "'Sons of Adam': Text, Context, and the Early Modern African Subject." *Representations* 92, no. 1 (Fall 2005): 16–41.

Berco, Cristian. "Textiles as Social Texts: Syphilis, Material Culture and Gender in Golden Age Spain." *Journal of Social History* 44, no. 3 (Spring 2011): 785–810.

Beusterien, John. *Canines in Cervantes and Velázquez: An Animal Studies Reading of Early Modern Spain*. Burlington, Vt.: Routledge, 2013.

———. *An Eye on Race: Perspectives from Theater in Imperial Spain*. Lewisburg: Bucknell University Press, 2006.

———. "Talking Black in Spanish: An Unfinished Black Spanish Glossary." *Bulletin of the Comediantes* 51, nos. 1–2 (1999): 83–104.

Beverley, John R. "On the Concept of the Spanish Literary Baroque." In *Culture and Control in Counter-Reformation Spain*, edited by Anne J. Cruz and Mary Elizabeth Perry, 216–30. Minneapolis: University of Minnesota Press, 1992.

Bhabha, Homi K. *The Location of Culture*. London: Routledge, 1994.

Biddle-Perry, Geraldine, and Sarah Cheang, eds. *Hair: Styling, Culture and Fashion*. Oxford: Berg, 2008.

Blackmore, Josiah. "Imagining the Moor in Medieval Portugal." *Diacritics* 36, nos. 3–4 (Fall–Winter 2006): 27–43.

———. *Moorings: Portuguese Expansion and the Writing of Africa*. Minneapolis: University of Minnesota Press, 2008.

Blackmore, Josiah, and Gregory S. Hutcheson, eds. *Queer Iberia: Sexualities, Cultures, and Crossings from the Middle Ages to the Renaissance*. Durham: Duke University Press, 1999.

Bloch, R. Howard. *Medieval Misogyny and the Invention of Western Romantic Love*. Chicago: University of Chicago Press, 1991.

Boehrer, Bruce, ed. *A Cultural History of Animals in the Renaissance*. Oxford: Berg, 2011.

———. *Parrot Culture: Our 2500-Year-Long Fascination with the World's Most Talkative Bird*. Philadelphia: University of Pennsylvania Press, 2004.

Bonilla-Silva, Eduardo, and David Dietrich. "The Sweet Enchantment of Color-Blind Racism in Obamerica." *Annals of the American Academy of Political and Social Science* 634, no. 190 (2011): 190–206.

Boose, Lynda. "'The Getting of a Lawful Race': Racial Discourse in Early Modern England and the Unrepresentable Black Woman." In *Women, 'Race,' and Writing in the Early Modern Period*, edited by Margo Hendricks and Patricia Parker, 35–54. London: Routledge, 1994.

Borrego Gutiérrez, Esther. "Libros de caballería y estas cortesanas para el recién coronado Felipe IV." In *Dramaturgia festiva y cultura nobiliaria en el Siglo de Oro*, edited by Bernardo García and María Luisa Lobato, 347–84. Madrid: Iberoamericana, 2007.

Bourdieu, Pierre. *Language and Symbolic Power*. Edited and with an introduction by John B. Thompson. Translated by Gino Raymond and Matthew Adamson. Cambridge: Harvard University Press, 1991.

Branche, Jerome C. *Colonialism and Race in Luso-Hispanic Literature*. Columbia: University of Missouri Press, 2006.

Braude, Benjamin. "The Sons of Noah and the Construction of Ethnic and Geographical Identities in the Medieval and Early Modern Periods." *William and Mary Quarterly* 54, no. 1 (1997): 103–42.

Braun, Harald E., and Jesús Pérez-Magallón, eds. *The Transatlantic Hispanic Baroque: Complex Identities in the Atlantic World*. London: Routledge, 2014.

Bravo-Villasante, Carmen, ed. *Villancicos del siglo XVII y XVIII*. Madrid: Editorial Magisterio Español, 1978.

Bristol, Joan Cameron. *Christians, Blasphemers, and Witches: Afro-Mexican Ritual Practice in the Seventeenth Century*. Albuquerque: University of New Mexico Press, 2007.

Brittan, Arthur, and Mary Maynard, eds. *Sexism, Racism, and Oppression*. Oxford: Blackwell, 1984.

Britton, Dennis Austin. *Becoming Christian: Race, Reformation, and Early Modern English Romance*. New York: Fordham University Press, 2014.

Brooks, Daphne A. "Afro-Sonic Feminist Praxis: Nine Simone and Adrienne Kennedy in High Fidelity." In DeFrantz and Gonzalez, *Black Performance Theory*, 204–22. Durham: Duke University Press, 2014.

———. "'All That You Can't Leave Behind': Black Female Soul Singing and the Politics of Surrogation in the Age of Catastrophe." *Meridians: Feminisms, Race, Transnationalism* 8, no. 1 (2008): 180–204.

———. *Bodies in Dissent: Spectacular Performances of Race and Freedom, 1850–1910*. Durham: Duke University Press, 2006.

Brooks, John. "Slavery and the Slave in the Works of Lope de Vega." *Romantic Review* 19, no. 3 (1928): 232–43.

Brooks, Kinitra D. *Searching for Sycorax: Black Women's Hauntings of Contemporary Horror*. New Brunswick: Rutgers University Press, 2017.

Bruzzi, Stella, and Pamela Church Gibson, eds. *Fashion Cultures Revisited: Theories, Explorations and Analysis*. London: Routledge, 2013.

Bryant, Sherwin K., Rachel Sarah O'Toole, and Ben Vinson III, eds. *Africans to Spanish America: Expanding the Diaspora*. Urbana: University of Illinois Press, 2012.

Budasz, Rogério. "Black Guitar-Players and Early African-Iberian Music in Portugal and Brazil." *Early Music* 35, no. 1 (February 2007): 3–21.

Buezo, Catalina. *Prácticas festivas en el teatro breve del Siglo XVII*. Kassel: Reichenberger, 2004.

Burke, Peter. *Popular Culture in Early Modern Europe*. Aldershot: Scolar Press, 1994.

Burshatin, Israel. "The Moor in the Text: Metaphor, Emblem, and Silence." *Critical Inquiry* 12, no. 1 (Fall 1985): 98–118.

———. "Playing the Moor: Parody and Performance in Lope de Vega's *El primer Fajardo*." *PMLA* 107, no. 3 (May 1992): 566–81.

Butler, Judith. *Bodies That Matter: On the Discursive Limits of "Sex."* New York: Routledge, 1993.

———. *Gender Trouble: Feminism and the Subversion of Identity*. New York: Routledge, 1999.

Caballero Bonald, José Manuel. *Sevilla en tiempos de Cervantes*. Barcelona: Planeta, 1991.

Cabrales Arteaga, José María. *La poesía de Rodrigo de Reinosa*. Santander: Institución Cultural de Cantabria, 1980.

Cabré, Montserrat. "Women or Healers? Household Practices and the Categories of Health Care in Late Medieval Iberia." *Bulletin of the History of Medicine* 82, no. 1 (2008): 18–51.

Cadden, Joan. *Meanings of Sex Difference in the Middle Ages: Medicine, Science, and Culture*. Cambridge: Cambridge University Press, 1993.

Callaghan, Dympna. *Shakespeare Without Women: Representing Gender and Race on the Renaissance Stage*. London: Routledge, 2000.

Cañizares-Esguerra, Jorge, Matt Childs, and James Sidbury, eds. *The Urban Black Atlantic in the Age of the Slave Trade*. Philadelphia: University of Pennsylvania Press, 2013.

Caponi, Gena Dagel, ed. *Signifyin(g), Sanctifyin', and Slam Dunking: A Reader in African American Expressive Culture*. Amherst: University of Massachusetts Press, 1999.

Carby, Hazel. "Policing the Black Woman's Body in an Urban Context." *Critical Inquiry* 18, no. 4 (Summer 1992): 738–55.

Castañeda, Vicente, and Amalio Huarte, eds. *Nueva colección de pliegos sueltos*. Madrid: Tipografía de Archivos, 1933.

Castellano, Juan R. "El negro esclavo en el Entremés del Siglo de Oro." *Hispania* 44, no. 1 (March 1961): 55–65.

Castillejo, David. *Guía de ochocientas comedias del Siglo de Oro: Para el uso de actores y lectores*. Madrid: Ars Millenii, 2002.

Castillo, David R. "Horror (Vacui): The Baroque Condition." In *Hispanic*

Baroques: Reading Cultures in Context, edited by Nicholas Spadaccini and Luis Martín-Estudillo, 87–104. Nashville: Vanderbilt University Press, 2005.

Castro de Moux, María E. "Tipos de discurso teatral en el *Entremés de los negros* de Simón Aguado." *Bulletin of the Comediantes* 45, no. 1 (Summer 1993): 53–66.

Certeau, Michel de. *The Practice of Everyday Life*. Berkeley: University of California Press, 1984.

Chamorro Fernández, María Inés, ed. *Segunda comedia de Celestina, Feliciano de Silva*. Madrid: Editorial Ciencia Nueva, 1968.

Chasca, Edmund de. "The Phonology of the Speech of the Negroes in Early Spanish Drama." *Hispanic Review* 14, no. 4 (1946): 322–39.

Chaudenson, Robert. *Creolization of Language and Culture*. New York: Routledge, 2001.

Chaves, Fernández, and Pérez García. "Las redes de la trata negrera: Mercaderes portugueses y tráfico de esclavos en Sevilla (c. 1560–1580)." In *La esclavitud negroafricana en la historia de España, siglos XVI y XVII*, edited by Aurelia Martín Casares and Margarita García Barranco, 5–34. Granada: Comares, 2010.

Chen, Mel Y. *Animacies: Biopolitics, Racial Mattering, and Queer Affect*. Durham: Duke University Press, 2012.

Childs, Matt D. "Gendering the African Diaspora in the Iberian Atlantic: Religious Brotherhoods and the *Cabildos de Nación*." In *Women of the Iberian Atlantic*, edited by Sarah E. Owens and Jane E. Mangan, 230–62. Baton Rouge: Louisiana State University Press, 2012.

Chireau, Yvonne. *Black Magic: Religion and the African American Conjuring Tradition*. Berkeley: University of California Press, 2003.

Clamurro, William H. *Language and Ideology in the Prose of Quevedo*. Newark, Del.: Juan de la Cuesta, 1991.

Clements, J. Clancy. *The Linguistic Legacy of Spanish and Portuguese: Colonial Expansion and Language Change*. Cambridge: Cambridge University Press, 2009.

Close, Anthony. *Cervantes and the Comic Mind of His Age*. Cambridge: Cambridge University Press, 2000.

Cobb, Martha. "Afro-Arabs, Blackamoors, and Blacks: An Inquiry into Race Concepts through Spanish Literature." *Black World* (February 1972): 32–40.

Cockrell, Dale. *Demons of Disorder: Early Blackface Minstrels and Their World*. Cambridge: Cambridge University Press, 1997.

Colish, Marcia L. "Cosmetic Theology: The Transformation of a Stoic Theme." *Assays* 1 (1981): 3–14.

Collins, Patricia Hill. *Black Feminist Thought: Knowledge, Consciousness, and the Politics of Empowerment*. New York: Routledge, 1990.

Comes, Juan Bautista. *Obras en lengua romance II: Villancicos a la natividad*. Translated by José Climent. Valencia: Institución Alfonso el Magnánimo, 1977.

Conquerwood, Dwight. "Between Experience and Expression: The Performed Myth." In *Essays on the Theory, Practice, and Criticism of Performance: Festschrift for Isabel Crouch*, edited by Wallace A. Bacon, 33–57. Las Cruces: New Mexico State University Press, 1988.

Contag, Kimberly. *Mockery in Spanish Golden Age Literature: Analysis of Burlesque Representation*. New York: University Press of America, 1996.

Cortés Alonso, Vicenta. *La esclavitud en Valencia durante el reinado de los Reyes Católicos*. Valencia: Ayuntamiento de Valencia, 1964.

———. "La población negra de Palos de la Frontera, 1568–1579." *XXXVI Congreso Internacional de Americanistas España: Actas y Memorias* 3 (1966): 609–18.

Cortés Cortés, Fernando. *Esclavos en la Extremadura meridional del siglo XVII*. Badajoz: Excelentísima Diputación Provincial de Badajoz, 1987.

Cortés López, José Luis. *La esclavitud negra en la España peninsular del siglo XVI.* Salamanca: Ediciones Universidad de Salamanca, 1989.

———. *Los orígenes de la esclavitud negra en España.* Madrid: Ediciones Mundo Negro, 1986.

Cossío, José María de, ed. *Rodrigo de Reinosa.* Santander: Librería Moderna, 1950.

Crenshaw, Kimberlé, Neil Gotanda, Gary Peller, and Kendall Thomas, eds. *Critical Race Theory: The Key Writings That Formed the Movement.* New York: New Press, 1995.

Cruickshank, Don W. *Don Pedro Calderón.* Cambridge: Cambridge University Press, 2009.

Cruz, Anne J., ed. *Approaches to Teaching* Lazarillo de Tormes *and the Picaresque Tradition.* New York: Modern Language Association of America, 2008.

Cruz, Anne J., and Mary Elizabeth Perry, eds. *Culture and Control in Counter-Reformation Spain.* Hispanic Issues 7. Minneapolis: University of Minnesota Press, 1992.

Culler, Jonathan. *Theory of the Lyric.* Cambridge: Harvard University Press, 2015.

Curtius, Ernst Robert. *European Literature and Latin Middle Ages.* Translated by Willard R. Trask. Princeton: Princeton University Press, 1973.

Dagel Caponi, Gena, ed. *Signifyin(g), Sanctifyin', and Slam Dunking: A Reader in African American Expressive Culture.* Amherst: University of Massachusetts Press, 1999.

Damiani, Bruno M. "Un aspecto histórico de *La Lozana Andaluza.*" *Modern Language Notes* 87, no. 2 (March 1972): 178–92.

Davis, Angela. *Blues Legacies and Black Feminism: Gertrude "Ma" Rainey, Bessie Smith, and Billie Holiday.* New York: Vintage Books, 1998.

Davis, David Brion. "Constructing Race: A Reflection." *William and Mary Quarterly* 54, no. 1 (January 1997): 7–18.

DeCosta-Willis, Miriam, ed. *Blacks in Hispanic Literature: Critical Essays.* Port Washington, N.Y.: Kennikat Press, 1977.

DeFrantz, Thomas F., and Anita Gonzalez. "Introduction: From Negro Expression to Black Performance." In *Black Performance Theory*, edited by Thomas F. DeFrantz and Anita Gonzalez, 1–18. Durham: Duke University Press, 2014.

Deleuze, Gilles, and Félix Guattari. *Kafka: Toward a Minor Literature.* Translated by Dana Polan. Minneapolis: University of Minnesota Press, 1975.

Delgado, Richard, and Jean Stefancic, eds. *Critical Race Theory.* New York: New York University Press, 2012.

Derrida, Jacques. *Writing and Difference.* Translated with an introduction and notes by Alan Bass. Chicago: University of Chicago Press, 1978.

D'Heur, Jean Marie. "L'Art de trouver du chansonnier Colocci-Brancuti." *Arquivos do Centro Cultural Português* 9 (1975): 321–98.

Diadié, Ismael, and Manuel Pimentel, eds. *Tombuctú: Andalusíes en la ciudad perdida del Sáhara.* Córdoba: Almuzara, 2015.

Diago, Manuel V. "Lope de Rueda y los orígenes del teatro profesional." *Criticón* 50 (1990): 41–65.

Díez Borque, José María. *Literatura, política y fiesta en el Madrid de los Siglos de Oro.* Madrid: Visor, 2007.

———. *Teoría y realidad en el teatro español del Siglo XVI: La influencia italiana.* Rome: Publicaciones del Instituto Español de Cultura y de Literatura de Roma, 1981.

Dillard, J. L. *Black Names.* Paris: Mouton, 1976.

Dolan, Frances E. "Taking the Pencil Out of God's Hand: Art, Nature, and the Face-Painting Debate in Early Modern England." *PMLA* 108, no. 2 (March 1993): 224–39.

Domínguez, Frank A. "Body and Soul: Jorge Manrique's 'Coplas por la muerte de su padre,' 13: 145–56." *Hispania* 84, no. 1 (March 2001): 1–10.

Domínguez Búrdalo, José. "Del ser (o no ser) hispano: Unamuno frente a la negritude." *Modern Language Notes* 121 (2006): 322–42.

Domínguez Ortiz, Antonio. "La esclavitud en Castilla durante la Edad Moderna."

Estudios de historia social de España 2 (1952): 369–428.

———. *La esclavitud en Castilla en la Edad Moderna y otros estudios de marginados.* Granada: Comares, 2003 [1952].

———. *The Golden Age of Spain, 1516–1659.* Translated by James Casey. New York: Basic Books, 1971.

Donnell, Sidney. *Feminizing the Enemy: Imperial Spain, Transvestite Drama, and the Crisis of Masculinity.* Lewisburg: Bucknell University Press, 2003.

Donoghue, Eddie. *Black Breeding Machines: The Breeding of Negro Slaves in the Diaspora.* Bloomington: Author House, 2008.

Dopico Black, Georgina. "The Ban and the Bull: Cultural Studies, Animal Studies, and Spain." *Journal of Spanish Cultural Studies* 11, nos. 3–4 (2010): 235–49.

———. "Ghostly Remains: Valencia, 1609." *Arizona Journal of Hispanic Cultural Studies* 7, no. 1 (2003): 91–100.

———. "Lengua e Imperio: Sueños de la nación en los *Tesoros* de Covarrubias." In *Sebastián de Covarrubias: Suplemento al Tesoro de la Lengua Española Castellana,* edited by Georgina Dopico Black and Jacques Lezra, ccvx–cclxxxiv. Madrid: Ediciones Polifemo, 2001.

———. *Perfect Wives, Other Women: Adultery and Inquisition in Early Modern Spain.* Durham: Duke University Press, 2001.

Dopico Black, Georgina, and Francisco Layna Ranz, eds. *USA Cervantes: 39 Cervantistas en Estados Unidos.* Madrid: Ediciones Polifemo, 2009.

Dopico Black, Georgina, and Jacques Lezra, eds. *Sebastián de Covarrubias: Suplemento al Tesoro de la Lengua Española Castellana.* Madrid: Ediciones Polifemo, 2001.

Dow, George Francis. *Slaves, Ships and Slaving.* New York: Dover, 1970.

Drabinski, John E. "Vernaculars of Home." *Critical Philosophy of Race* 3, no. 2 (2015): 203–26.

Drew-Bear, Annette. *Painted Faces on the Renaissance Stage: The Moral Significance of Face-Painting Conventions.* Lewisburg: Bucknell University Press, 1994.

Dufour de Pradt, Dominique. *Mémoires historiques sur la revolution d'Espagne.* London: G. Cowie and Company, 1822.

Duranti, Alessandro, ed. *Linguistic Anthropology: A Reader.* Malden, Mass.: Blackwell, 2001.

Dyer, Richard. *White.* London: Routledge, 1997.

Earle, T. F., and Kate Lowe, eds. *Black Africans in Renaissance Europe.* Cambridge: Cambridge University Press, 2005.

Ebert, Christopher. "European Competition and Cooperation in Pre-modern Globalization: 'Portuguese' West and Central Africa, 1500–1600." *African Economic History* 36 (2008): 53–78.

Ébora, Tony. *Orígenes de la música cubana.* Madrid: Alianza, 1997.

Egginton, William. *The Theater of Truth: The Ideology of (Neo) Baroque Aesthetics.* Stanford: Stanford University Press, 2010.

Elliot, John H. *Imperial Spain, 1469–1716.* New York: Penguin, 2002.

Enenkel, Karl A. E., and Paul J. Smith, eds. *Early Modern Zoology: The Construction of Animals in Science, Literature and the Visual Arts.* Leiden: Brill, 2007.

Erickson, Peter. "Invisibility Speaks: Servants and Portraits in Early Modern Visual Culture." *Journal for Early Modern Culture Studies* 9, no. 1 (Spring/Summer 2009): 23–61.

———. "Picturing Race: Early Modern Constructions of Racial Identity." *Journal for Early Modern Culture Studies* 13, no. 1 (Winter 2013): 151–68.

Erickson, Peter, and Kim F. Hall, eds. "'A New Scholarly Song': Rereading Early Modern Race." *Shakespeare Quarterly* 67, no. 1 (Spring 2016): 1–13.

Erickson, Peter, and Clark Hulse, eds. *Early Modern Visual Culture: Representation, Race, and Empire in Renaissance England.* Philadelphia: University of Pennsylvania Press, 2000.

Fairchild Ruggles, D. "Mothers of a Hybrid Dynasty: Race, Genealogy, and Acculturation in al-Andalus." *Journal of Medieval and Early Modern Studies* 34, no. 1 (Winter 2004): 65–94.

Falola, Toyin, and Matt D. Childs, eds. *The Yoruba Diaspora in the Atlantic World.* Bloomington: Indiana University Press, 2004.

Fernández Martín, Luis. *Comediantes, esclavos y moriscos en Valladolid: Siglos XVI y XVII.* Valladolid: Universidad de Valladolid, 1988.

Fernández Nieto, Manuel. "El falso humanismo de Lope de Vega." In *La Universidad Complutense Cisneriana: Impulso filosófico, científico y literario. Siglos XVI y XVII,* edited by Luis Jiménez Moreno, 313–28. Madrid: Editorial Complutense, 1996.

Fernández Olmos, Margarite, and Lizabeth Paravisini-Gebert. *Creole Religions of the Caribbean: An Introduction from Vodou and Santería to Obeah and Espiritismo.* 2nd ed. New York: New York University Press, 2011.

Fernández Valladares, Mercedes. "Biblioiconografía y literatura popular impresa: La ilustración de los pliegos sueltos burgaleses (o de babuines y estampas celestinescas)." *eHumanista* 21 (2012): 87–131.

Ferrara, Mario. "Linguaggio di schiave del quattrocento." *Studi di filologia italiana* 8 (1950): 320–28.

Ferraz, Luis Ivens. *The Creole of São Tomé.* Johannesburg: Witwatersrand University Press, 1979.

———. "The Substrate of Annobonese." *African Studies* 43 (1984): 119–36.

Ferrer Valls, Teresa. *Nobleza y espectáculo teatral (1535–1622): Estudio y documentos.* València: Colleciò Oberta, 1993.

Ferro, Gaetano. "Per una geografia storica degli insediamenti liguri in Portogallo e nella penisola iberica meridionale, nell'età delle scoperte." *Mare Liberum* 2 (1991): 37–41.

Few, Martha, and Zeb Tortorici, eds. *Centering Animals in Latin American History.* Foreword by Erica Fudge. Durham: Duke University Press, 2013.

Fineman, Joel. *Shakespeare's Perjured Eye: The Invention of Poetic Subjectivity in Sonnets.* Berkeley: University of California Press, 1986.

Fleetwood, Nicole R. *Troubling Vision: Performance, Visuality, and Blackness.* Chicago: Chicago University Press, 2011.

Fletcher, Richard. *The Quest for El Cid.* Oxford: Oxford University Press, 1989.

Forbes, Curdella. "Shakespeare, Other Shakespeares and West Indian Popular Culture: A Reading of the Erotics of Errantry and Rebellion in *Troilus and Cressida.*" *Small Axe* 9 (2001): 44–69.

Forbes, Jack D. *Africans and Native Americans: The Language of Race and the Evolution of Red-Black Peoples, Second Edition.* Urbana: University of Illinois Press, 1993.

Ford, Richard. *Handbook for Travellers in Spain.* London: J. Murray, 1878.

Foucault, Michel. *The Archaeology of Knowledge and the Discourse of Language.* Translated by A. M. Sheridan Smith. New York: Pantheon Books, 1972.

———. *The History of Sexuality, Vol. 1: An Introduction.* Translated by Robert Hurley. New York: Vintage Books, 1978.

———. *Language, Madness, and Desire: On Literature.* Edited by Philippe Artières, Jean-François Bert, and Mathieu Potte-Bonneville. Translated by Robert Bononno. Minneapolis: University of Minnesota Press, 2015.

———. *Power/Knowledge: Selected Interviews and Other Writings, 1972–1977.* Edited by Colin Gordon. Translated by Colin Gordon, Leo Marshall, John Mepham, and Kater Soper. New York: Pantheon Books, 1972.

———. *"Society Must Be Defended": Lectures at the Collège de France, 1975–1976.* Edited by Mauro Bertani and Alessandro Fontana. Translated by David Macey. New York: Picador, 2003.

Fracchia, Carmen. "Esclavo negroafricano en las imágenes españolas de los Santos Cosme y Damián." In *La esclavitud negroafricana en la historia de España, siglos XVI y XVII,* edited by Aurelia Martín Casares and Margarita García

Barranco, 127–49. Granada: Comares, 2010.
Fra-Molinero, Baltasar. "The Condition of Black Women in Spain During the Renaissance." In *Black Women in America*, edited by Kim Marie Vaz, 159–78. London: Sage, 1995.
———. "La formación del estereotipo del negro en las letras hispanas: El caso de tres coplas en pliegos sueltos." *Romance Languages Annual* 3 (1991): 438–43.
———. *La imagen de los negros en el teatro del Siglo de Oro*. Madrid: Siglo Veintiuno, 1995.
———. "Juan Latino and His Racial Difference." In *Black Africans in Renaissance Europe*, edited by T. F. Earle and K. J. Lowe, 326–44. Cambridge: Cambridge University Press, 2005.
———. "El negro Zaide: Marginación social y textual en el *Lazarillo*." *Hispania* 76, no. 1 (March 1993): 20–29.
———. "The Play of Race and Gender in Vélez de Guevara's *Virtudes vencen señales*." *Bulletin of the Comediantes* 49, no. 2 (1997): 337–55.
———. "Poetic Invention Against the Black Body: 'Retrata un galán a una mulata, su dama' by Salvador Jacinto Polo de Medina." *Calíope: Journal of the Society for Renaissance and Baroque Hispanic Poetry* 1, nos. 1–2 (1995): 96–110.
Fra-Molinero, Baltasar, Charles Isidor Nero, and Jessica B. Harris. "When Food Tastes Cosmopolitan: The Creole Fusion of Diaspora Cuisine: An Interview with Jessica B. Harris." *Callaloo* 30, no. 1 (Winter 2007): 287–303.
Franco Silva, Alfonso. *La esclavitud en Andalucía, 1450–1550*. Granada: Comares, 1992.
———. *La esclavitud en Sevilla y su tierra a fines de la Edad Media*. Sevilla: Diputación Provincial de Sevilla, 1979.
———. *Los esclavos de Sevilla*. Sevilla: Diputación Provincial de Sevilla, 1980.
———. *Registro documental sobre la esclavitud sevillana (1453–1513)*. Sevilla: Universidad de Sevilla, 1979.

Frankenberg, Ruth. *White Women, Race Matters: The Social Construction of Whiteness*. Minneapolis: University of Minnesota Press, 1993.
Frenk, Margit, ed. *Lírica española de tipo popular*. Madrid: Cátedra, 2015.
———. "Sobre los cantares populares del Cancionero Musical de Palacio." *Anuario de Letras* 25 (1997): 227.
Friedman, Edward H. "Afterword: Redressing the Baroque." In *Hispanic Baroques: Reading Cultures in Context*, edited by Nicholas Spadaccini and Luis Martín-Estudillo, 283–306. Nashville: Vanderbilt University Press, 2005.
Fromont, Cécile. *The Art of Conversion: Christian Visual Culture in the Kingdom of Kongo*. Chapel Hill: University of North Carolina Press, 2014.
Fuchs, Barbara. *Exotic Nation: Maurophilia and the Construction of Early Modern Spain*. Philadelphia: University of Pennsylvania Press, 2009.
———. *Mimesis and Empire: The New World, Islam, and European Identities*. Cambridge: Cambridge University Press, 2001.
———. *The Poetics of Piracy: Emulating Spain in English Literature*. Philadelphia: University of Pennsylvania Press, 2013.
Fudge, Erica, ed. *Renaissance Beasts: Of Animals, Humans, and Other Wonderful Creatures*. Urbana: University of Illinois Press, 2014.
Fuente, Alejandro de la. *Havana and the Atlantic in the Sixteenth Century*. Chapel Hill: University of North Carolina Press, 2008.
Fuentes Guerra, Jesús, and Armin Schwegler. *Lenguas y ritos del Palo Monte Mayombe: Dioses y sus fuentes africanas*. Madrid: Iberoamericana, 2005.
Fryer, Peter. *Rhythms of Resistance: African Musical Heritage in Brazil*. Hanover, N.H.: Pluto Press, 2000.
García, Bernardo, and María Luisa Lobato, eds. *Dramaturgia festiva y cultura nobiliaria en el Siglo de Oro*. Madrid: Iberoamericana, 2007.

García-Arenal, Mercedes, and Gerard Wiegers. *Los moriscos: Expulsión y diáspora; Una perspectiva internacional*. Valencia: Universitat de València, 2013.

García Barrientos, José Luis. *Drama y tiempo: Dramtología I*. Madrid: Consejo Superior de Investigaciones Científicas, 1991.

García Dini, Encarnación. *Antología en defensa de la lengua y la literatura españolas (siglos XVI y XVII)*. Madrid: Cátedra, 2007.

García Ivars, Flora. *La represión en el tribunal de Granada 1550–1819*. Madrid: Akal, 1991.

García Santo-Tomás, Enrique. *Espacio urbano y creación literaria en el Madrid del Felipe IV*. Madrid: Iberoamericana, 2004.

———. *The Refracted Muse: Literature and Optics in Early Modern Spain*. Translated by Vincent Barletta. Chicago: University of Chicago Press, 2017.

García Valdés, Celsa Carmen. "'El regidor': Mojiganga inédita de Francisco Bernardo de Quirós." In *Teatro del Siglo de Oro: Homenaje a Alberto Navarro González*, edited by Alberto Navarro González, 221–39. Kassel: Reichenberger, 1990.

———. "Sociedad y personajes en los *Pasos* de Lope de Rueda." *AISO Actas* 6 (2002): 853–62.

Gates, Henry Louis, Jr., ed. *"Race," Writing, and Difference*. Chicago: University of Chicago Press, 1985.

———, ed. *Reading Black, Reading Feminist: A Critical Anthology*. New York: Meridian, 1990.

———. *The Signifying Monkey: A Theory of African-American Literary Criticism*. Oxford: Oxford University Press, 1988.

Gaylord, Mary Malcolm. "How to Do Things with *Polimetría*." In Bass and Greer, *Approaches to Teaching Early Modern Spanish Drama*, 76–84.

———. "The Making of Baroque Poetry." In *The Cambridge History of Spanish Literature*, edited by David T. Gies, 222–37. Cambridge: Cambridge University Press, 2004.

Gerli, E. Michael. *Celestina and the Ends of Desire*. Toronto: University of Toronto Press, 2011.

Gestoso y Pérez, José. *Curiosidades antiguas de Sevilla II*. Sevilla: El Correo de Andalucía, 1910.

———. *Noticias inéditas de impresores sevillanos*. Sevilla: Universidad de Sevilla, 1924.

Gikandi, Simon. *Slavery and the Culture of Taste*. Princeton: Princeton University Press, 2001.

Gil, Juan. "De Sevilla a Lisboa: Aspectos de una relación secular." *Portuguese Studies* 8 (1992): 40–56.

Gilbert, Donald. "Playing to the Masses: Economic Rationalism in Lope de Vega's *Arte nuevo de hacer comedias en este tiempo*." *Comitatus: A Journal of Medieval and Renaissance Studies* 31 (2000): 109–36.

Gilroy, Paul. *Against Race: Imagining Political Culture Beyond the Color Line*. Cambridge: Harvard University Press, 2002.

———. *The Black Atlantic: Modernity and Double Consciousness*. Cambridge: Harvard University Press, 1993.

Goldberg, K. Meira. *Sonidos Negros: On the Blackness of Flamenco*. New York: Oxford University Press, 2018.

Goldenberg, David M. *The Curse of Ham: Race and Slavery in Early Judaism, Christianity, and Islam*. Princeton: Princeton University Press, 2005.

Gomez, Michael. "African Identity and Slavery in the Americas." *Radical History Review* 75 (1999): 111–20.

González Echeverría, Roberto. *Cuban Fiestas*. New Haven: Yale University Press, 2010.

González Ollé, Fernando, and Vicente Tusón, eds. *Pasos*. Madrid: Cátedra, 2013.

Gracia Boix, Rafael. *Brujas y hechiceras de Andalucía*. Córdoba: Real Academia de Ciencias, Bellas Artes y Nobles Artes, 1991.

Grady, Kyle C. "Moors, Mulattos, and Post-Racial Problems: Rethinking Racialization in Early Modern England." PhD diss., University of Michigan, Ann Arbor, 2017.

Granda, Germán de. *Estudios lingüísticos hispánicos, afrohispánicos y criollos*. Madrid: Gredos, 1978.

———. "Posibles vías directas de introducción de africanismos en el 'habla de negro' literaria castellana." *BICC* 24 (1969): 459–69, 467.

Graullera Sanz, Vicente. *La esclavitud en Valencia en los siglos XVI y XVII*. Valencia: Instituto Valenciano de Estudios Históricos, 1978.

Gray White, Deborah. *Ar'n't I a Woman? Female Slaves in the Plantation South*. Rev. ed. New York: Norton, 1999.

Grazia, Margreta de, Maureen Quilligan, and Peter Stallybrass, eds. *Subject and Object in Renaissance Culture*. Cambridge: Cambridge University Press, 1996.

Green, Lisa J. *African American English: A Linguistic Introduction*. Cambridge: Cambridge University Press, 2002.

Greenblatt, Stephen. *Marvelous Possessions: The Wonder of the New World*. Chicago: University of Chicago Press, 1991.

———. *Renaissance Self-Fashioning: From More to Shakespeare*. Chicago: University of Chicago Press, 2005.

Greer, Margaret R. *María de Zayas Tells Baroque Tales of Love and the Cruelty of Men*. University Park: Pennsylvania State University Press, 2000.

Greer, Margaret R., Walter D. Mignolo, and Maureen Quilligan, eds. *Rereading the Black Legend: The Discourses of Religious and Racial Difference in the Renaissance Empires*. Chicago: University of Chicago Press, 2007.

Grier, Miles P. "Inkface: The Slave Stigma in England's Early Imperial Imagination." In *Scripturalizing the Human: The Written as the Political*, edited by Vincent Wimbush, 193–220. New York: Routledge, 2015.

———. "The Only Black Man at the Party: Joni Mitchell Enters the Rock Canon." *Genders Journal* 56 (Fall 2012): n.p.

———. "Staging the Cherokee *Othello*: An Imperial Economy of Indian Watching." *William and Mary Quarterly* 73, no. 1 (January 2016): 73–106.

Griffin, Clive. *The Crombergers of Seville: The History of a Printing and Merchant Dynasty*. Oxford: Clarendon Press, 1988.

Gubar, Susan. *Racechanges: White Skin, Black Face in American Culture*. Oxford: Oxford University Press, 1997.

Gumbs, Alexis Pauline. *Spill: Scenes of Black Feminist Fugitivity*. Durham: Duke University Press, 2016.

Günther, Wielfried. *Das portugiesische Kreloisch der Jlha do Príncipe*. Marburg an der Lahn: Selbatverlag, 1973.

Gutiérrez Arranz, L. "La mitología en *La Gloria de Niquea*, del conde de Villamediana." In *Paraninfos, segundones y epígonos de la comedia del Siglo de Oro*, edited by Ignacio Arellano Ayuso, 97–103. Madrid: Anthropos, 2004.

Hall, Gwendolyn Midlo, *Slavery and African Ethnicities in the Americas: Restoring the Links*. Chapel Hill: University of North Carolina Press, 2005.

Hall, Kim F. "Beauty and the Beast of Whiteness: Teaching Race and Gender." *Shakespeare Quarterly* 47, no. 4 (Winter 1996): 461–75.

———. "Object into Object? Some Thoughts on the Presence of Black Women in Early Modern Culture." In *Early Modern Visual Culture: Representation, Race, and Empire in Renaissance England*, edited by Peter Erickson and Clark Hulse, 346–79. Philadelphia: University of Pennsylvania Press, 2000.

———. *Things of Darkness: Economies of Race and Gender in Early Modern England*. Ithaca: Cornell University Press, 1995.

Haney, Ian. "Is the Post in Post-Racial the Blind in Colorblind?" *Cardozo Law Review* 32, no. 3 (January 1, 2011): 807–31.

Hartikeinen, Elina. "African Accents, Speaking Child Spirits and the Brazilian Popular Imaginary: Permutations of Africanness in Candomblé." In *Africas of the Americas: Beyond the Search for*

Origins in the Study of Afro-Atlantic Religions, edited by Stephan Palmié, 323–50. Leiden: Brill, 2008.

Hartman, Saidiya V. Scenes of Subjection: Terror, Slavery, and Self-Making in Nineteenth-Century America. New York: Oxford University Press, 1997.

Hazañas y la Rúa, Joaquín. La imprenta en Sevilla. Sevilla: Universidad de Sevilla, 1945.

Hendricks, Margo, and Patricia Parker, eds. Women, "Race," and Writing in the Early Modern Period. London: Routledge, 1994.

Heng, Geraldine. The Invention of Race in the European Middle Ages. Cambridge: Cambridge University Press, 2018.

———. "The Invention of Race in the European Middle Ages I & II: Race Studies, Modernity, and the Middle Ages." Literature Compass 8, no. 5 (2011): 258–93.

Herbert, Robert. Language Universals, Markedness Theory, and Natural Phonetic Processes. Berlin: de Gruyter, 1986.

Hernández Araico, Susana. "Las inverosimilitudes imaginativa de Calderón y su función dramática teatral: El castillo de Lindabridis." Teatro de Palabras: Revista sobre teatro áureo 1 (2007): 67–77.

Herrera García, Miguel. Ideas de los españoles del siglo XVII. Madrid: Gredos, 1966.

Higginbotham, Evelyn Brooks. "African-American Women's History and the Metalanguage of Race." Signs 17, no. 2 (Winter 1992): 251–74.

Hill, Jane H. "Language, Race, and White Public Space." In Duranti, Linguistic Anthropology, 450–64.

Hitti, Philip. History of the Arabs. 8th ed. New York: St. Martin's Press, 1963.

Holloway, Joseph E., ed. Africanisms in American Culture. Bloomington: Indiana University Press, 1991.

Holmes, David G. Revisiting Racialized Voice: African American Ethos in Language and Literature. Carbondale: Southern Illinois University Press, 2004.

Hornback, Robert. "Emblems of Folly in the First Othello: Renaissance Blackface, Moor's Coast, and 'Muckender.'" Comparative Drama 35, no. 1 (Spring 2001): 69–99.

———. "'Extravagant and Wheeling Strangers': Early Blackface Dancing Fools, Racial Impersonation, and the Limits of Identification." Exemplaria 20, no. 2 (July 2008): 197–222.

———. "The Folly of Racism: Enslaving Blackface and the 'Natural' Fool Tradition." Medieval and Renaissance Drama in England 20 (2007): 46–84.

Howe, Elizabeth Teresa. "The Feminine Mistake: Nature, Illusion, and Cosmetics in the Siglo de Oro." Hispania 68, no. 3 (September 1985): 443–51.

Hutchinson, Stephen. Cervantine Journeys. Madison: University of Wisconsin Press, 1992.

Ireton, Chloe. "'They Are Blacks of the Caste of Black Christians': Old Christian Black Blood in the Sixteenth- and Early Seventeenth-Century Iberian Atlantic." Hispanic American Historical Review 97, no. 4 (November 2017): 579–612.

Irigoyen-Garcia, Javier. Moors Dressed as Moors: Clothing, Social Distinction and Ethnicity in Early Modern Iberia. Toronto: University of Toronto Press, 2017.

———. "'La música ha sido hereje': Pastoral Performance, Moorishness, and Cultural Hybridity in Los baños de Argel." Bulletin of Comediantes 62, no. 2 (2010): 45–62.

———. The Spanish Arcadia: Sheep Herding, Pastoral Discourse, and Ethnicity in Early Modern Spain. Toronto: University of Toronto Press, 2013.

James, Joy, and T. Denean Sharpley-Whiting, eds. The Black Feminist Reader. Oxford: Blackwell, 2000.

Jeffries, Michael P. Thug Life: Race, Gender, and the Meaning of Hip-Hop. Chicago: University of Chicago Press, 2011.

Jiménez Belmonte, Javier. Las obras en verso del Príncipe de Esquilache: Amateurismo y conciencia literaria. London: Támesis, 2007.

Johnson, Lemuel. *The Devil, the Gargoyle, and the Buffoon: The Negro as Metaphor in Western Literature*. Port Washington, N.Y.: Kennikat Press, 1971.

Jones, Douglas A., Jr. "Black Politics but Not Black People: Rethinking the Social and 'Racial' History of Early Minstrelsy." *The Drama Review* 57, no. 2 (Summer 2013): 21–37.

Jones, Nicholas R. "Cosmetic Ontologies, Cosmetic Subversions: Articulating Black Beauty and Humanity in Luis de Góngora's 'En la fiesta del Santísimo Sacramento.'" *Journal for Early Modern Cultural Studies* 15, no. 1 (Winter 2015): 26–54.

———. "Nuptials Gone Awry, Empire in Decay: Crisis, *Lo Cursi*, and the Rhetorical Inventory of Blackness in Quevedo's 'Boda de negros.'" *Arizona Journal of Hispanic Cultural Studies* 20 (2016): 29–47.

Jones, R. O., ed. *Studies in Spanish Literature of the Golden Age*. London: Támesis, 1973.

Jones, Steve, ed. *Antonio Gramsci*. London: Routledge, 2007.

Johnson, E. Patrick. *Appropriating Blackness: Performance and the Politics of Authenticity*. Durham: Duke University Press, 2003.

———. *No Tea, No Shade: New Writings in Black Queer Studies*. Durham: Duke University Press, 2016.

Jordan, Winthrop D. *White over Black: American Attitudes Toward the Negro, 1550–1812*. Chapel Hill: University of North Carolina Press, 1968.

Kallendorf, Hilaire, ed. *A Companion to Early Modern Hispanic Theater*. Leiden: Brill, 2014.

Kaminsky, Amy. "Gender, Race, *Raza*." *Feminist Studies* 20, no. 1 (Spring 1994): 7–31.

Kaplan, Gregory B. "Rodrigo de Reinosa's Sympathetic Attitude Toward African Slaves." *Ojáncano* 41 (October 2012): 61–88.

Karim-Cooper, Farah. *Cosmetics in Shakespearean and Renaissance Drama*. Edinburgh: Edinburgh University Press, 2006.

Katzew, Ilona. *Casta Painting: Images of Race in Eighteenth-Century Mexico*. New Haven: Yale University Press, 2005.

Katzew, Ilona, and Susan Deans-Smith, eds. *Race and Classification: The Case of Mexican America*. Stanford: Stanford University Press, 2009.

Kelley, Mary Jane. "Reading Góngora's *Habla de negros* in a Literary Attack Poem." *Calíope: Journal of the Society for Renaissance and Baroque Hispanic Poetry* 23, no. 1 (Spring 2018): 115–34.

King de Ramírez, Carmen. "(Mis)representations of Female Slaves in Golden Age Spain: Mariana de Carvajal's Recovery of the Black Female Slave in *La industria vence desdenes*." *Hispania* 98, no. 1 (March 2015): 110–22.

Kubik, Gerhard. "O intercâmbio cultural entre Angola e Portugal no domínio da música desde o século XVI." In *Portugal e o encontro de culturas na música*, 381–405. Lisbon, 1987.

Labov, William. *Language in the Inner City: Studies in the Black English Vernacular*. Philadelphia: University of Pennsylvania Press, 1972.

Labrador Herraiz, José, and Ralph Di Franco. "Villancicos de negros y otros testimonios al caso en manuscritos del Siglo de Oro." In *De la canción de amor medieval a las soleares*, edited by P. M. Piñero Ramírez, 163–87. Sevilla: Fundación Machado y Universidad de Sevilla, 2004.

Lane, Jill. "Becoming Chocolate: A Tale of Racial Translation." *Theatre Journal* 59, no. 3 (2007): 382–87.

———. *Blackface Cuba, 1840–1895*. Philadelphia: University of Pennsylvania Press, 2005.

Lanehart, Sonja L., ed. *Sociocultural and Historical Contexts of African American English*. Amsterdam: John Benjamins, 2001.

Larrea, Arcadio. "Sobre el posible origen americano de algunos cantes y bailes flamencos." In *Actas de la Reunión*

Internacional de estudios sobre las relaciones entre la música andaluza, la hispanoamerica y el flamenco, 83–91. Madrid: n.p., 1972.

Lawner, Lynne. *Harlequin on the Moon: Commedia dell'Arte and the Visual Arts.* New York: Harry N. Abrams, 1998.

Lawrance, Jeremy. "Black Africans in Renaissance Spanish Literature." In *Black Africans in Renaissance Europe,* edited by T. F. Earle and K. J. P. Lowe, 70–93. Cambridge: Cambridge University Press, 2005.

Lea, K. M. *Italian Popular Comedy: A Study in Commedia dell'Arte, 1560–1620.* 2 vols. Oxford: Clarendon Press, 1934.

Legarda, P. Anselmo de. *Lo "vizcaíno" en la literatura castellana.* San Sebastián: Biblioteca Vascongada de los Amigos del País, 1953.

Leibsohn, Dana, and Jeanette Favrot Peterson, eds. *Seeing Across Cultures in the Early Modern World.* Burlington, Vt.: Routledge, 2012.

Leong, Elaine. "Collecting Knowledge for the Family: Recipes, Gender and Practical Knowledge in the Early Modern English Household." *Centaurus* 55 (2013): 81–103.

Levy, Evonne, and Kenneth Mills, eds. *Lexikon of the Hispanic Baroque: Transatlantic Exchange and Transformation.* Austin: University of Texas Press, 2013.

Lewis, Bernard. *Race and Slavery in the Middle East: An Historical Enquiry.* Oxford: Oxford University Press, 1990.

Lewis, Laura A. *Chocolate and Corn Flour: History, Race, and Place in the Making of "Black" Mexico.* Durham: Duke University Press, 2012.

Lichtenstein, Jacqueline. "Making Up Representation: The Risks of Femininity." "Misogyny, Misandry, and Misanthropy." Special issue of *Representations* 20 (Fall 1987): 77–87.

Lihani, John. *El lenguaje de Lucas Fernández: Estudio del dialecto sayagués.* Bogotá: Instituto Caro y Cuervo, 1973.

Lionnet, Françoise, and Shu-mei Shih, eds. *The Creolization of Theory.* Durham: Duke University Press, 2011.

———, eds. *Minor Transnationalism.* Durham: Duke University Press, 2005.

Lipski, John M. "El español *bozal.*" In *América negra: Panorámica actual de los estudios lingüísticos sobre variedades criollas y afrohispanas,* edited by Matthias Perl and Armin Schwegler, 293–327. Frankfurt: Vervuert, 1998.

———. *A History of Afro-Hispanic Language: Five Centuries, Five Continents.* Cambridge: Cambridge University Press, 2005.

———. *Latin American Spanish.* New York: Longman Group, 1994.

Little, Arthur L., Jr. "Re-historicizing Race, White Melancholia, and the Shakespearean Property." *Shakespeare Quarterly* 67, no. 1 (Spring 2016): 84–103.

Liu, Benjamin M. "'Affined to Love the Moor.'" In *Queer Iberia: Sexualities, Cultures, and Crossings from the Middle Ages to the Renaissance,* edited by Josiah Blackmore and Gregory S. Hutcheson, 48–72. Durham: Duke University Press, 1999.

———. *Medieval Joke Poetry: The Cantigas d'Escarnho e de Mal Dizer.* Cambridge: Harvard University Press, 2004.

Loomba, Ania. *Shakespeare, Race, and Colonialism.* Oxford: Oxford University Press, 2002.

Lorde, Audre. "A Burst of Light: Living with Cancer." In *A Burst of Light: Essays by Audre Lorde,* 49–134. Ithaca, N.Y.: Firebrand, 1988.

———. "Transformation of Silence into Language." In *Sister Outsider: Essays and Speeches by Audre Lorde,* 40–44. Freedom, Calif.: Crossing Press, 1984.

Lott, Eric. *Love and Theft: Blackface Minstrelsy and the American Working Class.* Oxford: Oxford University Press, 1993.

Lovejoy, Paul E. "The African Diaspora: Revisionist Interpretations of Ethnicity, Culture and Religion Under Slavery." *Studies in the World History of Slavery, Abolition and Emancipation* 2 (1997): 1–23.

———. "The Context of Enslavement in West Africa." In *Slaves, Subjects, and Subversives: Blacks in Colonial Latin America,* edited by Jane Landers, 9–38.

Albuquerque: University of New Mexico Press, 2006.

———. *Transformations in Slavery: A History of Slavery in Africa*. 3rd ed. Cambridge: Cambridge University Press, 2012.

Low, Jennifer A., and Nova Myhill. "Introduction: Audience and Audiences." In *Imagining the Audience in Early Modern Drama, 1558–1642*, edited by Jennifer A. Low and Nova Myhill, 1–17. New York: Palgrave Macmillan, 2011.

MacDonald, Joyce Green. *Women and Race in Early Modern Texts*. Cambridge: Cambridge University Press, 2002.

Mahar, William J. "Black English in Early Blackface Minstrelsy: A New Interpretation of the Sources of Minstrel Show Dialect." *American Quarterly* 37, no. 2 (Summer 1985): 260–85.

Makoni, Sinfree, Geneva Smitherman, Arnetha Ball, and Arthur K. Spears, eds. *Black Linguistics: Language, Society, and Politics in Africa and the Americas*. London: Routledge, 2003.

Maldonado-Torres, Nelson. "AAR Centennial Roundtable: Religion, Conquest, and Race in the Foundations of the Modern/Colonial World." *Journal of the American Academy of Religion* 82, no. 3 (September 2014): 636–65.

Manning, Susan, and Andrew Taylor, eds. *Transatlantic Literary Studies: A Reader*. Baltimore: Johns Hopkins University Press, 2007.

Maravall, José Antonio. *Culture of the Baroque: Analysis of a Historical Structure*. Translated by Terry Cochran. Minneapolis: University of Minnesota Press, 1986.

Mariscal, George. "The Role of Spain in Contemporary Race Theory." *Arizona Journal of Hispanic Cultural Studies* 2 (1998): 7–22.

Márquez-Villanueva, Francisco. "*La Celestina* as Hispano-Semitic Anthropology." *Revue de littérature comparée* 61 (1987): 425–53.

Martín, Adrienne L. *An Erotic Philology of Golden Age Spain*. Nashville: Vanderbilt University Press, 2008.

Martin, Kameelah L. *Conjuring Moments in African American Literature: Women, Spirit Work, and Other Such Hoodoo*. New York: Palgrave Macmillan, 2012.

Martín Casares, Aurelia. "Comba y Dominga: La imagen sexualizada de las negroafricanas en la literatura del cordel de la España Moderna." In *La esclavitud negroafricana en la historia de España, siglos XVI y XVII*, edited by Aurelia Martín Casares and Margarita García Barranco, 173–88. Granada: Comares, 2010.

———. *La esclavitud en la Granada del siglo XVI: Género, raza y religión*. Granada: Universidad de Granada, 2000.

———. "La hechicería en la Andalucía Moderna: ¿Una forma de poder de las mujeres." In *Pauta históricas de sociabilidad feminina: Rituales y modelos de representación*, edited by Mary Nash and María José de la Pascua, 101–12. Cádiz: Asociación Española de Investigación de Historia de las mujeres, 1999.

———. *Juan Latino: Talento y destino*. Granada: Universidad de Granada, 2016.

Martín Casares, Aurelia, and Margarita García Barranco, eds. *La esclavitud negroafricana en la historia de España, siglos XVI y XVII*. Granada: Comares, 2010.

———. "The Musical Legacy of Black Africans in Spain: A Review of Our Sources." *Anthropological Notebooks* 15, no. 2 (2009): 51–60.

———, eds. "Popular Depictions of Black African Weddings in Early Modern Spain." *Renaissance and Reformation/Renaissance et Réforme* 31, no. 2 (2008): 107–21.

Martín Casares, Aurelia, and Rocío Periáñez Gómez, eds. *Mujeres esclavas y abolicionistas en la España de los siglos XVI al XIX*. Madrid: Iberoamericana, 2014.

Martínez, José María. "Las farsas profanas de Diego Sánchez de Badajoz." *Criticón* 66–67 (1996): 225–42.

Martínez-Góngora, Mar. "La invención de la 'blancura': El estereotipo y la mímica en 'Boda de negros' de Francisco de Quevedo." *Modern Language Notes* 120 (2005): 262–86.

Martínez-San Miguel, Yolanda. *From Lack to Excess: "Minor" Readings of Latin American Colonial Discourse*. Lewisburg: Bucknell University Press, 2008.

Mason Vaughan, Virginia. *Performing Blackness on English Stages, 1500–1800*. Cambridge: Cambridge University Press, 2005.

Mbembe, Achille. "Necropolitics." Translated by Libby Meintjes. *Public Culture* 15, no. 1 (2003): 11–40.

McCaw, R. John. "The Liberated Word: Africans and Carnivalesque Imagery in Francisco de Quevedo's 'Boda de negros.'" *Afro-Hispanic Review* 18, no. 2 (1999): 1–14.

McKendrick, Melveena. *Theatre in Spain, 1490–1700*. Cambridge: Cambridge University Press, 1989.

McKnight, Kathryn Joy, and Leo J. Garofalo, eds. *Afro-Latino Voices: Narratives from the Early Modern Ibero-Atlantic World, 1550–1812*. Indianapolis, Ind.: Hackett, 2009.

McWorter, John. *The Missing Spanish Creoles: Recovering the Birth of Plantation Contact Languages*. Berkeley: University of California Press, 2000.

Méndez Rodríguez, Luis. "Visiones iconográficas de la esclavitud en España." In *La esclavitud negroafricana en la historia de España, siglos XVI y XVII*, edited by Aurelia Martín Casares and Margarita García Barranco, 95–126. Granada: Comares, 2010.

Merrim, Stephanie. *The Spectacular City, Mexico, and Colonial Hispanic Literary Culture*. Austin: University of Texas Press, 2010.

Mignolo, Walter D. *The Darker Side of the Renaissance: Literacy, Territoriality, and Colonization*. Ann Arbor: University of Michigan Press, 1994.

Miguel Magro, Tania de. "Los bailes históricos de Agustín Moreto: La intertextualidad como máscara." *Hipertexto* 14 (2011): 126–38.

Miller, Monica. *Slaves to Fashion: Black Dandyism and the Styling of Black Diasporic Identity*. Durham: Duke University Press, 2009.

Mills, Charles W. *Blackness Visible: Essays on Philosophy and Race*. Ithaca: Cornell University Press, 1998.

———. *The Racial Contract*. Ithaca: Cornell University Press, 1997.

Miñana, Rogelio. "Los márgenes del poder, el poder de los márgenes: El marco narrativo en *La Gloria de Niquea* de Villamediana." *Bulletin of the Comediantes* 52, no. 1 (2000): 55–81.

Mira Caballos, Esteban. *Indios y mestizos americanos en la España del siglo XVI*. Prologue by Antonio Domínguez Ortiz. Madrid: Iberoamericana, 2000.

Mitchell-Kernan. Claudia. "Signifying, Loud-Talking and Marking," In *Signifyin(g), Sanctifyin', and Slam Dunkin: A Reader in African American Expressive Culture*, edited by Gena Dagel Caponi, 314–15. Amherst: University of Massachusetts Press, 1999.

Molineux, Catherine. *Faces of Perfect Ebony: Encountering Atlantic Slavery in Imperial Britain*. Cambridge: Harvard University Press, 2012.

Monahan, Michael J. *The Creolizing Subject: Race, Reason, and the Politics of Purity*. New York: Fordham University Press, 2011.

More, Anna. *Baroque Sovereignty: Carlos Sigüenza y Góngora and the Creole Archive of Colonial Mexico*. Philadelphia: University of Pennsylvania Press, 2013.

Moreno, Isidoro. *La antigua hermandad de "Los negros" de Sevilla: Etnicidad, poder y sociedad en 600 años de historia*. Sevilla: Universidad de Sevilla/Junta de Andalucía, 1997.

Morgan, Jennifer L. *Laboring Women: Reproduction and Gender in New World Slavery*. Philadelphia: University of Pennsylvania Press, 2004.

Morgan, Marcyliena. *Language, Discourse, and Power in African American Culture*. Cambridge: Cambridge University Press, 2002.

———. "'Nuthin' but a G Thang': Grammar and Language Ideology in Hip Hop Identity." In *Sociocultural and Historical Contexts of African American English*, edited by Sonja L. Lanehart, 187–209. Amsterdam: John Benjamins, 2001.

———. *The Real Hip Hop: Battling for Knowledge, Power, and Respect in the LA Underground*. Durham: Duke University Press, 2009.

Morínigo, Marcos A. *América en el teatro de Lope de Vega*. Buenos Aires: Revista de Filología Hispánica, 1946.

Morrison, Toni. *Playing in the Dark: Whiteness and the Literary Imagination*. New York: Vintage Books, 1992.

Moten, Fred. *In the Break: Aesthetics of the Black Radical Tradition*. Minneapolis: University of Minnesota Press, 2003.

Mourão, Manuela. "Whitewash: Nationhood, Empire, and the Formation of Portuguese Racial Identity." *Journal for Early Modern Cultural Studies* 11, no. 1 (Spring/Summer 2011): 90–124.

Mudimbe, V. Y. *The Invention of Africa: Gnosis, Philosophy, and the Order of Knowledge*. Bloomington: Indiana University Press, 1988.

Mujica, Barbara. "Golden Age/Early Modern Theater: Comedia Studies at the End of the Century." *Hispania* 82, no. 3 (September 1999): 397–407.

———. *Shakespeare and the Spanish Comedia: Translation, Interpretation, Performance*. Lewisburg: Bucknell University Press, 2013.

Mullen, Edward J. "Simón Aguado's *Entremés de los negros*: Text and Context." *Comparative Drama* 20, no. 3 (Fall 1986): 231–46.

Munro, Martin. *Different Drummers: Rhythm and Race in the Americas*. Berkeley: University of California Press, 2010.

Murray, Pauli. "The Liberation of Black Women." In *Voices of the New Feminism*, edited by Mary Lou Thompson, 87–102. Boston: Beacon, 1970.

Nadeau, Carolyn A. *Food Matters: Alonso Quijano's Diet and the Discourse of Food in Early Modern Spain*. Toronto: University of Toronto Press, 2016.

Nash, Elizabeth. *Seville, Córdoba, and Granada: A Cultural History*. Oxford: Oxford University Press, 2005.

Nash, Jennifer C. *The Black Body in Ecstasy: Reading Race, Reading Pornography*. Durham: Duke University Press, 2014.

Navarrete, Ignacio. *Orphans of Petrarch: Poetry and Theory in the Spanish Renaissance*. Berkeley: University of California Press, 1994.

Navarro García, José Luis. *Historia del baile flamenco*. Sevilla: Signatura Ediciones, 2010.

Navarro González, Alberto. *Teatro del Siglo de Oro: Homenaje a Alberto Navarro González*. Kassel: Reichenberger, 1990.

Navarro Tomás, Tomás. *Métrica española: Reseña histórica y descriptiva*. Syracuse: Syracuse University Press, 1956.

Nelson, Dana D. *The Word in Black and White: Reading "Race" in American Literature, 1638–1867*. Oxford: Oxford University Press, 1993.

Newman, Karen, and Jane Tylus, eds. *Early Modern Cultures of Translation*. Philadelphia: University of Pennsylvania Press, 2015.

Nichols, Tom, ed. *Others and Outcasts in Early Modern Europe: Picturing the Social Margins*. Aldershot: Ashgate, 2007.

Ocasio, Rafael. *Afro-Cuban Costumbrismo: From Plantations to the Slums*. Gainesville: University Press of Florida, 2012.

Omi, Michael, and Howard Winant, eds. *Racial Formation in the United States: From the 1960s to the 1980s*. New York: Routledge, 1989.

Orozco, Emilio. *Introducción a Góngora*. Barcelona: Editorial Crítica, 1984.

Orr, Bridget. *Empire on the English Stage, 1660–1714*. Cambridge: Cambridge University Press, 2001.

Owens, Sarah E., and Jane E. Mangan, eds. *Women of the Iberian Atlantic*. Baton Rouge: Louisiana State University Press, 2012.

Páez Granados, Octavio. "El villancico de negro y su pertinente abordaje sociológico y literario." *Romance Notes* 54, no. 2 (2014): 177–85.

Palmer, Colin. "Defining and Studying the Modern African Diaspora." *Perspectives* 36 (1998): I, 22–25.

Palmié, Stephan. "Creolization and Its Discontents." *Annual Review of Anthropology* 35 (2006): 433–56.

———. "Introduction: On Predications of Africanity." In *Africas of the Americas: Beyond the Search for Origins in the Study of Afro-Atlantic Religions*, edited by Stephan Palmié, 1–37. Leiden: Brill, 2008.

———. Panagia, Davide. *The Political Life of Sensation*. Durham: Duke University Press, 2009.

Parkvall, Mikael. *Out of Africa: African Influences in Atlantic Creoles*. London: Battlebridge, 2000.

Paz, Octavio. *Sor Juana Inés de la Cruz o las trampas de la fe*. 3rd ed. Mexico City: Fondo de Cultura Económica, 1983.

Peñafiel Ramón, Antonio. *Amos y esclavos en la Murcia del setecientos*. Murcia: Real Academia Alfonso X el Sabio, 1992.

Penas Ibáñez, María Azucena. "El habla vizcaína en el teatro de Lope de Vega." *Anuario del Seminario de Filología Vasca "Julio de Urquijo"* 27, no. 3 (1993): 815–20.

Penny, Ralph. *Variation and Change in Spanish*. Cambridge: Cambridge University Press, 2000.

Pensado, J. L. *Una crisis en la lengua del imperio: El "Diálogo de las lenguas" de Damasio de Frías*. Salamanca: Ediciones Universidad de Salamanca, 1982.

Pérez de Tudela, Almudena, and Annemarie Jordan Gschwend. "Renaissance Menageries: Exotic Animals and Pets at the Habsburg Courts in Iberia and Central Europe." In *Early Modern Zoology: The Construction of Animals in Science, Literature and Visual Arts*, edited by Karl A. E. Enenkel and Paul J. Smith, 419–47. Leiden: Brill, 2007.

Perry, Mary Elizabeth. *Gender and Disorder in Early Modern Seville*. Princeton: Princeton University Press, 1990.

Pharies, David A. *A Brief History of the Spanish Language*. Chicago: University of Chicago Press, 2007.

Phillippy, Patricia. *Painting Women: Cosmetics, Canvases, and Early Modern Culture*. Baltimore: Johns Hopkins University Press, 2006.

Piedra, José. "The Black Stud's Spanish Birth." *Callaloo* 16, no. 4 (Fall 1993): 820–46.

———. "Literary Whiteness and Afro-Hispanic Difference." *New Literary History* 18, no. 2 (Winter 1987): 303–32.

Pike, Ruth. *Aristocrats and Traders: Sevillian Society in the Sixteenth Century*. Ithaca: Cornell University Press, 1972.

———. "Sevillian Society in the Sixteenth Century: Slaves and Freedmen." *Hispanic American Historical Review* 47, no. 3 (1967): 344–59.

Pinto, Samantha. *Difficult Diasporas: The Transnational Feminist Aesthetic of the Black Atlantic*. New York: New York University Press, 2013.

Portús Pérez, Javier. *La antigua procesión del Corpus Christi en Madrid*. Madrid: Consejería de Educación y Cultura, 1993.

Post, Anike. "Fa d'Ambu." In *Pidgins and Creoles: An Introduction*, edited by Jacques Arends, Pieter Muysken, and Norval Smith, 191–204. Philadelphia: John Benjamins, 1995.

Pratt, Mary Louise. *Imperial Eyes: Travel Writing and Transculturation*. New York: Routledge, 1992.

———. "Language and the Afterlives of Empire." *PMLA* 130, no. 2 (March 2015): 348–57.

Pulido Serrano, Juan Ignacio. *Injurias a Cristo: Religión, política y antijudaísmo en el siglo XVII: Análisis de las corrientes antijudías en durante la Edad Moderna*. Alcalá de Henares: Universidad de Alcalá de Henares, Servicio de Publicaciones, 2002.

Pym, Richard J. *The Gypsies of Early Modern Spain, 1425–1783*. New York: Palgrave Macmillan, 2007.

Rabinow, Paul, ed. *The Foucault Reader*. New York: Pantheon Books, 1984.

Rasmussen, Birgit Brander, Eric Klinenberg, Irene J. Nexica, and Matt Wray, eds. *The Making and Unmaking of Whiteness*. Durham: Duke University Press, 2001.

Reed, Alison. "The Whiter the Bread, the Quicker You're Dead: Spectacular Absence and Post-Racialized Blackness in (White) Queer Theory." In Johnson, *No Tea, No Shade*, 48–65.

Reid, Michele. "The Yoruba in Cuba: Origins, Identities, and Transformations." In *The Yoruba Diaspora in the Atlantic World*, edited by Toyin Falola and Matt D. Childs, 111–29. Bloomington: Indiana University Press, 2004.

Reyes Peña, Mercedes de los. *El vestuario en el teatro Español del Siglo de Oro*. Madrid: Cuadernos de Teatro Clásico, 2000.

Rickford, John R. *African American Vernacular English: Features, Evolution, Educational Implications*. Oxford: Blackwell, 1999.

Río Parra, Elena del. *Una era de monstruos: Representaciones de lo deforme en el Siglo de Oro español*. Madrid: Iberoamericana, 2003.

Roach, Joseph. *Cities of the Dead: Circum-Atlantic Performance*. New York: Columbia University Press, 1996.

Robinson, Cedric. *Black Marxism: The Making of the Black Radical Tradition*. London: Zed Press, 1983. Reprint, Chapel Hill: University of North Carolina Press, 2000.

Rodríguez Cuadros, Evangelina. "El hato de la risa: Identidad y ridículo en el vestuario." In *El vestuario en el teatro Español del Siglo de Oro*, edited by Mercedes de los Reyes Peña, 109–37. Madrid: Cuadernos de Teatro Clásico, 2000.

Rodríguez-Moñino, Antonio. *Los pliegos de la colección del Marqués de Morbecq: Siglo XVI*. Madrid: Estudios Bibliográficos, 1962.

Roger, Charles C. "The Role of Semantics in the Study of Race Distance in Puerto Rico." *Social Forces* 22, no. 4 (May 1944): 448–53.

Roncero López, Victoriano. "*Lazarillo, Guzmán*, and Buffoon Literature." *Modern Language Notes* 116, no. 2 (2001): 235–49.

Root, Deborah. "Speaking Christian: Orthodoxy and Difference in Sixteenth-Century Spain." *Representations* 23, no. 1 (Summer 1998): 118–34.

Rosa, Jonathan, and Nelson Flores. "Unsettling Race and Language: Toward a Raciolinguistic Perspective." *Language in Society* 46, no. 5 (2017): 621–47.

Ross, Jill. *Figuring the Feminine: The Rhetoric of Female Embodiment in Medieval Hispanic Literature*. Toronto: University of Toronto Press, 2008.

Rout, Leslie B., Jr. *The African Experience in Spanish America*. Introduction and bibliographical update by Miriam Jimenez Roman and Juan Flores. Princeton, N.J.: Markus Warner Publishers, 2003.

Rowe, Erin Kathleen. "After Death, Her Face Turned White: Blackness, Whiteness, and Sanctity in the Early Modern Hispanic World." *American Historical Review* 121, no. 3 (June 2016): 727–54.

Royster, Francesca T. "The 'End of Race' and the Future of Early Modern Cultural Studies." *Shakespeare Studies* 26 (1998): 59–69.

Ruano de la Haza, José María. *La puesta en escena en los teatros comerciales del Siglo de Oro*. Madrid: Castalia, 2000.

Ruano de la Haza, José María, and John J. Allen. *Los teatros comerciales del siglo XVII y la escenificación de la comedia*. Madrid: Castalia, 2011.

Rudlin, John. *Commedia dell'Arte: An Actor's Handbook*. London: Routledge, 1994.

Ruiz, Teofilo F. *A King Travels: Festive Traditions in Late Medieval and Early Modern Spain*. Princeton: Princeton University Press, 2012.

Russell, Craig H. *Santiago de Murcia's Códice Saldívar IV*. Urbana-Champaign: University of Illinois Press, 1995.

Russell, Peter E. "Towards an Interpretation of Rodrigo de Reinosa's *'poesía negra.'*" In *Studies in Spanish Literature of the Golden Age Presented to Edward M. Wilson*, edited by R. O. Jones, 225–45. London: Támesis, 1973.

Said, Edward W. *Orientalism*. New York: Vintage Books, 1978.

Salvador, Francisco. *La neutralización l/r explosivas agrupadas y su área andaluza*. Granada: Universidad de Granada, 1978.

Sandoval, Prudencio de. *Biblioteca de Autores españoles: Historia de la vida y hechos del emperador Carlos V*. Edited by Carlos Seco Serrano. Madrid: Atlas, 1956.

Santamaría, Carolina. "Negrillas, negros y guineos y la representación musical de lo africano." *Cuadernos de música, artes visuales y artes escénicas* 2, no. 1 (2005): 4–20.

Santos Domínguez, Luis Antonio. "El lenguaje teatral del morisco." *Boletín de la Biblioteca de Menéndez Pelayo* 63 (1987): 5–16.

Santos Morillo, Antonio. "Caracterización del negro en la literatura española del XVI." *Lemir* 15 (2011): 23–46.

———. "La expresión lingüística de los esclavos negros según Alonso de Sandoval." *Actas: Congreso Internacional América Latina; La autonomía de una región. XV Encuentro de Latinoamericanistas Españoles* (2012): 1086–1093. https://halshs.archives-ouvertes.fr/halshs-00876365/document/.

Saunders, A. C. de C. M. *A Social History of Black Slaves and Freedmen in Portugal, 1441–1555*. Cambridge: Cambridge University Press, 1982.

Scarry, Elaine. *The Body in Pain: The Making and Unmaking of the World*. Oxford: Oxford University Press, 1985.

Schlueter, Jennifer. "'How You Durrin?': Chuck Knipp, Shirley Q. Liquor, and Contemporary Blackface." *The Drama Review* 57, no. 2 (Summer 2013): 163–81.

Schuchardt, Hugo. "Kreolischen Studien VII: Ueber das Negerportugiesische von Annobom." *Sitzungsberichte der kaiserlichen Akademie der Wissenschaften zu Wien* 116, no. 1 (1888): 193–226.

Selden, Raman, Peter Widdowson, Peter Brooker. *A Reader's Guide to Contemporary Literary Theory*. 4th ed. Essex, UK: Prentice Hall, 1997.

Shepard, Sanford. *El Pinciano y las teorías literarias del Siglo de Oro*. Madrid: Gredos, 1962.

Shergold, N. D. "Ganassa and the '*Commedia dell'arte*' in Sixteenth-Century Spain." *Modern Language Review* 51, no. 3 (July 1956): 359–68.

Silleras-Fernández, Núria. "Nigra sum sed formosa: Black Slaves and Exotica in the Court of a Fourteenth-Century Aragonese Queen." *Medieval Encounters: Jewish, Christian, and Muslim Culture in Confluence and Dialogue* 13, no. 3 (2007): 546–65.

Silva, Feliciano de. *Segunda comedia de Celestina*. Edited by Consolación Baranda and prologue by Fernando Arrabal. Madrid: Cátedra, 1988.

Sloman, Albert. "The Phonology of Moorish Jargon in the Works of Early Spanish Dramatists and Lope de Vega." *Modern Language Review* 44, no. 2 (1949): 207–17.

Smedley, Audrey. *Race in North America: Origin and Evolution of a Worldview*. 3rd ed. Boulder, Col.: Westview Press, 2007.

Smith, Cassander L. *Black Africans in the British Imagination: English Narratives of the Early Atlantic World*. Baton Rouge: Louisiana State University Press, 2016.

Smith, Ian. *Race and Rhetoric in the Renaissance: Barbarian Errors*. New York: Palgrave Macmillan, 2009.

———. "White Skin, Black Masks: Racial Cross-Dressing on the Early Modern Stage." *Renaissance Drama* 32 (2003): 33–67.

Smith, Marlene K. *The Beautiful Woman in the Theater of Lope de Vega: Ideology and Mythology of Female Beauty in Seventeenth-Century Spain*. New York: Peter Lang, 1998.

Smith, Paul Julian. *Writing in the Margin: Spanish Literature of the Golden Age.* Oxford: Oxford University Press, 1988.

Smitherman, Geneva. *Talkin and Testifyin: The Language of Black America.* Detroit: Wayne State University Press, 1985.

Snook, Edith. *Women, Beauty and Power in Early Modern England: A Feminist Literary History.* London: Palgrave Macmillan, 2011.

Solà-Solé, Josep M. *Sobre árabes, judíos y marranos y su impacto en la lengua y literatura española.* Barcelona: Puvill Libros, S.A., 1983.

Spadaccini, Nicholas, and Luis Martín-Estudillo, eds., *Hispanic Baroques: Reading Cultures in Context.* Nashville: Vanderbilt University Press, 2005.

Sparks, Randy J. *Where the Negroes Are Masters: An African Port in the Era of the Slave Trade.* Cambridge: Harvard University Press, 2014.

Spicer, Joaneath, ed. *Revealing the African Presence in Renaissance Europe.* Baltimore: Walters Art Gallery, 2013.

Spillers, Hortense J. *Black, White, and in Color: Essays on American Literature and Culture.* Chicago: University of Chicago Press, 2003.

———. "Mama's Baby, Papa's Maybe: An American Grammar Book." In *Black, White, and in Color*, 203–29.

———. "Peter's Pans: Eating in the Diaspora." In *Black, White, and in Color*, 1–64.

Stafford, A. O. "The Tarik É Soudan." *Journal of Negro History* 2, no. 2 (April 1917): 139–46.

Stallybrass, Peter. "Worn Worlds: Clothes and Identity on the Renaissance Stage." In *Subject and Other in Renaissance Culture*, edited by Margreta de Grazia, Maureen Quilligan, and Peter Stallybrass, 289–320. Cambridge: Cambridge University Press, 1996.

Stallybrass, Peter, and Ann Rosalind Jones. "Fetishizing the Glove in Renaissance Europe." *Critical Inquiry* 28, no. 1 (2001): 114–32.

Stephens, Michelle Ann. *Skin Acts: Race, Psychoanalysis, and the Black Male Performer.* Durham: Duke University Press, 2014.

Stevens, Andrea Ria. *Inventions of the Skin: The Painted Body in Early English Drama, 1400-1642.* Edinburgh: Edinburgh University Press, 2013.

Stevenson, Robert. "The Afro-American Musical Legacy to 1800." *Musical Quarterly* 54, no. 4 (1968): 475–502.

Stoever, Jennifer Lynn. *The Sonic Color Line: Race and the Cultural Politics of Listening.* New York: New York University Press, 2016.

Stoichita, Victor. "The Image of the Black in Spanish Art: Sixteenth and Seventeenth Centuries." In *The Image of the Black in Western Art: From the "Age of Discovery" to the Age of Abolition: Artists of the Renaissance and Baroque*, vol. 3, part 1, edited by David Bindman and Henry Louis Gates Jr., 191–234. Cambridge: Harvard University Press, 2010.

Stone, Rob. "'Quiero llorar': Lorca and the Flamenco Tradition in *Poeta en Nueva York.*" *Bulletin of Hispanic Studies* 77, no. 5 (2000): 493–510.

Suárez, Juan Luis, and Estefanía Olid-Peña. "Hispanic Baroque: A Model for the Study of Cultural Complexity in the Atlantic World." *South Atlantic Review* 72, no. 1 (Winter 2007): 31–47.

Surtz, Ronald. *The Birth of a Theater: Dramatic Convention in the Spanish Theater from Juan del Encina to Lope de Vega.* Madrid: Castalia, 1979.

Sutcliffe, David. "The Voice of the Ancestors: New Evidence on 19th-Century Precursors to 20th-Century African American English." In *Sociocultural and Historical Contexts of African American English*, edited by Sonja L. Lanehart, 129–68. Amsterdam: John Benjamins, 2001.

Sweet, James H. *Domingos Álvares, African Healing, and the Intellectual History of the Atlantic World.* Chapel Hill: University of North Carolina Press, 2011.

———. "The Iberian Roots of American Racist Thought." *William and Mary*

Quarterly 54, no. 1 (January 1997): 143–66.

———. *Recreating Africa: Culture, Kinship, and Religion in the African-Portuguese World, 1441–1770*. Chapel Hill: University of North Carolina Press, 2003.

———. "Teaching the Modern African Diaspora: A Case Study of the Atlantic Slave Trade." *Radical History Review* 77 (2000): 106–22.

Swiadon Martínez, Glenn. "Los villancicos de negro en el teatro breve un primer acercamiento." In *La literatura popular impresa en España y en la América colonial: Formas y temas, géneros, funciones, difusión, historia y teoría*, edited by Eva Belén Crro Carbajal, Laura Mier, Laura Puerto Moro, and María Sánchez Pérez, 161–68. Madrid: Seminario de Estudios Medievales y Renacentistas, 2006.

Talton, Benjamin, and Quincy T. Mills, eds. *Black Subjects in Africa and Its Diasporas: Race and Gender in Research and Writing*. New York: Palgrave Macmillan, 2011.

Tejerizo Robles, Germán. *Villancicos barrocos en la Capilla Real de Granada (500 letrillas cantadas la noche de Natividad 1673–1830)*, vol. 1. Seville: Junta de Andalucía, Consejería de Cultura, 1989.

Terry, Arthur. *Seventeenth-Century Spanish Poetry: The Power of Artifice*. Cambridge: Cambridge University Press, 1993.

Teyssier, Paul. *A Língua de Gil Vicente*. Lisbon: Imprensa Nacional-Casa da Moeda, 2005.

Thacker, Jonathan. *A Companion to Golden Age Theatre*. Woodridge, UK: Támesis, 2007.

Thacker, Jonathan, and Alexander Samson, eds. *A Companion to Lope de Vega*. Woodbridge, UK: Támesis, 2008.

Thompson, Ayanna. *Performing Race and Torture on the Early Modern Stage*. London: Routledge, 2008.

Thompson, Peter E. *The Outrageous Juana Rana Entremeses: A Bilingual and Annotated Selection of Plays Written for This Spanish Golden Age Gracioso*. Toronto: University of Toronto Press, 2009.

———. *The Triumphant Juan Rana: A Gay Actor of the Spanish Golden Age*. Toronto: University of Toronto Press, 2006.

Tinsley, Omise'eke Natasha. "To Transcender Transgender: Choreographies of Gender Fluidity in the Performances of Mildred Gerestant." In Johnson, *No Tea, No Shade*, 131–46.

Tobar, María Luisa. "Los disfrazados de mujer de la *Floresta de engaños* de Gil Vicente." In *Actas de las XVII Jornadas de Teatro Clásico, julio de 1994*, edited by María Luisa Tobar, 141–54. Almagro: Universidad de Castilla–La Mancha, 1994.

Toll, Robert. *Blacking Up: The Minstrel Show in Nineteenth-Century America*. New York: Oxford University Press, 1974.

Tompkins, Kyla Wazana. *Racial Indigestion: Eating Bodies in the 19th Century*. New York: New York University Press, 2012.

Tortorici, Zeb. *Sins Against Nature: Sex and Archives in Colonial New Spain*. Durham: Duke University Press, 2018.

Trambaioli, Marcella. "Apuntes sobre el guineo o baile de negros: Tipologías y funciones dramáticas." *Actas* 6 (2002): 1773–83.

Tranberg Hansen, Karen, and D. Soyini Madison, eds. Introduction to *African Dress: Fashion, Agency, Performance*. London: Bloomsbury, 2013.

Valkhoff, Marius, ed. *Miscelânea Luso-Africana*. Lisbon: Junta do Ultramar, 1975.

Van Dijk, Teun A., ed. *Racismo y discurso en América latina*. Barcelona: Editorial Gedisa, S.A., 2007.

Vaz, Kim Marie. *Black Women in America*. London: Sage, 1995.

Vélez-Sainz, Julio. "Mitología, caballería y espejo de príncipes en *La Gloria de Niquea* del Conde de Villamediana." *Compostella Áurea, Actas del VIII Congreso de la AISO* (2011): 525–34.

Veres, Ernesto. "Juegos idiomáticos en las obras de Lope de Rueda." *Filología Española* 34 (1950): 195–217.

Vila, Isidro. *Elementos de la gramática ambú o de Annobón*. Madrid: Imprenta de A. Pérez Dubrull, 1891.

Vila Vilar, Enriqueta. *Hispanoamérica y el comercio de esclavos*. Seville: Escuela de publicaciones hispano-americanos de Sevilla, 1977.

Vilches, Elvira. *New World Gold: Cultural Anxiety and Monetary Disorder in Early Modern Spain*. Chicago: University of Chicago Press, 2010.

Villa-Flores, Javier. *Dangerous Speech: A Social History of Blasphemy in Colonial Mexico*. Tucson: University of Arizona Press, 2006.

Vodovozova [Operstein], Natalie. "A Contribution to the History of the *villancico de negros*." Master's thesis, University of British Columbia, 1996.

Voigt, Lisa. "Imperial Celebrations, Local Triumphs: The Rhetoric of Festival Accounts in the Portuguese Empire." *Hispanic Review* 79, no. 1 (Winter 2011): 17–41.

———. *Writing Captivity in the Early Modern Atlantic: Circulations of Knowledge and Authority in the Iberian and English Imperial Worlds*. Chapel Hill: University of North Carolina Press, 2009.

Watkin, William. *The Literary Agamben: Adventures in Logopoiesis*. London: Continuum, 2010.

Weber de Kurlat, Frida, ed. *Servir a señor discreto*. Madrid: Castalia, 1975.

———, "El tipo cómico del negro en el teatro prelopesco: Fonética." *Filología* 8 (1962): 139–68.

———. "El tipo del negro en el teatro de Lope de Vega: Tradición y creación." *Nueva Revista de Filología Hispánica* 19, no. 2 (1970): 337–59.

———. "Sobre el negro como tipo cómico en el teatro español del siglo XVI." *Romance Philology* 17, no. 2 (1963): 380–91.

———. "Sobre el portuguesismo de Diego Sánchez de Badajoz: El portugués hablado en farsas españolas del siglo XVI." *Filología* 13 (1968): 349–59.

Weheliye, Alexander G. "Engendering Phonographies: Sonic Technologies of Blackness." *Small Axe* 18, no. 2 (July 2014): 180–90.

———. *Habeas Viscus: Racializing Assemblages, Biopolitics, and Black Feminist Theories of the Human*. Durham: Duke University Press, 2014.

———. *Phonographies: Grooves in Sonic Afro-Modernity*. Durham: Duke University Press, 2005.

Weinreich, Uriel. *Language and Contact: Findings and Problems*. New York: Mouton, 1968.

Weiss, Julian. "Renaissance Poetry." In *The Cambridge History of Spanish Literature*, edited by David T. Gies, 159–77. Cambridge: Cambridge University Press, 2005.

Wheat, David. *Atlantic Africa and the Spanish Caribbean, 1570–1640*. Chapel Hill: University of North Carolina Press, 2016.

Wickersham Crawford, J. P. *Spanish Drama Before Lope de Vega: A Revised Edition*. Philadelphia: University of Pennsylvania Press, 1967.

Williamsen, Vern. *The Minor Dramatists of Seventeenth-Century Spain*. Boston: Twayne, 1982.

———. "Women and Blacks Have Brains Too: A Play by Diego Ximenez de Enciso." In *Studies in Honor of Everett W. Hesse*, edited by William C. McCrary and José A. Madrigal, 199–205. Lincoln: Society of Spanish and Spanish-American Studies, 1982.

Williams-Farrier, Bonnie J. "Signifying, Narrativizing, and Repetition: Radical Approaches to Theorizing African American Language." *Meridians: Feminism, Race, Transnationalism* 15, no. 1 (2016): 218–42.

Wilson, Leslie. "*La Poesía Negra*: Its Background, Themes and Significance." In *Blacks in Hispanic Literature: Critical Essays*, edited by Miriam DeCosta-Willis, 90–104. Port Washington, N.Y.: Kennikat Press, 1977.

Wimbush, Vincent, ed. *Scripturalizing the Human: The Written as the Political*. New York: Routledge, 2015.

Wittgenstein, Ludwig. *Philosophical Investigations*. Translated by G. E. M. Anscombe. Oxford: Basil Blackwell, 1958.

Woolard, Kathryn A. "Bernard de Aldrete and the Morisco Problem: A Study in Early Modern Spanish Language." *Comparative Studies in Society and History* 44, no. 3 (July 2002): 446–80.

Wright, Elizabeth R. *The Epic of Juan Latino: Dilemmas of Race and Religion in Renaissance Spain*. Toronto: University of Toronto Press, 2016.

Wright, Michelle M. *Becoming Black: Creating Identity in the African Diaspora*. Durham: Duke University Press, 2004.

———. *Physics of Blackness: Beyond the Middle Passage Epistemology*. Minneapolis: University of Minnesota Press, 2015.

Wynter, Sylvia. "Eye of the Other." In *Blacks in Hispanic Literature: Critical Essays*, edited by Miriam DeCosta-Willis 1–17. Port Washington, N.Y.: Kennikat Press, 1977.

Yancy, George. "Geneva Smitherman: The Social Ontology of African-American Language, the Power of *Nommo*, and the Dynamics of Resistance and Identity Through Language." *Journal of Speculative Philosophy* 18, no. 4 (2004): 273–99.

Ynduráin, Francisco. *Los moriscos en el teatro en Aragón: Auto de la destruyción de Troya y Comedia pastoril de Torcato*. Zaragoza: Artes Gráficas Librería General, 1986.

Index

Page references to images are indicated with italics.

Abd al-Rahman I, 165n3, 169n42
abjection, 20, 33, 41, 57, 120–21, 133
aesthetics
    adornment, 40, 43, 126, 141, 145, 147, 149, 161 (*see also* cosmetics)
    black African, 4–5, 7, 15, 25, 95, 115, 149
    black female, 119, 121, 129, 139, 149
    European, 133–34, 139, 149
    White, 128
African American Vernacular English (AAVE), xxiii, 109, 116, 177n10
African Diaspora, xxii, 14–18, 29, 51, 60, 67, 91–94, 110, 123
    culture of, 2, 5–6, 15, 24, 53, 55, 67–68, 75, 86, 96, 116, 118
diasporic language, 24, 26, 87, 89, 162
    diasporic studies, xiii, 2, 4, 14, 16, 123
    folklore (*see* folklore)
African ethnonyms
    Akan, 16, 22
Arará, 51–53, 161
    Berbasina, 151–52, 154, 157
    Bucamandé, 99, 102, 107

"Gelofe Mandinga," 98, 103, 106, 116
Guineo, 9, 46, 48, 103 (*see also* bailes de negros: guineo)
Jolof, 100, 102, 106, 109, 112, 154
Mandé, 107
Mandinga, 98–101, 103, 106, 111–12, 116
Serer, 154
Wolof, 22, 106–9, 114, 154
Yoruba, xvi, 52, 55, 161–62
Africanity, 17–18, 90, 96–97
Africanized Castilian. See *habla de negros*
African spiritual systems
    Ifá, 162
    La Regla de Osha, xvi, 161–62
    lumbe, 54–55, 57
    mpungo zarabanda, 53–54
    nganga, v, 54
    nkisi, 161, 163
    orisha, 161, 163
    Palo Mayombe, xvi, 63, 80, 161
Afro-Cuba, xvi, 50, 55, 63, 159, 161–62
Agamben, Giorgio, 20

agency
    Black African (*see* Black Africans: agency)
    black female, xv, 71, 117, 119, 123–24, 126, 128, 134, 140, 142, 148, 156 (*see also* Eulalla: agency; Guiomar: agency)
    European (white) female, 124
Aguado, Simón, 2, 5, 10, 17, 26, 69–79
Al-Andalus. *See* Spain
alcohol. *See* cosmetics: kohl
aljamiado, 26
    See also Barletta, Vincent
Angola, 3, 17, 50, 61, 63–65
animal studies, 134
Aranjuez, 30–31
Arará, 51–53, 161
Auerbach, Erich, 166n6
authority, 105, 117, 121, 128, 132, 139, 151, 157
Avellaneda, Francisco, 5, 10, 70

bailes de negros, xiv, 5, 26, 28, 47–49, 50–60, 66–68
    cumbé, 61
    guineo, 5, 9, 28, 48, 54, 56–57, 59–60, 101
    gurumbé, 5, 55, 57–58
    paracumbé, 55, 61, 63
    zarabanda, 5, 54, 56, 58–60, 67, 73 (*see also* African spiritual systems: mpungo)
    zarambeque (zumbé), 5, 10, 54, 56, 60–61, 63, 67
    See also dance
Bakhtin, Mikhail, 6
Balibar, Étienne, 159–60
Banerjee, Bobby, 55
Barletta, Vincent, 170n76
Barranco, Marga G., 49, 170n76
    Battle of Lepanto, 91
Belo, André, 4
Benavente, Luis Quiñones de, 2, 11, 26, 48
Benston, Kimberly W., 117
Berbasina, 151–52, 154, 157
Beusterien, John, 19, 33, 36, 50, 108, 176n122, 176n124

Beyoncé, 142, 144, 145–47
bible, 2, 39, 66, 72
Black Africans
    agency, xiii–xiv, 6, 8, 15, 20, 28, 68–69, 72, 154
    in the Americas, xiii, xxii, 2, 16, 68, 94–95, 105, 115, 156
    in early modern Iberia, 3–4, 6, 15–18, 29–32, 49–50, 69
    European depictions of, 5, 7–9, 28, 146–47, 160–61
    language of, 19–23, 25 (*see also* habla de negros)
    stereotypes of, 6, 9, 16, 28, 42, 72, 75, 89, 91, 107
Black coolness, 24–25
blackface
    black actors in, 35, 61, 67
    and black skin, 27–29
    definition of, 36–38
    implicating white gaze, 33–34
    "inkface," 38–39
    materiality of, 47
    minstrelsy, 33–35, 67, 75
    whiteface, 35, 172n31
    See also Blackness: materiality of; cosmetics: representing blackness
Black feminism, 121–22, 154–57
    theoretical framework, xv–xvi
Blackmore, Josiah, 116
black mouth. *See* bozal
Blackness
    Castilian, 4, 13
    corporeality, xiv, 26, 28, 38, 122–23
    linguistic, xiii–xiv, 6, 13, 23, 161
    materiality of, xiii, 6, 39, 47, 84 (*see also* blackface)
    performance of, xv, 87, 91, 142 (*see also* blackface)
    sartorial, 45–47
    skin, xiv, 26, 28–29, 38, 41–44, 108–9
Blaxploitation, 89
Boose, Lynda, 124
Brooks, Daphne A., 120, 180n5
Brooks, Kinitra D., 51

Bourdieu, Pierre, 19, 21, 23–25, 147
    cultural capital, 147
    symbolic capital, 21, 23, 148
bozal, xiv, 9, 26–28, 42, 69–72, 79–82, 150, 162
    See also habla de negros: as bozal speech
Budasz, Rogério, 50–51

cabildos de nación, 52
Cádiz, 49, 51, 61, 165n3
Calderón de la Barca, Pedro, 10, 23, 26, 28, 30, 63, 65–66, 119, 157
Camos, Fray Marcos Antonio, 58
Campo Tejedor, Alberto del, 68
Cáncer, Jerónimo de, 61
Candomblé, 162–63
capital. See Bourdieu, Pierre; symbolic capital
Carabajal, Mariana de, 9
Carby, Hazel, xv, 148
carnivalesque. See Bakhtin, Mikhail
carnival, 28
    See also Bakhtin, Mikhail
Carrillo, Alonso, 3
Castro, Francisco de, 61
Catholicism, 9, 16, 49, 55, 86, 112, 115–16, 118, 166n10
celebrity, 121–22
Cervantes, Miguel de, 2, 9, 11, 25, 51, 58, 60, 67, 119, 121–22
chapbooks, 12, 62, 90
Chireau, Yvonne, 51
Christian, Barbara, 123
Christianity, 16, 42–43, 66, 72, 114–15, 165n3, 180n62
Claramonte, Andrés de, 11, 30
clothing, xiii, 15, 39, 46–47, 88, 108, 122–23, 126, 161, 180n50
    See also costumes
Collins, Patricia Hill, 123, 148–49
colonialism, 15, 76, 103, 105, 129, 142, 161
    colonial Spain, 136, 156 (see also Spain: imperialism)
Columbus, Christopher, 105, 136
Cone, James, 53

"Conguitos" candy, 79–84
conversos, 168n34
cool, 24–25
Córdoba, 16, 39, 59, 165n3, 169n42
Correa, Gaspar, 88
Cortés de Tolosa, Juan, 36
cosmetics
    kohl, 39–41
    representing blackness, 36–46, 83, 120
    and self-fashioning, xv
    and white women, 41–42
    See also costumes; material culture
cosmology, xvi, 51, 55, 57
    See also African spiritual systems
Cossío, José María, 115
costumes
    blackness as, 35, 47
    imitating skin, 44–47
    See also clothing
Cotarelo y Mori, Emilio, 44
Covarrubias, Sebastián de, 38, 106, 108
    on bozal, 80–81
    on cosmetics, 40–41
    on dance, 56, 59, 67
    emblems, 133–34, 135, 136–37, 138
critical race studies, 8, 18, 72, 146, 160
Cromberger, Jacopo, 34, 38, 39
Cuba, xii, 49–50, 52–56, 80, 160–62
    See also Afro-Cuba
Cullen, Countee, 16
cumbé, 61

dance
    black (see bailes de negros)
    flamenco, 49, 53, 67–68
    as language, 47–49
Dávila, Gil González, 128
Davis, Angela, 51
DeFantz, Thomas F., 7
Deleuze, Gilles, 79–80
Delicado, Francisco, 9, 109
dialect, v, xii, 7, 14, 22, 89, 114, 162
Didascalia multiplex. See Fernández de Cordoba, Francisco
DiFranco, Ralph, 13

INDEX   215

diva
     behavior, 128–29, 133–34
     and blackness, 122, 128
     definition of, 128, 157
     See also Eulalla: as diva; Guiomar
Dolph, Steve, 166n6
Dujardin, Karel, 36, *37*
Dumas, Alexandre, 16

El Diablo Cojuelo. *See* Vélez de Guevara, Luis
Ellison, Ralph, 66, 93–94
enslaved peoples, xxi, 3, 17, 23, 55, 68, 87–88, 97, 106, 109, 117, 162, 164
     creative endeavors of, 57
     as curiosities, 139–40, 142
     language of, 12
     and literacy, 12–13, 80–81, 154–56
     trafficking of, 1–3, 17, 38, 106, 149, 155, 173n71, 179n44
entremés. *See* teatro breve
Equiano, Olaudah, 179n28
êres, 163
Erickson, Peter, 146
espiritismo, 162
     See also *mesa blanca*
Eulalia. *See* Eulalla
     See also *Peristephanon*
Eulalla
     agency, xv, 121, 126, 128, 134, 139–40, 142, 148
     authority, 121, 128, 132, 139
     beauty politics, 140–50
     as Beyoncé, 142, 145–47
     as diva, xv, 121, 128, 132–34, 136, 141
     as go-between, 141, 150

Fanon, Frantz, 21, 29, 33, 142
Felipe II, 1–2, 91
Felipe III, 30
Felipe IV, 30–31, *32*
Felipe V, 65
Ferdinand II of Aragon, 86
Ferdinand III of Castile, 16
Ferdinand VI, *58*
Fernández de Córdoba, Francisco, 59

flamenco, 49, 53, 67–68
folklore, 7, 12, 47–48, 50, 54, 56, 68, 94
Fontana, Julio César, 30
food studies, 72
     culinary distinction, 5, 90, 106, 112–15, 161
Forbes, Curdella, 35
Foucault, Michel, 18, 105
Fra-Molinero, Baltasar, 133, 168n40, 172n43, 178n11, 182n40
Fryer, Peter, 50
Fuchs, Barbara, 19, 169n41, 169n46

Gama, Vasco da, 88
games, xv, 24, 91, 108
García Lorca, Federico, 68
Gates Jr., Henry Louis, 92–94
Gaylord, Mary Malcolm, 13
Gelofe, 98, 103, 106, 116
gender
     ideology, 110, 150
     and politics, 124, 129, 141, 151
     and race, xv, 13, 32, 110, 122, 142, 148, 150–51, 157, 167n16
     See also performance theory: gendered
genre, 9, 12–13, 24, 27–28, 72, 128, 167n26
     See also habla de negros: as genre
Ghana, 22, 94, 166n44, 179n45
     See also African ethnonyms: Akan
Gilroy, Paul, 29
Goldberg, K. Meira, 67–68
Gómez de Toledo, Gaspar, 9
Góngora y Argote, Luis de, 10, 21–25, 39–44, 66, 70, 119
Gonzalez, Anita, 7
Granada, 8, 13, 26, 69, 142
Granados, Octavio Páez, 12
Granda, Germán de, 108
Graves, Yinka Esi, 68
Greenblatt, Stephen, 129
Grier, Miles P., 38–39
Guattari, Félix, 79–80
guineo. *See* African ethnonyms: guineo; bailes de negros: guineo

216 INDEX

Guiomar
    agency, xv, 123, 154, 156
    authority, 151, 157
gurumbé, 5, 55, 57–58

habla de negros
    and blackface, 28, 34–35 (see also blackface)
    as bozal speech, 27, 79–82 (see also bozal)
    construction(s) of, 5, 9, 11, 13, 15, 48, 52, 80
    as genre, 9, 13
    imitations, 9, 53
    influences, xvi, 9, 163
    literary, xi–xii, xiv, xvi, 5, 13, 23, 89
    musicality of, 27, 48–58
    orthography, 5–6, 104
    poetry, xiv, 11–13, 24, 89, 96–97
    and signifying, xv, 90–95, 103–4, 108, 110–18
    speaking to black audiences, 95–96
    white European appropriation, 21–25
    women's use of, 120–24, 137, 139, 148, 150, 154–55, 157
Hall, Gwendolyn Mildo, 103, 107
Hall, Kim F., 124, 146
Harlem Renaissance, 16, 93–94
Hartikainen, Elina, 162–63
Hartman, Saidiya, 34–35
Havana, 49–50, 56
Herraiz, José Labrador, 13
heteroglossia. See Bakhtin, Mikhail; speech
hip-hop, 24–25
Hispanic Studies, 56, 82, 120–25
Hurston, Zora Neale, v, 7, 54, 93–94
Hurtado de Mendoza, Antonio, 31

Ifá, 162
Inquisition, 13–14, 174n73
Irigoyen-García, Javier, 67
Isabella I of Castile, 48, 86
Islam, 2, 55, 67, 103, 113–16
    Islamic Iberia, 16–17

Jeffries, Michael, 25
Joanna of Austria (Juana de Austria), Princess of Portugal, 139, *140*
João II, King of Portugal, 85–86, 88–89
Jolof, 100, 102, 106, 109, 112, 154
    Juan Danzante (character), 64

Kubik, Gerard, 50
Kunstkammer, 134, 136, 139
Kyeser, Konrad, *143*

ladino, 81–82, 150
Latino, Juan, 91
La Celestina. See Rojas, Fernando de
La Gloria de Niquea, 30–32
La Peste, 3, 52
La Regla de Osha, xvi, 161–62
    Las Reglas Congas. See African spiritual systems: Palo Mayombe
lengua, 162
letter writing, xv, 122–23, 154, 156
Lipski, John M., 4, 9, 17, 88
Lisbon, 24, 30, 86, 145, 154, 173n71, 174n73
    See also Portugal
literacy, 13, 39, 66, 80–81, 93, 150, 154–56, 170n1
literature
    canonical, xiv, 25, 41, 69, 93, 109
    early modern Spanish, xiii, xvi, 4, 15, 21, 103, 128, 133, 159
López de Mendoza, Íñigo, marqués de Santillana, 11
López Pinciano, Alonso, 58
Lorca, Federico García, 67–68
Lorde, Audre, xxii, 8
Lovejoy, Paul E., 15–16, 115
"lower frequencies," 66–67
    See also bailes de negros; Tavia Nyong'o
Lukumí. See African spiritual systems: La Regla de Osha
lumbe, 54–55, 57

MacDonald, Joyce Green, 124–25
makeup. See cosmetics
Málaga, 53

Mali, 17, 71, 94, 107
  See also Timbuktu
Mandé, 107
  See also African ethnonyms:
    Bucamandé
Mandinga, 98–101, 103, 106, 111–12, 116
Ma(a)ngana. *See* Reinosa, Rodrigo de
manuscript culture, 12, 21
  See also print culture
Maravall, José Antonio, 147
  María Luisa of Savoy, 65
marriage, 69, 72, 79, 86, 128–29, 131
  See also women
Martin, Kameelah L., 51
Martín, Luis Fernández, 30
Martín Casares, Aurelia, 43, 49
Martínez, Domingo, 58
material culture, 15, 38–39, 41, 47, 84, 88, 120, 123, 150
  See also cosmetics; costumes
Mbembe, Achille, 55
mediumship, 162
mesa blanca, 162
  See also *espiritismo*
Mialhe, Frédéric, 55
Microcosmia, 58
Middle Passage, 94
  See also slavery
Miller, Monica L., xiii
Mitchell-Kernan, Claudia, 113–14
mojiganga, 27–28, 44, 61, 63–64, 66, 70
mona. See monkey
  See also Covarrubias, Sebastián de
monkey, 132–34, 136, 139, 148
Montaigne, Michel de, 92
Moors, 67, 88, 115–16
Morais, Cristóvão de, 139, 140
Morgan, Marcyliena, 24
Moriscos, 14, 26, 67, 173n153
Moten, Fred, v, 8,
mpungo (zarabanda), 53–54
Muñoz, José Esteban, xiv
music
  African traditional, 3, 5, 26–27, 29, 34, 48–57, 64–68, 77, 86
  antiphony, xv, 61, 111
  and faith, 52
  hip-hop, 24–25
  as language, 48, 50, 66, 77, 112
  Nativity, 17, 26, 51, 61
  and theater, 12, 30, 34, 70, 75, 77

Navarrete, Ignacio, 41
Navarro García, José Luis, 49, 53, 61, 64
Nebrija, Antonio de, 19, 104–5
necromancy, 55–56
nganga, v, 54
nkisi, 161, 163
Nyong'o, Tavia, 66

opacity (politics of), 120
opera, 30
orality, 72, 75
  See also speech
Orientalism, 17
orisha, 161, 163
Orr, Bridget, 33
Ortiz, Fernando, 56
Otherness, xii, 17, 32–33, 43, 83, 116, 148, 159, 161

Palmié, Stephan, 17
Palo Mayombe, xvi, 63, 80, 161
pamphlets. *See* chapbooks
papagayo. See parrots
paracumbé, 55, 61, 63
parrots, 65, 132–34, 136–37, 139, 148, 150
  parrot culture, 139
Peraza, Luis de, 3
Peréz de Montoro, José, 51–53
performance theory
  Black, 7
  gendered, xiii, 6
Peristephanon, 128
Petrarchism, 41
pliegos sueltos. See chapbooks
  See also print culture, speech
poetry
  Baroque, 13, 23, 41, 97
  and civic engagement, 11
  habla de negros (*see* habla de negros: poetry)

218

INDEX

lyric, 21, 41, 97
Renaissance, 12, 89
villancico, 12–13, 17, 51–53, 56, 61, 68, 168n31 (*see also* music: Nativity)
Portugal, 2, 11, 31, 61, 63, 179n45
    Luso-African society, 85–89, 116, 153–55, 174n73
    slave trade, 1–3, 15–17, 106
postcolonial studies, 35, 75
Pratt, Mary Louise, 87–88
print culture, 12, 25, 34, 38, 150
    See also manuscript culture
Puerto Rico, xii, 153, 155–56, 160

Queen of Sheba, 142, *143*
queer studies, 72
Quevedo y Villegas, Francisco de, 5, 9, 21, 38, 47–48, 56, 69–70, 119
Quint, David, 22
Quirós, Francisco Bernardo de, 10, 26, 63–65

race
    political positions, xiii, xxii, 141
    skin color v imposed definitions, xxi–xxii, 12, 28–29, 42–43, 139–41, 148–49, 161
    social categories, xii, xxi–xxii, 6, 16, 67, 80–81, 105–6, 116, 134, 145, 148, 156
    stereotypes, xiii, 6, 20, 28, 42, 89, 91, 148, 159
    See also racism
racial impersonation. *See* blackface
racism, 19, 108, 121, 142, 148, 155, 159
    essentialism, 109
    ideology, 92, 154
    intraracism, 178n26
radical, xiv, 7–8, 66, 121–22
Rebelo, Manuel Coelho, 36
Reinosa, Rodrigo de
    audience, 95–96, 111, 115, 117
    black female characters, 91, 106–8, 114–15
    as go-between, 110–11, 116
    Muslim characters, 104–5, 114–16

    poesía negra, 160
    representing habla de negros, 91–97, 110–11
    use of obscenity, 96–97, 104–6, 116–17
Resende, Garcia de, 12, 86–89, 113
resistance, v, xiii, 6, 14–15, 18, 58, 70, 77, 121–25, 141–42, 161
    See also agency
rhetoric, 23, 32, 39, 105, 111, 117, 120, 141, 155
    in black literature, 93–94
    chiasmus, 41
    classical Western, 91–93
    hyperbole, 80
Rivers of Guinea. *See* Senegambia: Rivers of Guinea
Rodríguez Cuadros, Evangelina, 46
Rojas, Fernando de, 110–11, 141
Rosales, Miguel Ángel, 68
Ruano de la Haza, José María, 29–30
Rueda, Lope de
    acting as black woman, 121
    audience, 122, 125, 137, 156
    black women characters, xv, 2, 5, 119–25, 157–58 (*see also* Eulalla; Guiomar)
    celebrity, 121–22
    classical influence, 128
    on race relations, 151
    racial appropriation, 141–42
    representing habla de negros, 137, 139, 154–56
Ruiz, Juan, 110
Russell, Peter E., 159–60, 177n10

Santería. *See* African spiritual systems: La Regla de Osha
Santiago de Compostela, 83
"Santísimo Sacramento," 10, 39–43
satire, 42, 48, 69, 72, 103
Savall, Jordi, 68–69
scribes, 13–14, 41
self-fashioning, xv, 120, 126, 128–29, 134
Senegambia, 3, 24, 56–57, 103, 106–7, 112–13, 180n62
    Rivers of Guinea, 3, 24, 56, 88, 97, 157
Serer, 154

Seville
  Arenal, 1–2
  black community, 2–3, 5, 30, 49, 52, 70–71, 89–91, 95–96, 103, 110–11, 119
  Castilian Reconquest of, 16
  early modern, 2, 24, 52, 63–64, 70–71, 110, 119
  enslaved people in, 38, 49, 70, 89, 145
  first black residents, 154–55
sex, 59, 108, 128
sexuality, 61, 104–5, 124, 128–29
  hypersexualization, 66–67, 70, 120
Shakespeare, 6, 35, 146
Shelton, Ron, 93
Siglo de Oro. *See* Spain: Golden Age
Silva, Feliciano de, 9, 30
Silveira, Fernão da, 85–89, 113
slavery, 5, 15, 25, 38, 40, 70, 79, 122
  Atlantic slave trade, 2–3, 15–17, 103, 106–7, 142
  creative responses to, 57, 68–69
  familial relationships, xxi, 155
  and movement of culture, 94–95
  political policies, xxi, 179n44
  and race, 23, 149, 161
  slave trade (*see* enslaved peoples: trafficking of; *see also* Portugal: slave trade)
  See also enslaved peoples
sonic, xiv, 26–29, 34, 66, 69, 75, 77, 128
  Blackness, 52, 60, 69, 120
Soplillo, 31, 32
Soto, Catalina de, 142
Spain
  Al-Andalus, 3, 16–17
  Andalusia, 9, 53, 56, 60, 75, 168n35
  Caliphate of Córdoba, 16
  Golden Age, 28, 30, 46, 48, 124 (*see also* theater: Spanish Golden Age)
  imperialism, 33, 38, 82, 105, 125, 134, 136–37, 147, 155–56
  slave trade, 2–3, 17, 142

speech.
  Black, xv, xix, 4, 6, 13–14, 91
  heteroglossia, 6 (*see also* Bakhtin, Mikhail)
  and social ordering, 19
  unwritten, xiv, 6
  See also orality
Spillers, Hortense J., 108–10, 119
Stone, Rob, 67–68
subjectivity, v, 8, 20, 90, 106, 122–23, 128, 136, 156
subversion, 5, 41–42, 110, 128, 155, 158
  See also cosmetics; genre
Sweet, James H., 14–15
symbolic capital, 21, 23, 148
  See also Bourdieu, Pierre

Tasso, Torquato, 22
Tertullian, 43
theater
  comedia/comedia nueva, 27–29, 33–34, 36, 121, 124, 157
  commedia dell'arte, 36
  Spanish Golden Age, 5, 33, 46, 124
  theater studies, 5, 121
  See also teatro breve
teatro breve, xiv, 27–28, 34, 61, 66
  baile, 27–28, 44, 61, 66 (*see also* bailes de negros)
  entremés, 5, 17, 27–28, 44, 48, 60–61, 64, 66, 69–72, 121, 149
  loa, 27, 44, 61
  mojinganga, 27–28, 44, 61, 63–64, 66, 70
Thacker, Jonathan, 27–28
Timbuktu, 17
Tompkins, Kyla Wazana, 72, 180n5
Trambaioli, Marcella, 28
trance, xvi, 58–59, 162–63
transatlantic, 36, 49, 56, 60, 63, 125, 157
  colonialism, 15, 156
  slavery, 38, 94
translation, xxi–xxiii, 117, 145, 177n10, 180n68
Truth, Sojourner, 122–23, 125

Vega y Carpio, Félix Lope de (Lope de Vega), 2, 11, 21, 23, 25, 28, 119
Velázquez, Bernardino, 30
Velázquez, Diego, 31
Vélez de Guevara, Luis, 2, 11, 36, 56, 58
vernacular, xvi, xxii, 68, 75, 80, 87, 91, 94, 161, 181n7
    Castilian, 19
    Latin, 81
    See also African American Vernacular English
Villamediana, Conde de, 30–32
Villandrando, Rodrigo de, *32*
Villaviciosa, Sebastián de, 60–61, 174n72
Virgil, 91

Weheliye, Alexander G., 75
Wheat, David, xxi–xxii, 80, 88, 154, 156
White Men Can't Jump (film), 93
white supremacy, 6, 77

Whiteness, xii, 6, 33–34, 43, 50, 81, 146
    performance of, xiv, 122, 134, 139, 141, 145, 148
    representations of, 112
Williamsen, Vern, 30
witchcraft, 13, 56–57, 141
Wolof, 22, 106–9, 114, 154
women
    and the Church, 42–43, 118
    misogynist representations, 93–94, 108, 117–18, 121, 158
    prostitution, 89, 108–10
    See also black feminism; diva; marriage
Wright, Richard, 93–94

zarabanda. *See* bailes de negros: zarabanda
    See also African spiritual systems: zarabanda
Zayas y Sotomayor, María de, 120, 157

www.ingramcontent.com/pod-product-compliance
Lightning Source LLC
Chambersburg PA
CBHW021943290426
44108CB00012B/937